THE EVERYTHING® PARENT'S GUIDE TO CHILDREN AND DIVORCE

Reassuring advice to help
your family adjust

Carl E. Pickhardt, Ph.D.

Adams Media
Avon, Massachusetts

Dedication

May this book help parents heal some of the necessary wounds that children of divorce commonly suffer, and help parents prevent some unnecessary injuries from happening at all.

• • •

I would like to express my appreciation to Grace Freedson's Publishing Network for creating the opportunity to write this book.

• • •

Publishing Director: Gary M. Krebs
Associate Managing Editor: Laura M. Daly
Associate Copy Chief: Brett Palana-Shanahan
Acquisitions Editor: Kate Burgo
Development Editors: Karen Johnson Jacot, Jessica LaPointe
Associate Production Editor: Casey Ebert

Director of Manufacturing: Susan Beale
Associate Director of Production: Michelle Roy Kelly
Cover Design: Paul Beatrice, Erick DaCosta, Matt LeBlanc
Layout and Graphics: Colleen Cunningham, Holly Curtis, Sorae Lee

An Everything® Series Book.
Everything® and everything.com® are registered trademarks of F+W Publications, Inc.

Published by Adams Media, an F+W Publications Company
57 Littlefield Street, Avon, MA 02322 U.S.A.
www.adamsmedia.com

ISBN: 1-59337-418-6

Printed in the United States of America.

J I H G F E D C B A

Library of Congress Cataloging-in-Publication Data

Pickhardt, Carl E.
The everything parent's guide to children and divorce : reassuring advice to help your family adjust / Carl Pickhardt.
p. cm. -- (The everything parent's guide series)
ISBN 1-59337-418-6
1. Children of divorced parents. 2. Divorced parents. 3. Divorce. I. Title. II. Series.

HQ777.5.P53 2005
306.874--dc22
2005026454

This publication is designed to provide accurate and authoritative information with regard to the subject matter covered. It is sold with the understanding that the publisher is not engaged in rendering legal, accounting, or other professional advice. If legal advice or other expert assistance is required, the services of a competent professional person should be sought.

—From a *Declaration of Principles* jointly adopted by a Committee of the American Bar Association and a Committee of Publishers and Associations

Disclaimer: All the examples and dialogues used in this book are fictional and have been created by the author to illustrate psychological challenges that parents and children face adjusting to divorce.

di•vorce (dĭ-vôrs′) ▶ *n.* 1. When two adults choose to legally, socially, physically, and emotionally end the marriage connection between them and proceed to lead separate lives.

Contents

Introduction

All children are both beneficiaries and victims of choices their parents make, because a mixed performance is the best that parents can give—a mix of strength and frailty, of wellness and illness, of wisdom and stupidity, of consideration and selfishness. In consequence, children develop partly because of and partly in spite of how their parents choose to act.

In the case of parental divorce, children are more victims than beneficiaries of this decision. Now children must continue to grow up in light of and in spite of a choice by parents that forever alters children's lives. Now children are left to answer many troubling questions that divorce creates.

- How can parents who commit to get married choose not to stay married?
- If the commitment of marriage is made to be broken, then what commitments can you trust?
- If parents can lose their love for each other, can they also lose their love for their children?
- If one parent can leave the family, can the other parent leave too?
- If love is not forever, then how long is love for?

Divorce is a life-changing event. It violates children's basic sense of trust because it breaks two contractual commitments they took for granted: (1) that their

parents would always stay together for the sake of the marriage, and (2) that they would stay together for the sake of the family they created. So for many children, divorce represents a multiple loss—of love between parents, of faith in love's enduring commitment, and of trust in parents who now put adult self-interest before family responsibility.

Although not meaning to, when parents divorce each other, they also divorce their children. Divorce may feel necessary or right for parents, but it usually feels wrong for children, who to some degree feel anxious, injured, betrayed, abandoned, and rejected. Where the parent or parents wanting the divorce see a prospect for life improvement, children experience only a broken promise, family dislocation, an uncertain future, and personal loss.

That divorce is so common (some statistics estimate about fifty percent of marriages made today will end in divorce) does not mean divorce is a casual event. It is not. It is a far-reaching choice made by parents usually for their own self-interest at the expense of their children's happiness. This doesn't mean that parents are divorcing in order to hurt their children, only that parents cannot divorce without their children's getting hurt. This doesn't mean that parents can't divorce out of a troubled marriage and make a lasting happy remarriage thereafter. They can. This doesn't mean that children of parents who remain well married do not have their share of family hurt. They do. This doesn't mean that parents who remain unhappily married spare children from the consequences of that unhappiness. They don't.

But divorce is a surgical strike at the family. It cuts that unit apart. One household is divided into two. For the children, there is permanent parental separation where living with one parent precludes living with the other at the same time. "When I'm with one, I miss the other, and I can never have them both together again!" For the divorced mother or father, there is a new sense of solitude. Becoming a single parent means he or she no longer has a partner with whom to share child care, understanding, work, and responsibility. "I'm on my own; I have to go it alone."

The *Everything® Parent's Guide to Children and Divorce* addresses the emotional impact and the adjustment demands on single parents and children in the wake of divorce.

- It describes some of the emotional impact and adjustment demands created for children when parents divorce.
- It describes common role and responsibility changes that are part of becoming a single parent.
- And it describes the transition from single-household to dual-household family living and what it takes to make this new arrangement work for children.

Traumatic as parental divorce can sometimes be, it rarely "ruins" a child's life in the long term. Certainly it can mark that life and it can hurt a lot, but the pain is passing, not permanent. It is an influential part of the child's history, but it is not all of the child's history. There are far worse adversities (like deprivation, neglect, violence, catastrophic events, or death of a parent) that a child can suffer. Most children are resilient enough to weather parental divorce and grow on with their lives.

CHAPTER 1

How Marriage Ends Is How Divorce Begins

T he foundation of each divorce is a broken marriage, and just as no two marriages are identical, the same is true for divorces. The shape of parental marriage shapes how children grow— the concerns they develop, the emotions that predominate, and the behaviors they develop to take care of themselves.

Common Ways Marriages Fail

Marriages fail in an infinite variety of ways. Consider just several common scenarios. First, there is the estranged marriage. A couple marries, partners pursue separate occupational paths, have children, juggle competing demands of parenting and career, take insufficient time to nourish partnership in marriage, become personally disinterested in each other, grow apart, and mutually decide to let the marriage go.

Then there is the abandoned marriage. A couple marries, partners both work until they have children, the wife stops her job to stay home to take care of the children, the husband financially supports the family, each partner feels his or her family contribution is unappreciated by the other, more quarreling engenders more desire to be apart, the husband spends more time at his job, the husband leaves marriage for an outside relationship, leaving the wife without a job with children in her primary care.

Or consider the violent marriage. A couple marries, personal differences create unexpected conflict, high control needs or drinking or temper cause conflict to become abusive, abuse causes injury, the relationship becomes unsafe for one partner and children, victim partner and children flee the marriage for safety, to that end filing for divorce.

 **Fact**

How the marriage falls apart is how the divorce begins, so ending marriage well bodes best for a "working divorce"—where ex-partners are adequately communicative, emotionally reconciled, socially cooperative, continually supportive, personally respectful, and mutually committed as parents. The challenge of the early part of a divorce is to create a unified parental partnership out of a divisive marriage for the sake of the children.

Different parental marriages can socialize children to get used to different realities of family life. Children learn from their parents. In the estranged marriage, children can grow up with parents who have more to say to, and more affection to share with, their children than with each other. In the abandoned marriage, children grow up with parents who spend little time together, and when they are together, they quarrel a lot but resolve very little, resulting in ongoing friction that creates a constant stress in family life. In the violent marriage, children grow up around at least one parent who is dangerous and scary to live with and so must live in fear on a daily basis.

Marriages fail in many ways. How your particular marriage fell apart is important to understand because that history creates the dynamics of early divorce to which you and your children must initially adjust. The emotional recovery that you and your children will have to make, the relationship with your ex-spouse that you must reestablish, changes in each parent that children must get used to, the quality of care each parent gives are all affected by the nature of the parental marriage and the state in which it ends. Where you've been in marriage has a lot to do with how you and your ex-spouse and your children enter early divorce.

Although children will still have a painful adjustment, the better the divorce between the parents, the less encumbered and influenced by ongoing parental pain and discord the children's adjustment tends to be.

Making a Working Marriage

So, why do people divorce? The answers are to be found in why people marry, and in the nature of a working marriage itself. What follows is a simple model that can help you understand the marriage you made and how that marriage may have fallen apart. Understanding how the marriage failed can help you make the divorce, for the sake of the children, succeed.

The decision to marry is usually motivated by desire from falling in love—a mood- and mind-altering experience. Attraction, infatuation, and romance all combine to create a euphoric sense of union in which the positives about each other are enhanced, while the negatives are often discounted. "Love is blind" is a true statement when it comes to describing how a person, caught up by heart's desire, can deny incompatibilities and unpleasant realities that conflict with what he or she wants to believe. Togetherness rules, commonalities bond, differences are amicable, agreements are easy, separations feel lonely, and conflicts can be frightening when opposition feels like loss of love.

Alert!

When divorced people remarry, the basic conditions that must be met for the relationship to be a happy one are no different than they were before. Thus the first chapter in this book, about how marriage can unhappily fall apart, also bears on the last chapter, about how remarriage can happily be made.

As time passes, and as that feeling of being in love gradually fades, a more sober sense of caring takes its place. Now companionship based on familiarity begins to grow, confiding and reliance building trust, mutual appreciation leading the couple to consider joining their separate paths through life together, choosing to make a commitment to each other through marriage.

The Compromise of Marriage

But to what do they commit? To wedded bliss? To an everlasting honeymoon? To unbroken harmony? No. Ideal isn't real. Commitment must be to reality, to a relationship ruled not by perfection but by compromise, which is as good as a good marriage gets. And if they tend that compromise with vigilance and care, marriage shall be good enough to nourish love they want to share through the years ahead.

What is the compromise? It is how the couple must learn to manage the mix of three components in their relationship: payoffs, costs, and risks.

People enter marriage to enjoy two kinds of payoffs (or rewards) of a caring kind. There are payoffs of giving of themselves in ways they value—by providing and doing for, by sharing, by supporting, by tending, by confiding, by showing affection, for example. And there are payoffs of getting for themselves in ways they value—receiving companionship, appreciation, understanding, personal interest, sexual intimacy, empathy, for example. But in marriage, partners can't have payoffs only, because to get those payoffs, there are always costs to pay. When people marry, they must also incur two kinds of costs, each one demanding they give up some personal freedom in the form of responsibility in the relationship. (In marriage, there is no "free love.") There are costs of obligations, things each must do for the sake of the relationship—keeping the other adequately informed, contributing household labor or income or both, providing care when the other gets sick, for example. And there are costs of prohibitions, things each must not do for the sake of the relationship—breaking confidences, having affairs, indebting the other without consent, for example. But in marriage, partners can't just balance payoffs and costs only, because in managing that balance, there are also always risks to be taken.

When people marry, they expose themselves to two kinds of risks, because caring for each other creates vulnerability to hurt from actions by the other person. There are acts of commission, in which one person, for example, can inflict harm in a moment of anger or sullen withdrawal in a conflict. And there are acts of omission, in which the other person, for example, self-preoccupied or under stress, may not listen or may forget a promise.

 **Essential**

The compromise that comes with any marriage is a mix of payoffs that yield personal satisfaction, costs that limit personal freedom, and risks that can cause personal hurt. The goal in a working marriage is to maximize the payoffs, moderate the costs, and minimize the risks.

Managing the Mix

To stay happily married, a couple needs to manage this mix so that most of the time, for both partners, the payoffs outweigh the necessary costs and occasional risks. The importance of keeping the exchange of payoffs in marriage alive and well cannot be overstated. While commitment of love may be unconditional, caring is not. When the giving and getting of payoffs diminishes, feelings of active caring diminish too. The exchange of payoffs is what makes the marriage feel worthwhile.

The importance of sharing the costs of responsibility in marriage also cannot be overstated. Responsibility in marriage is the willing sacrifice of some personal freedom for the sake of each other's well-being and for the good of the relationship, and it must be shared. Refusal by one partner to take equal responsibility results in the other's doing too much and fosters resentment at the noncontributing partner on that account. The costs of responsibility constitute a lot of the work that supports a working marriage.

Safety within marriage is also important—the risk of emotional injury is greatest in a relationship as close as a marriage. The person you love the most can hurt you the worst because that person matters so much and knows you so well. In conducting marriage, as in practicing medicine, the first rule is "do no harm." The risks of hurt in marriage are ever present but can be moderated by active consideration. It is impossible to avoid all hurt totally, but hurting one another should be accidental, not intentional.

So in marriage, every couple is left with this compromise, this mix of payoffs, risks, and costs. The mix is not perfect, but it is the best a committed, caring relationship has to offer. "I don't have everything I want, you don't have everything you want, but we each have enough of what we want in this relationship to sustain our love." This is one key to happiness in marriage: some (not all) of what each wants is sufficient for both to feel content.

Alert!

Divorced partners must commit to "remarry" as parents for the sake of their common interest in the children—so important information can be shared, so major decisions can be deliberated, so visitation arrangements can be made. Still "married" in this sense, they must learn to manage the mix of payoffs, costs, and risks with each other in their divorced relationship to keep it working well. As before, a compromise will be the best that they can achieve.

How Marriage Can Fall Apart

To the degree that the compromise of marriage is not well kept, the relationship can deteriorate across four levels of increasing unhappiness. As unhappiness proceeds from one level to the next, one or both partners carry issues of discontent that accumulate as conditions worsen. The level of unhappiness that ends a marriage is the level of unhappiness that begins divorce.

Unwillingness to Communicate or Compromise

The goal in marriage is to keep the mix working as well as possible for both parties, which means maximizing the payoffs, moderating the costs, and minimizing the risks.

To achieve this goal, each partner must continually monitor the mix for himself or herself.

 **Fact**

Communication is key. If a couple ends their marriage because they can't or won't reasonably discuss differences, then that is how they begin divorce. If the divorce is to become a working one, it must enable parents to communicate better than they did before, particularly when inevitable disagreements over children, now resident in two separate households, arise.

When the mix starts not working well enough or is working badly for one partner, level-one unhappiness in marriage begins. Now he or she must speak up to renegotiate a more satisfactory mix of payoffs, costs, or risks. If the mix is currently working well for one party but not for the other, then the other must be willing to open up discussion and enter into that negotiation. Maybe one partner prefers more time together or apart, maybe parental duties need to be reallocated, perhaps one partner needs to choose different language during a disagreement to make it feel safe.

Relationships are flexible arrangements structured by choices each partner makes, and by agreements that they both support. Because life itself is ever changing, the mix is ever changing too. As personal growth alters each partner, the old mix may become unsatisfactory. As circumstances change—a new job, a move, an illness, having a child—the mix of payoffs, costs, and risks also changes.

When one or both partners refuse to discuss how the mix of payoffs, costs, and risks in the relationship is working, then necessary compromises to keep up with change cannot be made, and matters go from bad to worse. Or, when marriage is built on one party's self-serving terms, that party may insist that there be no basic compromise—"I want all the payoffs, I refuse to incur any costs, and I will not be exposed to any risks." Now a one-way marriage is in the making. Such terms do not a happy marriage make, at least not for the party getting fewer payoffs, bearing most of the costs, and suffering major risks from hurt.

The Bad Bargain

When the mix becomes unsatisfactory for one partner, but the dissatisfied party decides not to speak up, then level-two unhappiness begins. Perhaps the dissatisfied partner doesn't like disagreement, doesn't want to cause a problem, or feels foolish or selfish expressing discontent with the way things are. Or perhaps, she simply feels that if nothing is said, the problem will right itself. In either case, it causes delay, and the passage of time causes the problem to feel worse. Now the discontented partner has allowed unspoken dissatisfaction to build up into frustration and resentment.

Essential

Confrontation is key. If the couple ends their marriage with a habit of first avoiding and then resenting what is going wrong, that is how they begin divorce, which, if it is to become a working one, must enable parents to keep discussion current regarding inevitable child-related difficulties that arise.

Impelled by this accumulated emotion, the aggrieved partner now speaks up on level two, but does so with a force of feeling that would have been lacking had this declaration been made on level one in a timely manner. And what the partner has to say amounts to this: "I feel this relationship is a bad bargain. I have given up all this freedom, I have experienced all this hurt, and I am not receiving sufficient rewards to make my sacrifice worthwhile. I don't want to stay married on these terms!"

By letting a bad bargain stand, partners put the marriage in danger of neglect because significant differences are avoided or ignored, and adjustment to unhappiness threatens to become a way of married life. As for peace at any price ("It's not worth arguing about it"), that is usually too high a cost to pay. A good marriage is worth fighting (safely) for.

Chronic Complaints

If the couple elects not to speak up when their feelings of unhappiness are at level one, and if they refuse to contest the buildup on level two and thus begin living with a "bad bargain," then they begin to store up grievances that burden themselves and their relationship on level-three unhappiness. Chronic complaints now come to characterize how each feels about the relationship. These complaints are usually about:

- **Payoffs:** "My wants are not being met; this relationship is not worthwhile."
- **Costs:** "I have given up too much; this relationship is not fair."
- **Risks:** "I keep getting hurt; this relationship is not safe."

The compromise of marriage dictates that you won't always get all the payoffs you desire, you will sometimes have to give up more personal freedom than you like, and you will sometimes endure hurts and hardships from what your partner does and doesn't do.

**Fact**

Constructive change is the key. If the couple ends their marriage with a habit of lapsing into passive complaint without making an effort toward corrective action, that is how they begin divorce, which, if it is to become a working one, must enable parents to turn complaints about child-care practices into cooperative cause for change.

Long-Term Damage

If a couple continues to stay married in level-three unhappiness, resentment, not love, becomes the tie that binds. From here, it is only a matter of time before resignation and defeat drive the couple out of level three into level four.

Now the payoffs that were once so many become too few. Unattended and ignored, expressions of caring are allowed to diminish and disappear, while apathy begins to build: "There's nothing positive for me in this relationship." At this point, one or both parties have burned out—the marriage feels bankrupt of caring.

As payoffs disappear, each partner grows resentful of the costs, resentful at sacrificing personal freedom while receiving little positive return. They feel angry and express it strongly: "It's not right! I do too much and I get too little back." Now, in addition to burning out, they are burned up—enraged by the unfairness of the relationship.

 **Fact**

Correction is the key. If the couple ended their marriage feeling mistreated by each other, that is how they begin divorce, which, if it is to become a working one, must enable partners to correct old patterns of harmful interaction so they can helpfully get along.

Living in a state of abiding resentment, the partners become more insensitive to each other and oversensitive to mistreatment themselves, intolerant of minor risks in their relationship. A small discourtesy, a slight or oversight, becomes amplified by grievance into another major injury. They take offense quickly and hold grudges. Each feels abused and victimized in the relationship: "All I ever get in this relationship is hurt!" Now, in addition to burning out and burning up, they feel beaten down.

Summing Up

In summary, then, how do marriages commonly fail and how does the motivation to divorce develop? For a marriage to deteriorate from the bright promise with which it began in level one to the extreme unhappiness of level four is tragic. How did the marriage come to such a sorry state? The couple did not tend the compromise from the beginning. In level one, when the mix became unsatisfactory, rather than discussing and adjusting the mix through negotiation, they elected to let it go and not speak up. When accumulated tension from delay built up and brought them into level two, rather than contest the bad bargain in an atmosphere of emotional intensity, they avoided conflict, adjusted to a compromise they didn't like, storing up unspoken grievances, leading them to level three. Arriving there, instead of using the complaints each deeply felt to address the wrongs in their relationship, they accepted what they did not like as hopeless. Giving up all power to change, they entered level four, where they experience daily damage from each other, resigning themselves to suffering or at last deciding to get out.

Essential

Marriage is a mixed blessing—this mix the most that any couple can get. The "work" in a working marriage is maintaining a working dialogue about the mix, and making an ongoing effort to adjust the mix in response to personal and circumstantial changes that life continually creates. Compromise, not perfection, is the goal. Divorced parents also have a mixed relationship, with ongoing dialogue and effort required to make it work.

How Divorce Decisions Vary

The four levels of marital unhappiness presented here are oversimplifications. They describe a common process through which simple problems can become more severe as they are allowed to deteriorate with time and lack of adequate attention. There are, of course, an infinite variety of paths to the decision to divorce. However, using these four levels of unhappiness for starters, try to identify the dynamics of your own divorce. By doing so, you can begin to locate the personal and interpersonal issues that need to be addressed for you to turn an unworkable marriage into a working divorce for your own—and your children's—sake.

Unwillingness to Communicate and Compromise

Level-one divorce occurs because one or both partners is unable or unwilling to communicate about what is happening in the relationship and stubbornly refuses to make adjustments and concessions to help the marriage work well for both partners. "We never talked that much about what was going on between us; we weren't brought up that way. And neither of us was willing to make changes to accommodate the other person's needs when they conflicted with our own. We were each too selfish for our own good and for the good of the marriage. We each put ourselves first. The less we did for each other, the less loving and loved we felt. We knew things weren't going smoothly, but one reason we didn't talk about it was that we didn't like confrontation, and we hoped if we ignored them long enough, our disagreements would go away. Of course, they just got worse. Finally, divorce just seemed like the easiest way out—getting out of our troubles by getting out of the marriage, instead of working out the differences between us."

Common challenges for couples recovering from a level-one divorce are learning how to speak up about what is happening in their divorced relationship and negotiating differences so they can communicate and compromise with each other as parents for the sake of their children.

The Bad Bargain

Level-two divorce occurs because one or both partners feels he has given up too much for the sake of the marriage and is not getting enough positive return, or one partner feels he or she is living entirely on the other person's terms and refuses to do so any longer. At this point, one or both parties may passively leave the marriage by withdrawing communication and cooperation, even by investing primary caring somewhere else—in a job (putting in longer hours), in an outside recreation (getting away and staying away), or in another relationship (a flirtation or affair).

Essential

Common challenges for couples recovering from a level-two divorce are making peace with feelings of resentment over undue self-sacrifice for the marriage, or recovering from feelings of abandonment, rejection, or betrayal in response to extramarital actions the other partner took.

"We each felt the other person wasn't taking a fair share of responsibility or appreciating the responsibility the other took. It felt like one of us was getting to do all the play and the other having to do all the work. Finally we each went on strike in order to change the bad deal we each felt we were getting, demanding that before either one of us was going to give an inch to each other, we were going to get something from the other first. That's when we each got more interested in pursuing happiness meant for the marriage, outside of marriage. Divorce seemed like the best way to get out of a marriage that had become intolerably unfair."

Chronic Complaints

Level-three divorce occurs because problems are grudgingly accepted as unchangeable. The couple uses complaints to show how hopeless and helpless their plight is and how all problems are the other partner's fault. They use blame as evidence that there's too much wrong to make things right, there's nothing to be done, there's no point in even trying. Both agree on the futility of effort and in giving up on change.

"All the positives had gone out of our relationship. Putting up with each other was the best we could do. We had become married in mutual dislike and resignation. We each felt the other person wouldn't get any better to live with, but we kept complaining anyhow. And although we said complaints from each other didn't hurt, that wasn't true. They just made things worse and worse. We became wed to the bad between us and acted like that was okay. Finally, although we both wanted divorce, we each blamed it on each other."

 **Fact**

Common challenges for couples recovering from a level-three divorce include ceasing to complain about and criticize their ex-spouse now that they are no longer married, particularly not doing so to the children, who become torn between feeling sorry for the complaining parent and loyally defending the parent complained against.

Long-Term Damage

Level-four divorce occurs because treatment conditions in the relationship have become too harsh to bear. With no identifiable rewards in the relationship, the marriage has become bankrupt of caring. With intolerable responsibilities, anger, even rage, is a constant companion. With continuing hurt from how the other person acts, each partner comes to feel abused, and if the abuse is dangerous, can come to live in fear.

"It got extremely painful toward the end. There was nothing to look forward to except time apart and relief from each other's company. Absence from each other was the only break from hurt we had. Most of the damage we did came from how we fought our differences out, with no restraint for safety, using each conflict to repeat the awful things we felt, with no apologies after. Just more incentive for doing further harm. The relationship had become destructive. We had become enemies in marriage, so we divorced to end the damages."

Essential

> Common challenges for couples recovering from a level-four divorce are letting grievance from past mistreatment go, ceasing to engage in intentionally hurtful ways with one another, and avoiding the temptation of continuing to love hating each other more than they love their children, who are victimized by this ongoing animosity.

Premature Divorce

Somewhere along the four-level continuum of divorce specified above, you and your ex-spouse ended your marriage. In general, the further down the continuum you divorced, the more work will be required to create a working divorce for the sake of the children. Parents coming out of a level-one divorce may have to learn to communicate and compromise as they could not when married, but they don't have to contend with, and reconcile, the embittered feelings and ongoing hostility that often accompany a level-four divorce.

No matter what the level of divorce, shutting the door and not looking back on this painful personal history is not a good strategy for ex-partners to follow because they ignore important understanding and don't take appropriate responsibility, which can result in a premature divorce.

Self-Understanding and Personal Responsibility

It is premature to divorce without first identifying and claiming one's share of responsibility for the breakup of the marriage. Each partner should be willing to ask and able to answer this question: "What contributions did I make to the unhappiness we came to create?"

Unless each person can honestly make this assessment, he or she is likely to carry unacknowledged self-defeating or destructive behaviors into the post-marriage relationship with the ex-spouse, into subsequent caring relationships, into another marriage, and even with the children. For example, a spouse whose habit of not listening when her mind is made up (because she's usually sure she's right) was never willing to entertain differences of opinion with her partner, and this incapacity to talk about and resolve disagreements was one factor that led to divorce. Unless she identifies, owns, and corrects this behavior, her refusal to listen and discuss differences when in conflict will continue to trouble future caring relationships, the relationship with her ex-spouse, and the relationship with her children, particularly when their adolescence and the time for more conflict arrive.

Alert!

Divorce is always diagnostic. It illuminates how two people functioned and malfunctioned together in marriage, how the worst in them may have brought out the worst in each other. Ex-partners who refuse to take their share of responsibility and identify their own shortcomings in an unhappy marriage are likely to repeat the same mistakes in subsequent relationships.

To inventory contributions to divorce, a partner can ask himself:

- What payoffs did my partner need that I neglected to give? ("I took her efforts for granted and never expressed much appreciation.")
- What costs did I refuse to bear myself but expected her to pay? ("Even though we both had full-time jobs, I expected her to take care of the housekeeping and mostly raise the kids.")
- What risks of being hurt by me did I allow my partner to run? ("I criticized her for being so busy at home she never took the time to be romantic with me.")

Realizing he may have been self-centered at the expense of the relationship, he may decide to correct those behaviors by becoming more othersensitive as he builds a more equitable parenting partnership with his ex-spouse and enters into other significant relationships himself.

What's the Story of Your Divorce?

There is an exercise a divorced parent can do to help his or her recovery. Take some time to write "The Story of My Divorce." Start with Chapter 1, "Getting Married"; end with the last chapter, "The Decision to Divorce"; and write as many chapters in between that describe significant events, changes, and problems that led to the final breakup. In each chapter have two sections. First describe what your partner did or didn't do to harm the marriage (mistreatment he or she may have given, for example); then write what you did or didn't do to harm the marriage (mistreatment you may have accepted, for example). Because every marriage is the creation of two people, at each downward step of the way, claim your share of responsibility. By owning up to your part, you are in the best position to never play that part again—in your subsequent relationship with your ex-spouse or with anyone else. Totally blame the other person and you victimize yourself; take your share of responsibility and you empower yourself.

Constructing a Working Divorce

Since both adults share responsibility for the continued welfare of their children, divorce only ends their former relationship as partners, but not their future relationship as parents.

To continue to fulfill this joint commitment, they must "remarry" as parents who still share a common interest in their children, keeping that commitment foremost and subordinating personal differences in their relationship. "We saw things differently in marriage, and those differences have only grown since the divorce. We're not in the business of criticizing or changing each other's values. But we are in the business of translating our respective values into what we each want, and then negotiating those wants so we can reach a joint decision for the sake of the kids."

Components of a Working Divorce

Like a working marriage, a working divorce is a compromise between payoffs, costs, and risks. In the area of payoffs, ex-partners can let each other know what they are doing that has parenting value for the children, and that they want the children to have an ongoing and affirming relationship with the other parent. In the area of costs, ex-partners can try and be flexible with each other about child-care and visitation arrangements, and be willing to make changes to accommodate each other's changing needs when unexpected complications and conflicts arise. In the area of risks, ex-partners can suppress frustrations and irritations with who and how each other is, talking these tensions out with a supportive adult family member or friend (not with the children). When the compromise is not working, ex-partners can confront what needs to be discussed in a reasonable manner, sticking to specifics about what is wanted, and being willing to negotiate to reach a decision both can support.

Divorced parents need to "remarry" around their shared commitment to the children's welfare and support by creating a workable relationship for those children's sake. Just because ex-spouses no longer have a loving reationship does not mean they cannot now create an amicable one. They can, and many do.

CHAPTER 2

Divorce Is Family Change

E ven if parents have been able to achieve a working divorce, that accomplishment reduces, but does not eliminate, pressures on the children, who are still subject to the taxing demands created by a major family change. So it is helpful if parents understand something about the psychology of change. This chapter and the next provide parents with different ways to consider the change demands created by divorce so they can be sensitive to challenges their children face, and can make choices that help ease the children's hard adjustment.

The Nature of Change

Change, of course, is the law of all living things. It is the process that takes us from an old to a new reality, relationship, condition, or definition. Change revolutionizes people's lives, alters significant terms on which they have been used to living, and opens up their future to some uncertainty. Change raises a lot of questions. What is going to happen now? Will it be better, worse, or some mixture of both? To help your children through change created by divorce, try to answer their questions as honestly and specifically as you can.

Change Is a Mixed Blessing

Even those life changes that we choose to bring into our lives—like getting married, having children, getting a

new job—yield a mix of positive and negative outcomes. For example, consider your decision to divorce and become a single parent. You have gained some new freedoms of personal and social choice you did not have before, but you have given up some old marital support that you depended on.

Change Creates Conflict

A change like divorce usually creates more conflict between single parent and children and among the children themselves. The reason for this conflict is because change is selective, unfair, and divisive.

Divorce is selective. What feels like a positive loss for the parents (they wanted out of an unhappy marriage) feels like a negative loss for the children (they wanted their parents to stay together at home).

Divorce is unfair. It usually imposes the burden of unhappiness on family members in an unequal fashion. A younger child may be devastated by the loss of the family, which made up most of her social world, whereas the older teenager has already built an independent social base that remains unaffected by divorce.

Divorce is divisive. One or both parents usually decide to divorce because he or she has more to gain from this painful decision, whereas children usually have more to lose. Thus while a parent may look ahead with hope for a happier new life, a child may dread the future and miss the past. So when it comes to divorce, it can be hard for them both to get on the same emotional page. "Divorce is for the best," explains the parent. "No, it's not!" objects the child.

Change Is a Compromise

What parents and children discover is that a change like divorce is a compromise, a kind of broken promise—partly kept and partly not. It usually does not turn out as well as parents may have hoped or as badly as their children may have feared. The reason for this compromise is that divorce simply substitutes one set of problems and payoffs for another, the new set hopefully preferable to the old. Freedom from an unsatisfying marriage is replaced by the loneliness of going it alone. The single parent does get more relief from the old married state, but also gets more pressures of family responsibility than he or she had before.

Change Is More Same Than Different

Although the single parent may want to create a "new life," that life is actually more similar to, than different from, how it was before divorce. She has the same job, she has the same children, she is the same person, and she is still partnered with her ex-husband when it comes to parenting. Divorce changes a lot, but a lot more still stays the same, a fact that children need to be told. So to the distraught child who is frightened by the prospect that "divorce will make everything different," you can honestly reply, "Not so. You still have the same parents. You will still be loved as much by us as before. You and we will still be the same people. You will still live in the same community. You will still go to the same school. Even living in separate households, most of the old rules and routines will remain the same even though living arrangements have changed."

Question?

How can I quell my child's fears that divorce "will make everything different"?
Help the child understand how much of life will remain unaltered. Identify the continuity of life that the child can still count on by brainstorming together a list of what will continue to be the same.

The Challenge of Change: Managing Transition

Confusing as change can feel, particularly the change of parental divorce for children, it is a lawful process. A sequence of adjustment demands is created for children by divorce: they must transition from the old reality (the dual-parent family) to the new reality (the dual-household family). The job of parents is to be aware of this sequence so they can help children move step by awkward step from the loss of married family life to acceptance of, and finally adjustment to, divorced family life.

Full adjustment to parental divorce is not an overnight transformation for children. In most cases, parents should allow children up to a couple of years to progress through two stages of transition:

- Through the early adjustments of letting go of the beloved old reality that has been lost, and
- Through the later adjustments of moving on to accept the challenging new reality that has been created.

Fact

A child's active and passive resistance to the demands created by parental divorce (through refusal, argument, or delay) is normal and functional. The child is defending against an unwanted family change to protect the way things were; to buy time to adjust; to express opposition; or to slow down, moderate, or defeat some demands of change.

Letting go is the first half of transition. Moving on is the second half of transition. In each half, the strategies for helpful parenting will be somewhat different. In the first half of transition, parents should be emotionally supportive of the child's response to loss, particularly to the child's pain over what is missed. "Talk to me about how hard all these changes feel." Listening and comforting are very important. In the second half, parents should be gently but firmly insistent that adjustment to the new family reality must be made, gradually wearing down the child's resistance. "I know you don't like going back and forth between separate homes, but that is how things are now going to be, and you are going to have to get used to this new living arrangement." Clarifying new conditions and expecting accommodation are very important.

Letting Go

The first part of transition is the letting-go stage, including denial, holding on, and mourning. These early adjustments to divorce are the most painful ones because children must begin letting go of the way things used to be and what had been so familiar—parents and children all sharing a single household run by parents who lovingly get along, an arrangement that is now forever lost. The nuclear family is broken apart by divorce. Parents may manage to be cordial with each other, but they are no longer lovingly attached. All this takes some painful getting used to.

Denial

It is to avoid pain that children resist accepting the new reality of divorce. Rather than admitting right away that divorce is permanent, a child may resort to denial to protect himself from acknowledging the loss. So the eight-year-old insists, "I know my parents will get back together. They're just divorcing for a little while." And filled with parental reunion fantasies, fueled by hope every time he hears them talk on the phone and sees them meet together, he refuses to believe divorce is here to stay. He may tell his friends his parents are still married. He may even stage crises of getting hurt or getting sick to cause both parents to come and attend him together, believing he has the power to cause them to remarry out of concern for him. Denial keeps the fear and pain at bay.

Most single parents are familiar with denial of their own when, perhaps late one night and all alone, the shock of recognition breaks through the wall of hope and pretense that kept the reality of divorce at an emotional distance. "Oh no! We really are going to divorce! What am I going to do now?" And in the grip of future uncertainty and sense of past loss, the single parent emotionally confronts how this change is going to change his or her present life. "Now I will be a single, part-time parent and the children will no longer have only one home!"

The purpose of denial is to avoid what is painful. The decision to react immediately or delay emotionally responding is up to every child. Some want to deal with the pain of divorce right away and "fall apart" as soon as they hear that parents are going to separate from each other. Falling apart opens them up to let the loss in and the sorrow out. Others may act like they are unaffected emotionally by this family change at the time, and only later begin to let in and talk their feelings out. Assuming that a child in emotional denial is not acting out pent-up emotion in self-defeating or self-destructive ways (angrily refusing to do schoolwork or scratching himself to create pain to manage pain, for example), it is usually best to let the child process the divorce at his or her own individual emotional pace.

 **Fact**

Young children can hold on to fantasies of their parents' reuniting for several years, and parents who still create a joint presence for family gatherings and holidays and birthdays can end up encouraging this denial. Parental separation at such significant events signals that divorce is here to stay. It is no mercy to the child to support false hope for a parental reunion.

It also helps to understand that among your children, there will be variation in how deeply affected they are. The nine-year-old may take it harder than the one-year-old, who is too young to appreciate divorce's loss, or the nineteen-year-old, who is too engaged with creating a life apart to dwell on what is lost when parents no longer live together. The self-preoccupied child may take it less hard than the child for whom family is what matters most. The child whose same-sex parent moves out of the home may take it harder than the child for whom the same-sex parent remains. All childhood losses from divorce are not created equal.

Holding On

Once no longer in denial, the child may still hold on to the sense of family he or she knew, like the seven-year-old who continued to set the supper table with a place for her father even though it had been almost a year since he moved out. Instead of letting go, she acts like she did when he was still resident in the family. And yet, pointless as this act may seem to her mother, the girl is making the loss more bearable for herself by engaging in this "holding on" ritual each night, making gradual adjustment to her loss more bearable. Holding on can help letting go hurt less.

Essential

Don't be impatient when your child takes a long time grieving over the divorce. He or she needs time to feel it through and talk it out in order to accept a change he or she does not like, did not want, but cannot stop. The goal of grieving is to gain emotional acceptance of a painful loss.

Mourning

At last, having admitted the loss and not denied it, and having let go of the loss and not held on, a child is free to mourn the loss. Crying at night in bed as her mother comforts, she talks over and over about how much she misses the way things used to be, about how much she misses the daily presence of her father. After a month of these nightly expressions of sorrow, her mother wonders why the girl can't stop. When will the child mourn enough? The answer is, she will circle through the loss many times, each time gaining a little more emotional acceptance than she had before, ceasing to mourn only when she has mourned enough to accept the loss and let it go. The goal of grieving is to gain emotional acceptance of painful loss.

Moving On

The "moving on" adjustments are refusal, holding back, and accommodation. This second phase of transition requires the child to accept family life on different terms than he or she has known before. Because these terms are unwanted, a child may resist what's new to reduce the rate and nature of this change. He or she may "forget" or put off new chores assigned by the single parent who needs more assistance from children now that he or she is parenting alone. "With one less adult in the family, I have more to do, and you are going to have to give more household help now than you did before."

Refusal

By resistance, the child communicates "I'm not willing to move on" and seeks to slow down new demands to suit his or her tolerance for change. This refusal of some of the new reality created by divorce begins the second half of transition, as the child buys time until he or she feels ready to begin reaching out, relating, and rebuilding a life that to some degree feels like it has been broken.

So a single parent who has had to move to less expensive quarters after divorce, has to enroll the children in new schools, which her twelve-year-old refuses to go to. "I'll go to my old school, not this new one!" Attending a different school feels like a concession—moving on with divorce by going along with one of the changes this change has created. Refusing is like going on strike. So, for the first month, the single parent does patient morning battle with her son to get him up and ready and grudgingly off to school, until he finally relents and goes without a fight. Refusal to adjust to the new reality is both an expression of opposition and a stubborn effort to defeat unwanted change.

Holding Back

Having gradually, and sometimes grudgingly, accepted the new reality of living with a single parent in separate homes, the child may still hold back from fully committing to this new arrangement. So the twelve-year-old who no longer refuses to go to school, does refuse to make his former academic effort, doing only the minimum to get by instead of achieving highly. "You can make me go to school, but you can't make me work as hard!" Holding back his achievement is like holding back his commitment. Holding back is both a stubborn act of loyalty to what was lost, and an act of self-protection, to prevent getting hurt so badly again.

Accommodation

At last, having ceased to hold back, children begin to agree to live on life's altered terms. They start fully engaging with the new reality. They begin to accommodate. If they have had to move because of divorce, they start to explore their new surroundings and to make new friends. Now they begin to accommodate to the conditions of divorce, and to exploit new opportunities that change has created. Visiting with a noncustodial parent at first was a painful reminder of the daily family presence that has been lost. Now it becomes an opportunity to have fun with and attention from that parent in ways the child may not have had before. Accommodation is a matter of letting go of the old enough to advantageously engage with the new.

 **Fact**

Because divorce is a process of taking children through a major parental change, parents must not become so preoccupied with serving their own concerns that they neglect understanding and attending to the emotional and adjustment needs of their children. Most divorcing parents are insensitive to all the changes they are taking children through, and all the pain those changes cause.

CHAPTER 3

Clarifying the Demands of Change

Sometimes a parent will get impatient with a child's slow adjustment to divorce and single-parent household life. "It's been six months since the divorce and you're still acting like it was yesterday, moaning about how unhappy you are, acting angry, and dragging your feet when I need your help. It's time you got with the program, and I mean now!" With a full plate of new responsibilities, the parent's frustrations are understandable, but the parent really needs to attend to the message in the child's behavior: adjustment to divorce is still a struggle. The child doesn't need parental frustration. The child needs parental help—perhaps with some stage of transition, perhaps with one of the losses change creates. Or perhaps with coping with another set of problems associated with change: confusion from the multiplicity of change demands.

Divorce Is Not a Single Change

Divorce is not a single, simple change. Divorce is a compound change because it encompasses many changes under a single heading, and it sets in motion a host of subsequent life changes that continue to alter the child's life.

Many Changes in One

To young children, notification of parental divorce itself can mean many things.

- "My parents don't love each other anymore."
- "My parents aren't going to live together anymore."
- "I'm going to see each parent less than before."
- "We won't be doing things as a family anymore."
- "Whatever happens now, life won't be the same."

Essential

Preoccupied by their own concerns, divorcing parents can discount the power of divorce for their children, and then wonder why some children have such a difficult time adjusting to this simple family change. Divorce is *not* a simple change, because it is not a single change. It is a compound change that takes a lot of getting used to.

For one single child, all the above meanings can hold true. The child in this example is simultaneously trying to come to terms with loss of love between parents, the separation of parents into different homes, less frequent contact with both parents, the end of whole-family activities, and uncertainty about what happens next.

A Host of Other Changes

Divorce is a good example of how one change can create many others. For example, when parents divorce, the one with primary custody of the children is now faced with two immediate changes—less money to live on and more parenting responsibility for children and household decisions that were previously shared. Under duress from both sources, immediate changes follow: the major parent becomes busier and less available to the children, and becomes more tired from all there is to do. In response to these changes, children create changes of their own—complaining about now having to do without what they formerly took for granted, and clinging more to the remaining parent, whose undivided attention is now harder to get. In response to increasing demands from children, the parent may become irritable and stressed from feeling called upon to exceed the current maximum effort, and begins neglecting and sacrificing personal well-being in the process. Now another round of change occurs. As the single parent exhibits more signs of stress from self-neglect, children become more stressed and demanding in response. And on and on the changes go. Change begets more change in response before things settle down into a stable new routine.

Alert!

This is the parenting challenge of taking children through divorce: to be sensitive to the psychology of change so you can help them come to terms of emotional acceptance of, and make adjustments to, ongoing changes created by divorce. For the majority of divorced parents, and their children, these changes continue all the way into remarriage and the complexity and conflicts of step relationships.

A Great Divide

Parental divorce is a watershed in the lives of children. Younger children remember it less, but older children remember it well. Ask older children with an established sense of personal history (when divorce occurred after age five or six) to itemize the differences in family and personal life before and after divorce, and they can list many changes.

Before divorce:	After divorce:
We spent family time together.	We have two different family times.
We had one set of family rules.	We have two sets of family rules.
I could have both parents at home.	When I'm with one parent, I miss the other.
My parents were like I'd always known.	My parents changed when they lived apart.
I heard my parents argue a lot.	I don't hear my parents argue anymore.

Continue this comparison with your children and it can illuminate for you some major differences created by divorce in their lives that may have been invisible to you.

Recognizing Two Kinds of Change

Without awareness there is no understanding, and without understanding, functional choice is hard to make. So, when it comes to helping children cope with change, they must first be taught awareness: how to identify when change occurs. Then they can be taught how to cope with two kinds of demands—from discontinuous and continuous change.

Alert!

Keep track of the number of changes that divorce is demanding of your child, moderating the rate of change where you can to keep it from overwhelming the child—having to get used to too much, too fast. For many children of divorce, it's not any one particular change that causes most of the stress, but the amount of change to which the child is supposed to immediately adapt.

Discontinuous Change

The most abrupt kind of change is discontinuous change—when something either stops happening in the child's life (cessation) that was ongoing before, or when something starts happening in the child's life (initiation) that didn't happen before. Discontinuous life change requires the most energy to adjust to. Stopping old family rituals because of divorce creates loss and requires painful letting go that is not quick to accomplish. "I know it's a small thing, but I miss our Sunday restaurant dinners as a family because they made everyone feels so close." The energy required by cessation, of stopping something familiar, is having to give up a valued experience and reluctantly letting it go.

Starting new family patterns because of divorce creates demands for beginning the different and unfamiliar, and this takes learning over many repetitions to comfortably accomplish. "Going back and forth between two homes, living in two places, not one, takes a lot of getting used to." The energy required by beginning, of starting up what was not done or known before, can be enormous. Like a rocket during liftoff, it takes a disproportionate amount of energy just to get the new activity off the ground and up and running.

Continuous Change

Continuous changes are less energy expensive and abrupt than discontinuous changes, but they are taxing nonetheless. Subtle in nature, they either increase or decrease the incidence of what has been happening by adding to an existing amount or by cutting back. Instead of stop and start demands, people must deal with the demands of more and less.

The problem with continuous changes is their subtle cumulative power. They can be hard to track. It can take a while to identify how one is now doing more or doing with less than one wanted, but at the point of recognition the awareness can feel dramatic indeed. A lot of continuous changes come in "under the radar" of our immediate awareness, catching our notice only after a while, when the increase or decrease is suddenly strongly felt. "I didn't realize as a single parent I had been spending so much more!" "I'm finding it really hard to make do with less!" The power of discontinuous changes is that they are so dramatic and easy to identify, whereas the power of continuous changes is that they often are not, building surreptitiously until their impact surprises and is suddenly felt.

 **Fact**

Because of social inequities that cause men in general to have more earning power than women, when the custodial single parent is a mother, there is often a dramatic decrease in family income. Single-parent families headed by women usually encounter greater economic pressure than single-parent families headed by men.

Some continuous changes, however, may be picked up on right away. So the child finds living with a single parent "unfair" because on top of dislocation caused by the divorce, the child is now given more household responsibilities than was the case before. "Why should I have to do more work just because now you have more to do?" Then there can be objection to the decrease in contact with the noncustodial parent. "Now I get to see my dad even less than ever!" It is often easier for parents to honor discontinuous changes from divorce because they are so apparent and to ignore continuous changes because they are less disruptive. However, it takes a lot of effort to cope with increases and decreases, and parents need to credit the energy required by those efforts as well.

 *Question?*

When can a child tell that change is happening in his or her life?
When any of four kinds of events occur: some event stops happening that was ongoing before (cessation), some event starts happening that didn't happen before (initiation), the frequency of some event decreases (reduction), the frequency of some event increases (addition).

The greatest stress most children experience in the immediate wake of parental divorce is from feeling overwhelmed by excessive change. And the same is often true for parents. For those parents divorcing out of the "traditional marriage" (rare these days)—wife at home managing children and household care, husband at work devoting full attention to his job and financially supporting family—divorce can create somewhat different change demands.

For the at-home mother, taking custodial responsibility for the children may represent a continuous change (assuming more child-care responsibility), while going to work or back to work as a single parent creates discontinuous change demands (starting a new job). For the at-work father, maintaining a job demands continuous change (putting in fewer hours for the sake of family), while assuming custodial responsibility as a single parent represents a discontinuous change (setting up and running a household). So, in this scenario, stress for the custodial mother will be starting a job in addition to providing familiar child care, while stress for the father will be starting to be a full-time parent in addition to holding a familiar job. When divorce occurs, no one in the family gets off stress-free.

Specifying Changes with Your Child

Because multiple changes of the kind created by divorce can be so confusing, it can be hard for children to get a handle on just what is going on. "I feel overwhelmed but I don't know exactly why or what to do." The job of the parent is to help clarify this confusion by specifying and keeping track of the changes that occur.

Alert!

In every divorce, there are secondary divorces—extended family on both sides are divorced by proxy (although they were never given a vote). These family members may now have less contact with children, depending on proximity and status of relationship with the parents. Don't let divorce take loving extended-family contact from the lives of children who have already suffered loss enough and need all the love and support they can get.

Creating a Checklist of Changes

This tracking can be done by making a checklist of divorce-related changes (behaviors and events) going on in the child's life, helping the child fill it in, and updating it periodically as more changes occur. Using the four kinds of change listed above (two discontinuous and two continuous), a beginning list might look like this.

What is STOPPING in my life?

- *Being able to celebrate holidays all together.*
- *Leaving my old school behind.*
- *Leaving my old friends behind.*
- *Not seeing my other parent every day.*

What is STARTING in my life?

- *Going back and forth between two homes.*
- *Getting used to two different sets of rules.*
- *Having time alone at home after school.*
- *Having to make friends in a new neighborhood.*

What is happening MORE in my life?

- *My parent is busier.*
- *I have more chores to do.*
- *I have to take more responsibility for myself.*
- *My parents are living more differently from each other.*

What is happening LESS in my life?

- *I have less time with each parent.*
- *My parents are less patient with me.*
- *We can't afford to do as much as we used to.*
- *We live in a smaller space.*

Essential

The challenge of divorce for children is learning to deal with an enormous amount of family change that begins when parents choose to separate a marriage. The job of parents is to help this adjustment along by specifying as many of the changes attendant on divorce as possible so that the magnitude of the child's challenge becomes clear, the different kinds of changes are identified and specified, and strategies for coping with these changes are developed.

Using the Checklist of Changes

With so much change happening, it is easy for children of divorce to feel confused and out of control. A checklist of changes can be used in four helpful ways:

- To recognize the number of changes going on: "Just so you know that I know you have a lot going on right now," says the parent, "I want us both to stay mindful of all the changes that are happening in your life right now."
- To identify those changes that the child finds most challenging: "Tell me which of these changes you find hardest," asks the parent, "so I can be sensitive and supportive."
- To develop strategies for dealing with these hard changes: "Let's see if we can think out ways to get used to or get over the most difficult changes, or maybe even make them easier," suggests the parent.
- To appreciate adjustments to change the child has successfully accomplished: "Change is very hard to do, and look at all the changes from divorce you have already learned to deal with," congratulates the parent. "Good for you!"

Helping Children Cope with Pain

Why is divorce so painful for children? The reason is not because of any single sense of loss, but because of the multiple losses change creates. For different children, different losses may be more pronounced. Like a doctor when a patient comes in complaining of some distress, a parent needs to ask his or her child, "Where does it hurt?" You want to help your child localize the pain around whichever loss or losses are most significant so he or she can better work though the suffering going on.

Among the many losses change creates, consider seven, and inventory with your child which of these losses hurts the worst. Each type of loss requires some parental support for the child to cope.

 *Fact*

When parents divorce out of the unhappy marriage they have created, they cause disruption for their children who must each find their own way of understanding and adjusting to this adverse turn of events. In most cases, parental divorce and the family changes that follow cause children to feel worse, not better, at least for a while.

Loss of Understanding

One common loss from change arises when the child moves from a known into an unknown set of family circumstances, as parental marriage is over and divorce has begun. Now the child has a significant loss of understanding. There is an increased need to know about the new family situation, about what will happen now and next, about what in the past is lost forever or still in place, about what the future is going to bring. Fear in the face of ignorance is a natural emotional response. Worry, rumor, and gossip rush in to fill the vacuum of ignorance as worst case scenarios project unhappy outcomes that increase the child's anxiety. "First Daddy left, and soon you will too!" Fear of abandonment and fear of further abandonment are common with divorce.

A parent's job is to help the child bring his or her ignorance into focus by formulating questions, and then to dispel that ignorance with honest answers and the most reliable information the parent has to give.

When a parent has no honest answer to a child's anxious question, admit this ignorance and promise that when that information is available, the child will be told. "I don't know how to phone your father right now, but as soon as I hear where he can be reached in the new city where he has moved, I will immediately let you know."

A deeper loss of understanding than lack of information about changes in circumstance is struggling to comprehend how two adults who once loved each other, who love their child, whom the child loves, could make such a hurtful decision as divorce. This kind of human understanding will take the child years of reflection to sort out.

The inventory question to ask your child is, "What would you like to know about what is happening and going to happen that could help you feel less anxious and more secure?"

Answering questions about routines is very important because established routines create a sense of predictable family life. "Will you still read me to sleep at night?" "When will I get to visit my dad (or mom)?" "How am I going to get to my new school?" "How are we going to do Christmas this year?" Answers can help restore security.

Loss of Valued Connections

Another common loss that arises from change occurs when the child has to give up valued relationships, activities, and surroundings associated with the old way of family life. Now the child can suffer a significant loss of valued connections. Gone is the unified family. Not every significant friendship or involvement can always be carried into the new situation. When moves occur, old surroundings are left behind. Old connections to parents are also lost as the custodial parent becomes busier and less available, and the noncustodial parent becomes more physically separated and around less. Grief and loneliness are natural responses to this kind of loss. Now the child can miss old family unity, old playmates and classmates, old connections to parents, and can feel distanced from people and places he or she cared so much about. When parents divorce, a journey through loneliness begins for many children. Dislocation and disconnection are common experiences that accompany divorce.

A parent's job is to help the child retain contact with old friends, activities, and places to the degree that this is possible, and to help forge new connections that matter where the family is living now.

Maintaining adequate contact with the busier parent at home and with the parent who moved out or away are critical for keeping a major source of loneliness at bay.

The inventory questions to ask your child are, "What have you lost from before the divorce that you miss the most; can we help any of those losses hurt any less; and can we create new interests, activities, and relationships that could come to matter as much?"

 **Fact**

> For young children, having something old to cling to, like a literal or figurative security blanket, in someplace new can feel reassuring. Also, as parental contact becomes more disrupted by visitation, it often helps for grandparents to become increasingly involved in the child's life so a sense of extended-family continuity is strengthened during this fragile time.

Loss of Power

Another common loss that arises from change is how the child feels at the mercy of a decision beyond his or her control. "I didn't want it and I couldn't stop it!" Now the child feels a significant loss of power. In addition, in consequence of resulting changes, the boy or girl is in some ways less able to get what is wanted after divorce than before. There is often less power of access to both parents. The parent the child lives with is less available, busier with added responsibilities, and the other parent is seen only on visitation. In addition, more limited financial resources for the single parent (most common for the mother) often reduce what that parent can provide and what the child has been used to getting. Anger and feelings of helplessness are natural emotional responses to nonnegotiable losses that the child would not choose and in which he or she had no voice. A child's sense of victimization is a common response to parental divorce.

 ***Essential***

Using the change of divorce to open up some power of decision making for the child that he or she did not have before goes a long way in helping the child regain important sense of control in family life. "I never wanted my parents to divorce, but in some ways I get more choices now."

A parent's job is to find points in the process of adjustment following divorce where the child can have influential choice in order to regain some sense of control. If a move occurs, giving a choice of room or furnishings can feel empowering. If a child can now have a pet that was disallowed before, this can be empowering. If a child can be involved in designing new household routines and assigning responsibilities, this can feel empowering.

The inventory question to ask your child is: "Are there old freedoms and choices you used to have that you miss, and new ones that you might like put in their place?"

Loss of Acceptance

Another common loss that arises from change occurs when going from being the same to becoming different. Now your child is a child of divorce. What difference will this difference make? That depends upon how the child, and how others, treat this change. If either acts rejecting, the child can experience a significant loss of acceptance. Because something "bad" happened to the child, the boy or girl may think he or she is now a "bad" person, particularly if the child feels in any way implicated in the parental decision to divorce. "If I hadn't made them so unhappy with me, they wouldn't have become so unhappy with each other."

If married parents of friends, or teachers at school, now consider the child as "damaged goods," a broken or problem child from a broken home, this rejecting attitude can cost the child both self- and social acceptance. When a teacher now considers the child a potential troublemaker, or a married parent shies away from your child's continuing to play with children of her own, this prejudice can have a damaging effect. Or, if one parent not only initiates divorce of the other but also ceases regular or reliable contact with the child thereafter, then that child can experience rejection. Feeling rejected is a natural emotional response to loss of acceptance. It is common for children to feel "divorced" when parents divorce, less loved by parents than they were before.

 **Essential**

Always make clear to children that they had no role in causing the divorce, that they have no influence to prevent the divorce, and that they have no power to reunite parents after divorce. "The decision to divorce is about us, by us, and for us. None of it is about or up to you."

A parent's job is to help the child not self-reject by taking divorce personally, as a negative statement about his or her self-worth. "The divorce is not about how you are or anything you did, it is about how your parents can't get along and decided to end an unhappy marriage."

The inventory question to ask your child is, "Do you ever feel badly about yourself because of the divorce, and if you ever do, can you tell me when and in what ways?"

Loss of Confidence

Another common loss that arises from change occurs when your child feels less effective in coping with the new situation than the old. Now the child has a significant loss of confidence. Will the child be able to make successful adjustments to divorced family life? Will the child cope and perform as competently after the divorce as he or she did before the divorce? Will the child's skills be adequate to meet this new challenge? Feelings of inadequacy are a natural emotional response in the face of new and untried challenges that divorce has created. It is common for children to doubt their capacity to cope with changes caused by parental divorce.

 **Fact**

Emotional interference from divorce can temporarily reduce effort and concentration on work at school. Then as performance lowers, the child's self-confidence and self-esteem can lower too. So if you start to see an achievement drop in the wake of divorce, make sure you give your child extra supervisory support around getting home-work done, completing projects, and studying for tests.

A parent's job is to encourage the child to put faith in trying, learn-ing new ways of behaving in different life circumstances, pointing out when new adjustments are well made. "Good for you! You came home from school and by yourself, before I got home from work, completed all your homework. That's hard to do, and you never did it before!"

The inventory question to ask your child is: "What changes from divorce do you find most difficult and challenging to meet and that you sometimes doubt that you will be able to meet?"

Loss of Identity

Another common loss that arises from change occurs when sig-nificant self-definition is lost as a function of divorce. An adult's, but also a child's, social identity depends on such identifications as "I am what I do," "I am what I own," "I am where I live," "I am who I know." Divorce can disrupt many of these identity connections. Now the child has a significant loss of identity. Without the absent parent to spend time with, without friends from the old school because of mov-ing, without activities that were given up because of having to live more inexpensively, the child has lost social parts of who or how she was, and for a while feels less than she was. Deprived of old identity supports, confusion is a natural emotional response. To some degree, it is common for children to have to redefine who and how they are after parental divorce. A parent's job is to help the child develop fresh identity supports in a new circumstance, helping initiate new social contacts, helping the child get involved in new activities.

The inventory question to ask your child is, "Because of what you've had to stop doing, where you've had to stop living, or who you've had to stop seeing, are there any ways you feel less than you used to be, and are there things to start doing that would make up for the loss?"

Loss of Meaning

Another common loss, and perhaps the most serious, that arises from change occurs when the child, having lost the intact family, loses some faith in the worth of life itself. "What's the point of going on when I've lost my family? Who can I trust if I can't trust my parents to keep the family together?" Now the child has a significant loss of meaning. How can people as good as his or her parents do such a hurtful and bad thing? Sense of family loss shakes the child's faith in what life is supposed to be about. Despondency in the face of inexplicable and devastating change is a natural emotional response.

Perhaps the most serious loss of meaning suffered by children of divorce is distrust and loss of faith in loving commitment, a consequence of parents' having broken their marriage commitment to each other and to the family. A parent's job is to help the child reestablish belief in what endures in life, restore faith in what matters in life, and reclaim a future to look forward to in life.

The inventory question to ask your child is: "Do you ever feel so sad about the divorce that you wonder what there is in life that matters that you can really count on?"

Helping Children Gain Resilience

Fortunately the change of divorce is not only equivalent to pain. There are also benefits for growth as the child adjusts to living on new and different terms. Change can create the opportunity for your child to grow stronger not just in spite of what occurred, but also because of his or her resilient response to what occurred. There are gifts in most adversities, and this includes divorce. As parents, you want to recognize, value, and support the growth of this resilience. For example, in the words of one child of divorce now grown into adulthood: "My parents' divorce taught me not to panic in change, to roll with the unexpected, to live in the moment, and to make the best of hard times when they happen."

Children who are most resilient in their capacity to recover from parental divorce tend to have certain characteristics. They understand that the other side of loss is freedom and so look for opportunity from adversity. The harder life gets, the stronger they seem to become. They recognize what they can do and don't waste energy trying to change what they cannot. They don't give up trying, because they won't accept defeat. And they maintain a positive outlook to motivate themselves through a negative time.

It is true that initially there was a loss of understanding, but in time, the child gains new knowledge about himself and the family world that has been changed. Now he knows more than he did before. A parent can affirm this growth by saying, "You've learned more about yourself and your parents, and you've learned to find your way around a new neighborhood and a new school. You've learned a lot!"

 **Essential**

> For some resilient children, divorce becomes a door into a better time with each parent. The losses still hurt, but the gain soon outweighs the pain as these children come to better know their parents and feel closer to each than before, as relationships become more intimately defined. "I spend more time with my dad now than before the divorce, and my mom and I talk more than we did."

It is true that initially there was a loss of the familiar, but in time, the child is able to make new and different commitments of comparable value. Now she has created new interests and connections to care about. A parent can affirm this growth by saying, "You've made yourself find new friends to make and new things you like to do, and even some new ways to be with each of your parents."

It is true that initially there was a loss of power, but in time, the child establishes a new sense of control and feels stronger on that account. Now she has created new ways to get her needs met. A parent can affirm this growth by saying, "You make more of your own decisions, take care of yourself more than you used to do, and take more charge of your life."

It is true that initially there was a loss of acceptance, but in time the child develops a tolerance for adversity that at first felt insupportable. Now he is more able to accept the reality of hardship in life than he was before. A parent can affirm this growth by saying, "You've learned bad times can happen to anyone, including you, because that's just how life sometimes is."

It is true that initially there was a loss of confidence, but in time the child affirms a new sense of competence. Now she trusts more in her capacity to cope than before. A parent can affirm this growth by saying, "From dealing with hard times, you've discovered you're stronger than you thought you were."

It is true that initially there was a loss of identity, but in time, the child develops a new sense of clarity about the person he really is. Now he has more sense of himself, independent of old social supports. A parent can affirm this growth by saying, "You've learned that divorce changes a lot of circumstances, but not the person you are."

It is true that initially there was a loss of meaning, but in time, the child develops new faith in her capacity to carry on. Now she knows that great hurt need not destroy her. A parent can affirm this growth by saying, "You've learned that you can go through a really unhappy time and come out stronger on the other side."

CHAPTER 4

The Process of Divorce

I n most cases, hard feelings over intractable differences are what contribute to the decision to divorce. Although separating the marriage removes each partner from the daily abrasion of living with each other, there is often lingering pain that remains to be reconciled. It takes time and effort to heal the hurts of an unhappy history. But when old injuries are finally understood, accepted, and let go, and new lives are satisfactorily established, then there are no ongoing hard feelings within and between parents to make adjustment to divorce more difficult for themselves and the children.

Accepting Divorce

No matter how soon divorced parents are able to let go of their painful history with each other and create a working divorce, their children will still have several years to work through their individual adjustment to this family change. However, to the degree that ex-partners have ongoing difficulty recovering from divorce and working with each other as parents, this will make the children's adjustment only harder to accomplish.

Divorce is a legal, financial, social, and emotional separation of marital sharing, with the emotional part often dragging on the longest. In general, the longer it takes parents to accept and adjust to divorce, the longer it will take their children, because unresolved tensions within and between parents create conditions children must contend with and are unable to emotionally ignore. "Mom and Dad are still so angry at each other that they barely speak. I have to be careful not to talk to one about the other. And I never say anything good because that would sound like I am taking sides. I wish they would just stop all the blaming and get over each other. They say they're divorced, but it sure doesn't feel that way!"

Fact

Hard feelings within and between parents after divorce can slow down a child's adjustment to their divorce by continuing tensions that still marry parents to past unhappiness and stand in the way of the divided family moving freely on.

A Highly Contested Divorce

The divorce settlement, as specified in the decree, clarifies the division of marital sharing and sets forth the subsequent parental obligations. It becomes the legal basis for your relationship with your ex-spouse, but the process through which that settlement is reached can have an ongoing emotional effect. The more adversarial, bitter, and financially costly the court battle, the more hard feelings are likely to contaminate the relationship between ex-partners after divorce, and to retard the building of a comfortable and cooperative parenting partnership for the sake of the children.

Alert!

It does no service to children for parents to contest divorce to the point of creating enmity between angry, unforgiving, even revengeful adults. All this does is create an ongoing emotional crossfire in which children are at constant risk of becoming emotionally wounded.

Mediation

The more highly contested—over property, assets and liabilities, custody, and support—a divorce, the more hard feelings there may be, so try mediation before litigation. Divorce with children is both a separation of sharing and an assumption of responsibility. Better for the ongoing relationship between parents, and so for children, to work this division and assignment out through a collaborative process rather than an adversarial one.

Today it is more common for courts to mandate mediation for this reason—to use mediation to build a base of cooperation that parents can take into their divorced relationship, which will strengthen their capacity for partnership and mutual involvement in the lives of their children. Mediation is a structured dispute or conflict resolution process that allows partners to cooperatively settle differences and reach agreement both parties can support.

Mediated decisions strengthen the divorced relationship because they demonstrate that the couple has resolved hard differences in a mutually acceptable way. And having successfully gone through mediation once, the divorced couple can go back through mediation should divorce disagreements arise in the future (e.g., a new job or a remarriage that would require a custodial parent's moving away). There are mediation services that help couples collaboratively manage divorce. In addition, more and more family-law attorneys now have mediation training and offer that service as part of their practice. Look in your local phone book for "mediation services" or "divorce mediation."

 **Essential**

The recommendation here is simply this: for the sake of yourself, your future relationship with your ex-spouse, and your children, when divorcing, try mediation before litigation. Better to work through differences than to fight them out. Better to be collaborators than adversaries.

Taking Sides

Sometimes, divorce is not just legally contested, but emotionally contested as well. For example, out of anger at the parent who was initiator of the breakup or in sympathy for the parent who was reactor to the breakup, a child will initially feel obliged to ally with one parent against the other in the immediate painful aftermath of the divorce. "My dad was so broken up when she left to be with someone else, I refused to see my mom for over a year!" Of course, the cost of boycotting one parent to support the other is a significant loss—for the child and for the parent whom the child refuses to see.

Alert!

No child of divorce should be expected to take sides between warring parents, or be pressured to do so by siblings or extended family members who believe taking sides is an act of loyalty.

For the boycotted parent, she must not reject back and cut off communication with the child, but instead hold herself in loving readiness for a resumption of the relationship when the child feels ready. The parent must keep initiating invitations for communication and contact to signify that openness constantly exists.

This situation can be complicated when the hurt and angry parent, with whom the child sympathetically allies, treats the child's inclination to want to see the absent parent as a betrayal. "After how badly she treated me, and the family, running off with someone else, how could you bear to see her? If you really loved me and really cared about the family, you'd refuse to see her at all!" This kind of "you're either with me or against me" message demands that the child take the speaker's side or else appear supportive of or complicit in the other parent's hurtful behavior.

This injured parent is doing what no divorcing parent should ever do: he is using divorce between partners to justify a child's "divorcing" the other parent.

As the injured parent recovers from his hurt, he usually recovers his desire for the child to have the benefit of a loving relationship with two parents, not just one. "Just because your mother didn't want to stay married with me in no way meant that she wanted to stop being a present and loving parent with you."

Essential

> Divorcing one's partner, or being divorced by one's partner, should never lead to demanding that children divorce the other parent as well.

Divorce Role and Recovery

There are two kinds of roles in the decision to divorce that can prescribe predictable, short-term, emotional responses in the parents, to which children must first learn to adjust. They are:

- Which partner is primarily the initiator of the divorce and which partner is primarily the reactor
- Which partner is going to be the major or custodial parent and which partner is going to be the more occasional or non-custodial parent.

There are different role combinations possible, each combination with its own set of emotional challenges. What the parent initially goes through emotionally affects what the children have to adjust to when living with that parent during separation and immediately following divorce.

Custodial parents end up with more stress and fatigue from family demands, as a single parent now supporting child-care responsibilities that used to be shared. Children of this parent must get used to a mother or father who often is more impatient and tired than before.

Noncustodial parents end up with more grief from loss and loneliness from disconnection, now no longer enjoying daily contact with the children, often feeling outside of the primary family circle. Children of this parent must get used to a mother or father who is sadder and more insecure than before.

A parent who is the initiator of divorce has to contend with some degree of guilt for seeking personal happiness, or less unhappiness, at the emotional expense of the children. Children of this parent must get used to a mother or father who may sometimes feel defensive about, make compensation for, or even deny the hurt that the decision to divorce has caused.

Alert!

When it comes to adjustment, the divorce initiator has an advantage over everyone else in the family because he or she has had a head start to feel through, think through, desire, and get used to the decision to divorce. So the divorce initiator must be patient with partner and children as they take the adjustment time required to emotionally catch up to the decision the initiator has made.

A parent who is the reactor to divorce has to contend with some degree of rejection and anger because the other partner wanted to end the partnership and leave the marriage. Children of this parent must get used to a mother or father who may need reassurance and express resentment toward the other parent.

The custodial parent who is initiator has a burden of responsibility: "I wanted this." Children of this parent must get used to a mother or father who may be more selfish and controlling from wanting the divorce decision and then wanting primary care of the children as well.

The custodial parent who is reactor has a burden of helplessness and self-pity: "I was left to do it all." Children of this parent must get used to a mother or father who may be prone to complain about the injustice and hardship of his or her role.

The noncustodial parent who is initiator has a burden of regret: "I have abandoned them." Children of this parent must get used to a mother or father who may act sad to see them come and go, being reminded on each occasion of what the decision to divorce has cost. The noncustodial parent who is reactor has a burden of loneliness: "I am left without anyone." Children of this parent must get used to a parent who may be hard to reach, despondent at some times and clinging for attachment at other times.

By locating your role in the divorce—initiator or reactor, custodial or noncustodial, any combination of the two—you can begin to diagnose your emotional state in early recovery, the state in which the children find you and to which they must initially adjust.

The Breakup of a "Good" Marriage

In some ways, the easiest divorces for parents to make and children to understand come from marriages that are hard for both parents to bear. Each partner possesses and expresses sufficient sense of estrangement, incompatibility, or grievance, and both are so convinced of unrecoverable and irreconcilable differences, that the divorce is mutually supported. As for the children, they have seen ample evidence of discord between their parents. So, while they do not want their parents to separate the marriage, at least they understand that there are powerful issues forcing their parents apart.

The "No Data" Divorce

But what happens when the evidence of discord is largely hidden—either in the private, quiet desperation of one partner or in the couple's determination "not to fight" in front of the children to spare them emotional upset.

Shielded by ignorance or by well-intended parental protection, the children's response to the announcement of divorce is honest disbelief. "Why would you want to get divorced? You always acted so happy. We never saw anything wrong! Were you just pretending? Were you lying to us? We don't understand!"

Essential

While it is true that witnessing acute and unremitting parental conflict can be injurious to children, witnessing some degree of conflict between parents can give children some cause to understand divorce should it occur. Don't stage parental fights for your children to see, but don't conceal all evidence of honest discord either. "Sometimes your mother and I have a lot we disagree about."

What the children are given is a "no data" divorce, and they are shocked, as well they should be. They had no preparation for this possibility, and now they question their own perceptions. How could they have missed what must have been there, unless they were deliberately misled? Not only do they distrust their own perceptions; they distrust their parents. Feeling doubly betrayed, they are doubly angry. What else are their parents hiding from them?

Now the children have a lot of catching up to do, and parents must take the time to give them data that was withheld before—not in blame statements, but in objective terms describing disagreements that could not be overcome.

The "No Sense" Divorce

If in addition to having provided no data, the divorce also makes no sense, children can become really confused. In this case, the reason why they never saw any evidence of significant parental discord (disagreements or offenses, irritations or arguments) was because there wasn't any. By mutual admission, both parents would agree they parented well together and the partnership was not hard to bear. It just wasn't personally fulfilling, and each wanted more than the relationship could provide. Estrangement and dissatisfaction more than discord caused the decision to divorce.

So the parents explain how they are still good friends, that they have no deep divisions or hard feelings, that they just grew apart and now want to go their separate ways and maybe someday find a marriage based on love, not just friendly compatibility. In response to this explanation of an "amicable divorce," the children become really confused. "If you still like each other as friends, and nothing really bad happened between you, then you have no reason to divorce! Besides, if you didn't love each other, why did you get married in the first place? Why isn't getting on okay good enough?"

As with the "no data" divorce, the "no sense" divorce requires whatever honest explanation parents can give to help children understand.

Alert!

Do not fight over who is the most important or loved parent. Jealous competition of this kind between parents only feeds hostility between them, invites manipulation by the children, and creates the illusion that one parent can supplant the other. Not true. The father can no more supplant the mother than the mother can supplant the father. Each has something uniquely different to offer, and that is how it will always be (see Chapters 16 and 17). As for custody battles, they usually just tear children up.

What Works in a Working Divorce

Chapter 1 ended with a beginning description of the components of a working divorce. This chapter opens with an amplification of that discussion by specifying adult behaviors that build cooperation between ex-partners and sustain their cooperation as parents.

What Does a Working Divorce Look Like?

Here are six components to consider, or six objectives to work for, if you so choose.

- **Adequate communication.** Keep each other sufficiently informed about what is going on with the children when they are in your care, and deal with any disagreements in a nonevaluative, issue-specific, and cooperative way. "In this instance, I disagree with what you want for the children, this is why, and this is what I think might work better instead. I would like for us to talk and work something out that we can both support."

- **Emotional reconciliation.** Let go of any unrequited feelings of lingering love or hard feelings from past hurts so that both partners are emotionally free to move on, joined only by the common caring they share for their children. "Even at our worst, I believe we each did the best we could, and now it's time to treat each other differently, forgive, let go, and move on."

- **Social cooperation.** Keep parenting agreements so you both feel you can count on each other's commitment to share responsibility for the children's welfare and care, and still be flexible to make changes when unexpected parental or child need arises. "When I give you my word, I will keep it, and I appreciate being able to trust your word too."

- **Continual support.** Create consistency of significant family practices between households where a child has special need or the other parent needs to be backed up on a disciplinary decision with which you agree. "Let's unify parental expectations so our child knows that there is no escaping doing homework in whichever home he's at."

- **Personal respect.** Do not expect or demand that the ex-spouse's household be run in a precisely like fashion, with values, routines, and rules similar to your own. Unless child safety is at issue, accept diversity between the two households as reflecting honorable (and usually increasing) lifestyle differences between the two parents. "The longer we live apart, the more differently we live, and that's okay."

- **Mutual commitment.** Subordinate any personal dislikes or disagreements between you to working together for the larger good—the welfare of the children. "Divorced as marriage partners, we are still married as parents wanting to do what's best for the children."

Why work toward these objectives? For the sake of your children.

What Does a Nonworking Divorce Look Like?

Just consider what it is like for children who live between parents who have a nonworking divorce, as some parents unhappily do.

When it comes to communication, they either won't speak at all (sending all messages to each other through the child), won't speak in a civil manner when they do communicate, or charge the conversation with old accusations from past grievances to feed fresh arguments between them.

When it comes to emotional reconciliation, they hold on to past hurts and hard feelings that they will neither forgive nor let go, even acting to get back at each other for past injuries received.

When it comes to cooperation, rather than take each other into consideration when making arrangements, they make things more difficult by not honoring commitments and insisting on inconvenient arrangements, perhaps not sharing important information about the children and not sending belongings that should accompany children on visitation.

When it comes to support, they continually fault and undercut each other's parental stands and regimens with the children, and one parent may even delay child support payments to string the other parent out.

When it comes to respect, they criticize each other's lifestyle, parenting, and personal characteristics to demean each other in the children's eyes.

When it comes to commitment, they push only their own personal and parenting agendas at the expense of the other's, so ultimately at the expense of the children.

Alert!

Parents who truly love their children do not want to add additional suffering from a nonworking divorce to the existing pain from marital breakup that children are already suffering.

How Adults Help Children with Divorce

Separation can do wonders for some relationships. "When we were married, we were too abrasive and emotional for our own good. But now that we're divorced and have some distance from each other, and don't have to live together every day, we can be more relaxed and reasonable in how we parent the kids."

There are four major variables under adult control that significantly affect how well children adjust to parental divorce.

- How well parents individually emotionally recover from divorce.
- How amicably the divorced couple reconciles their differences after divorce.
- How actively they both choose to remain in the children's lives.
- How smoothly two-household family living is made to work for the children.

CHAPTER 5

Getting Communication in Working Order

I n the tension and discord leading up to divorce, parents often do not communicate with each other very constructively (casting blame or withholding information, for example), and they can create a family system in which communication to and from children may not work very well. During marital discord, parents may not tell children what they need to know and may not attend to what children have to say.

It's not that parents mean to be unkind. It's just that they are self-preoccupied and operating under duress. During the marital time leading up to divorce, parents are often absorbed by painful feelings, engaged in stubborn conflict, and pondering hard decisions. And most of this information they do not directly share with children, who, because they know their mother and father so well, sense that something is amiss between their parents, and wonder what.

Sharing the Data

What is communication and why is it so important? A simple way to appreciate the power of spoken communication is to think of it as an exchange of three kinds of verbal data: data about feelings, thoughts, and behaviors. Notice that unless a person shares this data about himself or herself, it remains private, accessible to other people only through guesswork or, in the case of behaviors, hearsay. So unless your child tells you what she is feeling, what she is thinking, and what she was doing when you were apart, you cannot know unless you are told, and even then you can know for sure only if you are told the truth. This is why the cardinal sin in communication is lying, because that falsifies the data upon which accurate understanding depends.

Alert!

Nonverbal communication trumps verbal communication every time. "Are you feeling okay?" asks the child. The single parent snaps back, "I'm fine! Nothing is wrong! Now leave me alone!" Answered thusly, the child credits tone over words and knows something is the matter, just not exactly what. Actions always speak louder than words.

Even among those who know us best, even among family, we are all strangers. Interpersonal ignorance is the harsh reality communication is meant to overcome. It takes continually sharing one's own data (talking) to inform and to be understood, and continually being receptive to other people's data (listening) to become informed and to understand. Through the continual sharing of data, communication keeps family members feeling connected. "This is how I feel." "This is what I am thinking about." "This is what I have been doing."

Fact

When divorcing parents become unable to talk with each other and too self-preoccupied to listen to what children have to say or want to know, children can feel frightened on four counts: they feel disconnected, cut off, lonely, and isolated. Just because two marriage partners stopped talking with each other is no reason for them to stop talking with their children. In fact, it is all the *more* reason to talk with the children.

In their significant relationships, people are information gatherers, constantly asking questions to satisfy their need to know. "How are you?" "What's going on?" "How was your day?" "Where were you?" "Why did you do that?" "How do you feel?" People strive to keep communication current so they can feel connected.

If people stop sharing and receiving sufficient or reliable information, they grow out of touch. Stop sharing this data for long enough and people can become estranged, which is one contributing factor to the demise of most marriages. "Once we stopped talking, intimacy vanished and our relationship just fell away."

Change and the Need to Know

Because change takes people from a known into an unknown situation, it creates ongoing information needs. The divorce is announced, and the child wonders, "What is going to happen now?" A parent moves out, and the child wonders, "What is going to happen now?" A parent starts dating a new "friend," and the child wonders, "What is going to happen now?"

Family change always increases children's need to know, always creating questions about what is happening, why it is happening, and what is going to happen next. The more changes parents take their children through, the more information they must provide those children with to reduce the ignorance that has been created.

 **Essential**

In divorce, as with any hard major family change, the well-being of children depends not so much on what they are going through as on how they are going through it—and that how depends on communication. Families in which spoken communication is handled well allow children to stay informed, keep parents informed, and feel connected during a disruptive time.

The Problem with Ignorance

There is no mind reading in relationships. Guessing games in communication are mostly played by guessing wrong and by creating false assumptions that lead to misunderstanding or conflict later on.

Coping with so much change themselves, it is tempting for divorcing parents to feel too busy to take time to keep children adequately informed about changes that continue to unfold. However, not to communicate and thus leave a child at the mercy of personal ignorance only encourages her to fill the voids with her own worst imaginings. "First my parents are going to stop living with each other; then they're going to stop living with us; then we'll be sent to live somewhere else!" Left in ignorance, a child can fill in the blanks with imagination by answering worst worries with worst fears, coming to believe what isn't so. "The reason my parents are divorcing is because they were always fighting over what to do about me!"

Alert!

Stay informed about how your child is processing the divorce, how he is answering such basic questions as why it happened, how it is going to work, and what will happen next. By hearing how the child answers these questions, parents can figure out what the child needs to know and, more important, where they can dispel erroneous and painful beliefs the child may hold. "When I don't know, I imagine the worst."

Restoring Broken Communication

When family communication breaks down before divorce from insufficient data being shared, it must be rebuilt once divorce is over. One way for a single parent to reestablish a practice of effective communication with children is to formally create one. On a nightly basis with each child, take some time at bedtime to play "Tell Me How You Are." First, the parent tells the child about how he or she is feeling.

Then, the child has a chance to follow the example of self-sharing that the parent set. And every week for the first six months after divorce, schedule a family meeting where current information about upcoming changes is shared, children ask questions, progress in adjustment is duly noted, and suggestions for improved family functioning are discussed. Make regular communication an established and expected part of single-parent family life.

Essential

A hard challenge for children of an intensely conflicted parental divorce is figuring out the truth about what really went wrong between the parents when each one has a different vision and version of what happened. Tell the child, "Because of things each of your parents did and didn't do, the marriage between us fell apart. We each had a part to play, we are both partly at fault, and we will never exactly agree about what contribution each of us made."

Speaking Up

Of concern to divorcing parents is staying informed about how children are adjusting to the change—how they are feeling, what they are thinking, how they are doing. Another definition of communication is "speaking up."

Five Ways of Speaking Up

If parents are to adequately monitor the children's journey through the divorce, children must be encouraged to share data by speaking up about themselves and for themselves in five different ways.

- A child needs to speak up to express the thoughts and feelings that make up his or her inner experience. "I miss the way our family used to be." Talking out hurt feelings with someone else allows the child to identify and process what is emotionally going on, and enables him to feel acknowledged and supported.

- A child needs to speak up to explain opinions and beliefs in order to declare his or her point of view. "Just because you weren't getting along doesn't give you the right to get divorced!" Sharing opinions and beliefs with someone else allows a child to have his or her position understood.

- A child needs to speak up to question what is happening, asking to find out. "So which of you will be coming to watch my games?" Requesting information from someone else allows a child to get answers that reduce anxiety caused by ignorance.

- A child needs to speak up to confront mistreatment by taking a stand when he or she feels wronged. "You changed my weekend visit with Mom without even asking or telling me, and that's not right!" Objecting to what feels hurtful or unjust from someone else allows the child to take up for his or her self-interest or well-being.

- A child needs to speak up to resolve disagreements with others. "Why should I have to give up going to a birthday overnight with friends just because it's my weekend to visit you?" Being able to discuss an honest difference with someone else allows the child to work out conflicts with others.

Alert!

Divorcing parents need to give their child permission to speak up and say, "Stop, I don't want to hear that" when either parent starts talking badly about the other. Parents need to keep their complaints about each other to themselves or to confide them to adult friends, not to children, for whom such attacks only cause pain.

Through all five ways of speaking up—expressing, explaining, questioning, confronting, and resolving—a child is empowered to make himself or herself known, and parents are kept aware of what the child feels and thinks and wants and needs. So it is in the best interests of both parents and child to encourage these communication behaviors. Most children possess each of the five speaking-up behaviors to differing degrees—perhaps finding asking questions easier than expressing feelings, for example. It is the job of parents to positively reinforce speaking up where the child is strong, and to encourage development of speaking up where the child is less practiced and secure.

 **Fact**

Every child of divorce has to redefine the relationship with each single parent in light of what has been lost and gained through this family change. By speaking up, the child can influence what he or she needs to have to stay the same, and what he or she needs to have happen differently than how things worked before.

The Risks of Speaking Up

Deprive a child of the five tools for effective speaking up, and he or she will not only become less knowable and less socially well defined, but will be less able to address and take care of his or her adjustment needs moving through parental divorce. How could a child come to not develop these tools?

Suppose the parent with whom the child most identifies is an untalkative person who keeps thoughts, feelings, explanations, questions, dislikes, and conflicts to himself or herself? Or suppose the child encountered consequences of speaking up when parents were married, such as temper or abusive anger? If speaking up felt unsafe, the child, for protection's sake, may have learned to communicate very little.

Or suppose the risks were less dramatic but still inhibiting. Suppose expressing thoughts or feelings created vulnerability to teasing? Suppose explaining opinions provoked sarcasm? Suppose questions were criticized as statements of ignorance? Suppose confronting what was hurtful or unfair was considered talking back? Suppose efforts to resolve a difference was considered to be picking a fight?

Essential

Although a few children resolve to be outspoken no matter what the response, in most cases, it takes emotional safety in a family for a child to risk speaking up.

The Perils of Shutting Up

If you have a child who, for whatever cause, is prone to shutting up instead of speaking up, for your own sake and for that of your child, help that child learn to communicate more openly. Why? Consider how a shutting-up child acts and what it costs.

- Rather than express thoughts and feelings, the child may learn to withhold and withdraw, to remain silent. The cost: others' ignorance may cause the child to be misunderstood.
- Rather than voice personal opinions and beliefs, the child may learn to defer to the views of others. The cost: lack of input leads to loss of influence.
- Rather than question to find out, the child may wait to be told (or not told). The cost: refusing to request information can result in anxious ignorance.
- Rather than object to harmful or unjust treatment, the child may learn to passively accept any response. The cost: taking any treatment without objection leads to accepting what is not okay.
- Rather than contest significant differences, the child may learn to concede to avoid conflict. The cost: agreeing when not in agreement leads to living on other people's terms.

Alert!

> Shutting-up children have a harder time recovering from the hurts of divorce and adjusting to the changes it creates than do speaking-up children, who can communicate their hard experience, express their wants, and assert their needs.

Discouraging Shutting Up

Parents cannot make a shutting-up child speak up, nor should they try to force such a transformation. However, parents can explain to the uncommunicative child some family consequences that often come from shutting up.

- "If you don't talk about your emotions, then I can't know what's going on inside you, so I may act unmindfully of how you feel."
- "If you don't explain your point of view, then I can't know how you see the situation, and so may assume you have no strong opinion either way."
- "If you don't ask, then I can't know what you need to know, and so may not think to give you information you need to understand."
- "If you don't confront me when you feel I'm mistreating you, then I can't know when my actions are offensive, and so may not change what you wish I would correct."
- "If you don't openly disagree with me over some difference between us, than I can't know we are in conflict, and so may not be able to work out the issue you would like to get resolved."

Encouraging Speaking Up

To encourage their child to speak up, there are three simple steps parents can take. First, model speaking up. Parents who routinely use all five tools of speaking up—expressing, explaining, asking, confronting, and resolving—often have children who learn to do the same for themselves. Second, support speaking up. Parents who take the time to pay attention to speaking up by listening with interest often have children who value being known. And third, keep speaking up safe. Parents who are careful to refrain from criticism, anger, ridicule, or sarcasm in response to their children's communication often have children who have no fear of speaking up.

Adolescents, particularly, can speak up forcibly in response to parental divorce, so be prepared. "All this time I thought we had a loving family, and now it turns out the whole thing wasn't real. Nothing but a big pretense! A bunch of lies!" Or, "You're not just walking out on Mom, you're walking out on the whole family. You're walking out on me!" One of the hardest parts of divorcing is listening nondefensively to what adolescents, in grief or anger, may have to say.

Alert!

One kind of shutting up that children of divorce often do is protective communication. "Because I know my dad would just get sad or mad if I talked about my mom, I don't talk to him about her at all." The child is shutting up to spare her father hurt and spare herself discomfort over seeing him upset. To some degree, most children of divorce engage in protective communication (shutting up) to avoid injuring emotionally vulnerable parents and to stay out of their conflicts.

Breaking the News about Divorce

In general, if both parents have agreed on divorce (even if one parent wants it more than the other does), it is best to tell the children together. This show of unity signifies that although the connection between them as marriage partners is soon to be over, the connection between them as parents is unbroken. They still share a common interest in the children and will continue to work together to help the children grow.

If you cannot make this joint announcement without breaking down, bickering, and blaming, then agree to have one parent do the telling or, with multiple children, take turns doing the telling. If you choose the latter option, do not delay your announcements, so that one child hears the news from another. Your children should not hear, or overhear, the news secondhand, because that will only add insult to injury: "Why didn't they tell me themselves?"

Telling Children the News

In general, keep your presentation as simple and specific as possible. Remember: breaking the news of the divorce is not a final announcement; it is a beginning explanation. Unfolding actions will operationally define what divorce experience will actually come to mean. The words you speak should help children to understand the decision you have made and to anticipate further actions to come. Your announcement sets the framework and the tone for ongoing communication to follow.

Essential

Regardless of your children's age, pitch what you have to say to about age five. You want to keep it that direct and that simple. For older children, their questions will allow you to elaborate if more complete or complicated information is desired.

Think before you speak. What about the nature of your decision do you want the children to understand (basic assurances), and what specifics do you want them to know (basic information) about what is going to happen? Basic assurances generally include:

- Assignment of responsibility: "Divorce is all our fault because it is all our decision. You did not cause it and you cannot change it."

- Sensitivity to injury: "We know divorcing hurts you a lot. We want to listen to whatever hard feelings you have whenever you have them."
- Commitment to care: "We will work as hard as ever to take care of you as always."
- Openness to questions: "Anytime there are things you want to know about what is happening or what is going to happen, please ask. We will always answer as best we can."
- Freedom to communicate: "Anytime you're with one of us and you want to talk with the other, that will be able to happen."

Alert!

When you end the announcement meeting, be sure to schedule a follow-up time to meet again within a day. At first hearing the news, most children cannot process it all and don't know what to say. In twenty-four hours, however, they are likely to have responses they want to make and questions they want to ask. And you want to get the process of two-way communication under way.

Basic information generally includes:

- Why divorce is happening: "We have decided to get divorced because we are so unhappy living together, and we believe we can be happier living apart."
- How divorce will work: "We will each have a separate place to live, and you will travel back and forth to spend time living with each of us."
- Who will be in charge: "If something happens at school and they need to contact a parent, they will call me first."
- Which will be the place of primary residence: "Your dog and most of your belongings will stay with me."

- When things will happen: "You will visit with me every other weekend and one night during each week."
- What else will change: "Because of my new job, you will be staying in day care after school."

Under each category, list additional information your children need to know.

Telling Others the News

Part of a parent's job is figuring out who else in the child's world needs to be told the news, and what information that news should contain. In general, consult with your child before doing this. Explain that people like the family doctor, the minister, the scout leader, the coach, the child-care person, neighbors, the classroom teacher, the school counselor, and significant relatives and friends are good to tell because they can be of help both by being sensitive and supportive and by being there to listen if the child wants to talk.

 *Fact*

At first, some children, believing that divorce makes them different in some socially unacceptable or self-conscious way, may not want anybody told. Should this occur, help the child understand that divorce is about the parents, not the child, and that secrecy will only make a hard situation more uncomfortable, not less. Offer to notify those people yourself that the child would find hard to tell, if that is what the child wants.

Also explain that what people are told can be kept very simple, and that these people can be told not to question the child about it, or make a public fuss over the divorce out of sympathy for the child. Children vary widely in how much information they want let out and how much special attention they desire.

When it comes to telling the child's friends, that is usually best left to the child, although a lot of times the child will want help in deciding what to say.

The Child's Emotional Response

There is no soft way to break the hard news of divorce to children, no matter how much they have been led to expect it by parental discord, by angry arguments that culminate in threats to end the marriage, by being told about marriage counseling, or even by seeing a trial separation. Most children are still emotionally unprepared for the change. In addition, hearing the words only begins awareness and understanding that subsequent actions will make real through unfolding experience—as parents physically separate, as two households are established, and as visitation begins.

The most painful part of divorce for many parents is seeing the sorrow it causes children. So it is natural that parents, having given the sad news, want to provide comfort to empathetically respond to and shore up unhappy children.

Children respond to being told about divorce in many emotional ways. What is important is for parents not to force feelings from their child ("You must be really sad") but to accept whatever state the child is in as he or she begins to process news of divorce. There is no one "right" response. Parental acceptance is the key. Understand the range of emotional responses, and parents can not only be more accepting of the child's felt reactions to divorce, but they can help the child be accepting too. Emotions are often cloaked in common statements children make or questions that they ask. Be alert to some of these common statements and questions, and you can open the door for the child to talk some feelings out. "It sounds to me like you might be feeling _____." Consider a few common examples:

- "I don't feel anything." (The child may be in a state of shock or denial.)
- "I don't understand why this is happening." (The child may be in a state of confusion.)

- "I never thought this would happen." (The child may be in a state of surprise.)
- "I was hoping you were going to work things out." (The child may be in a state of disappointment.)
- "I don't care if you divorce." (The child may be in a state of apathy.)
- "I'll never have us all together again." (The child may be in a state of loss.)
- "I feel like crying all the time." (The child may be in a state of mourning.)
- "I feel all alone." (The child may be in state of abandonment.)
- "Why couldn't you try harder to be happy?" (The child may be in a state of frustration.)
- "How do I know you'll take care of us?" (The child may be in a state of distrust.)
- "How could you do this to us?" (The child may be in a state of anger.)
- "I feel like you don't love me anymore." (The child may be in a state of rejection.)
- "If it wasn't for me, none of this would be happening." (The child may be in a state of guilt.)
- "What's going to happen to us now?" (The child may be in a state of fear.)
- "There's nothing I can do!" (The child may be in a state of helplessness.)
- "There's nothing good to look forward to!" (The child may be in a state of hopelessness.)
- "What's the point of going on?" (The child may be in a state of despondency.)

Somewhere along this range of emotional response, your child will begin to register the news of divorce, and after that, he or she may visit other emotional locations along the way. Your job, to the degree your child discloses his or her feelings, is to empathetically listen to what is said and to encourage the child to talk those feelings out as the news and then the new situation sink deeper in.

Alert!

> One role of the parent is to help the child honor feelings but not let feelings substitute for thought in determining action. So help your child declare emotional independence when it comes to making decisions. Ask the child, "If you were not angry, sad, afraid, frustrated, disappointed, depressed, or however you are feeling, what would you choose to do that would be in your best interest?"

Don't argue, don't defend, and don't correct. Simply reflect back what you have heard. "What I heard you say was how angry you are at both of your parents for splitting up the family, and I can certainly see why you would feel that way. If I were you, I would feel the same way too. Can you tell me any more?" The parent goal here goes beyond providing emotional support. By helping the child speak up about these feelings, the dangers of shutting up are reduced— dangers like blocking out, building up, and then acting out emotion. By talking out feelings, identifying and expressing them, the child is given a chance to work through the emotional experience and feel that he or she has been heard.

If your child appears to get stuck at either end of the continuum for a month after the news is first told, then get him or her some counseling. The danger of protracted denial is the buildup of unacknowledged feelings, which may cause the child to act out in self-defeating ways. The danger of protracted despondency is the possibility of turning depression into self-destructive behavior. It's all right to resort to denial or succumb to despondency for a short while, to emotionally start there, but it is not okay to stay there.

Guarded Feelings

Is it realistic to expect a child to speak up to parents about the emotional impact of divorce? In many cases, the answer is no. Suppose having broken the news to your child, and seen the anguish on her face, you find she stubbornly refuses to speak up and tell you how she feels and so refuses the listening support you are prepared to provide? Why the refusal?

 **Essential**

In general, it is not always realistic for parents to expect full emotional disclosure from their child in response to divorce, because by divorcing, they have usually earned some amount of the child's distrust. You can offer openness and receptivity, but only children can decide to what degree they want to take it.

There are usually two reasons. First, the child may find it hard to entrust the people who perpetrated this unhappiness with more emotional honesty. "It's like your parents hitting you as hard as they can and then expecting you to say how it feels afterward so they can comfort you. It's not going to happen!" Feeling injured by people loved and trusted the most, it is not uncommon for children to become more guarded with parents and less emotionally open. This is why siblings, friends, and even outside helpers may feel more comfortable for children to confide in.

The second factor that inhibits children from sharing divorce-related feelings with parents is the fear of making a bad situation worse. "If I told my parents how angry I really felt at them, I would just drive them further away!" Having seen hard feelings break up the parental marriage, children may not dare express hard feelings of their own. "I'd just make an unhappy situation worse."

Peer support groups for children of divorcing or divorced parents are extremely helpful. Often offered by school counselors, churches, and social agencies or family services, these groups allow children to share feelings with other children who understand what parental divorce feels like, to feel emotionally supported, and to get strategies for coping with a hard experience. Definitely see what's available in your community.

Question?

When should parents seek counseling to help a child talk out hard feelings?

When the child is experiencing emotionally disturbed behavior (recurrent nightmares or daily anxiety, for example), is engaging in self-defeating behavior (failing in school from lack of effort or getting into fights and getting into trouble, for example), or is engaging in self-destructive behavior (withdrawing into isolation or escaping into substance use, for example).

CHAPTER 6

Childhood and Divorce

For the purposes of this book, childhood is defined as ending around age nine or ten, which is when early adolescence and the separation from childhood usually begin. Adolescence is the time when parents experience their child's doing more pushing against them, more pulling away from them, and more getting around parental authority in order to get more independence from family and more freedom to explore the larger world with like-minded friends.

The Child's Age Matters

To anticipate the larger impact of divorce on their son or daughter, parents need to factor in whether that boy or girl is in childhood or in adolescence when the marital breakup occurs. Stage of development can make a difference, the dependent child often reacting primarily in a sad, clinging way, and the more independent adolescent often reacting primarily in a mad, more autonomous way.

Childhood Versus Adolescence

Childhood is usually characterized by a strong dependence on family, parents, and home. Adolescence is usually characterized by an increased independence from family, parents, and home. In this sense, the child feels more strongly connected to family whereas the adolescent, through social separation, feels more disconnected.

During the childhood years, the boy or girl tends to be family focused (it is the center of his or her social world); to treat parents as favored company (parents are viewed as playmates); to treat home as the preferred place to be (for its comfort, familiarity, and security). During the adolescent years, the young person tends to be more self-centered (self-preoccupation becomes the major focus); to treat peers as favored companions (parents now obstruct personal freedom); to treat home as a base of operations (a stepping-off point to explore the larger world).

 ***Essential***

Growing up requires giving up, every gain costing some degree of loss. To enter the more independent stage of adolescence, the boy or girl must let go of some old dependencies that went with being defined and treated as a child. This is why adolescents can be ambivalent about growing up. They wonder if the gain is worth the pain. Hence the mixed messages they send: "I can do it!"/"Do it for me!"

Divorce and the Problem of Timing

If the boy or girl is still in childhood and strongly connected to (and dependent on) family, parents, and home, then parental divorce threatens those connections, creating grief and insecurity caused by family loss. If the young person is now in adolescence, already to some degree disconnected from family, parents, and home because of the desire for more social freedom, then parental divorce tends to increase and intensify that push for independence (and reliance on peers) to compensate for family loss.

For the child, as opposed to the adolescent, insecurity and anxiety tend to predominate as the issues of primary concern when parents divorce. "My greatest fear is having my parents split up over some stupid argument and break my world apart."

Alert!

Because family feels so out of control when parents divorce, both children and adolescents strive to get some control back. However, where the child will often seek control by engaging in more regressive behavior (acting dependent to get taken care of), the adolescent will often seek control by engaging in more aggressive behavior (acting independent of parental authority to get his or her way).

Coping with the Fears Created by Loss

For the boy or girl still in childhood, feeling so safely anchored to home, so closely connected to parents, and so dependent on them for happiness and well-being, divorce can feel extremely frightening. There is fear of rejection: "If my parents can stop loving each other, can they stop loving me?" There is fear of the future: "What will happen to me now?" There is fear of abandonment: "If my parents can leave each other, they can also leave me." In the face of these uncertainties, a child may regress by acting more immature and dependent in order to receive more attention and caretaking support. Now he or she may cling to the single parent who is the only parent left at home.

Fact

Divorce is so frequent today that it is among children's most common fears. And that fear can be triggered when parents of friends get divorced, or when parents have recurrent bickering or extremely loud or intense arguments. To the fearful child, angry conflict is equated with loss of love, and loss of love with the marriage's ending. Thus, for many contemporary children, parental divorce is a bad dream come true.

The Importance of Rituals

For a single parent, coping with a child's repeated need for ritual can seem pointless and become irritating. "Why must I go through the same order of reassurance again and again? What's the point when she knows I'll be back in twenty minutes? I always am." But the four-year-old, consigned to an older sibling while the mother goes for her usual evening walk, gives the departing parent this warning each and every time: "Watch out for cars. Don't die. Don't get lost. Come back soon. And don't forget that!" By repeatedly giving this warning, the child gives herself something she can do to create a sense of safety in a family world that divorce has made insecure.

 *Question?*

Don't these rituals of reassurance have a superstitious quality?
Yes, they often do. And that's okay. The child may ascribe magical protection to these repeated words and acts, even becoming upset when the ritual is not completely accomplished. Best for the parent to respect these rituals. As the child becomes more secure in the new situation, the need for them will naturally subside.

Young children may find their departure for day care or school more frightening than before, now unsure that they will be picked up or that a parent will be at home at the end of the day. The single parent needs to be patient with this insecurity and the ritual questions and assurances the child wants—usually at times of departure and reunion when the parental connection is interrupted or restored—to help structure a safe passage through uncertainty and fear. Remember, this little person is a child whose faith and trust in the constancy of family connections has been injured by divorce, who needs stability over time to restore that faith and trust in the new family situation.

The Importance of Routines

The basic fear that divorce arouses in children is fear of abandonment. "If my mom and dad can leave each other, can they also leave me?" Abandonment fears can run deep in children after divorce. (Adult children of divorce often carry this fear into committed relationships later on.)

To help quell such anxieties, the single parent needs to establish a clear family structure, consistent adherence to that structure, and put in place routines for household operation that the child can count on from one day to the next. A predictable schedule for all to follow, an organized way that daily household events are handled, an understood set of responsibilities that the child is expected to assume, these all provide the basis for familiarity, continuity, and stability in the new family situation.

One critical routine to establish as early as possible is a regular visitation schedule with the absent parent. It is often in this relationship that the child feels most abandoned. The child needs to know that the absent parent is there for him, and the best way to instill that confidence is through regular visitation contact and interim communication the child can rely upon.

 **Essential**

The anxious child of divorce needs to be reassured that even though the parental marriage is over, family structure is still firmly in place. To give the child a sense of family to count on, answer questions patiently, honor rituals and organize routines, and establish reliable visitation that the child can count upon.

Do not criticize or punish the child for feeling afraid. Fear needs to be respected, accommodated, and talked out, not driven into concealment by parental disapproval, into hiding by the child's embarrassment or shame.

Scaring the Child with Safety

It is normal for a child to have fears of further loss as a consequence of parental divorce and to act more anxious, insecure, and clinging on that account. It is also normal for a single parent to want to reassure the child by making the new family situation as safe as possible. What the parent has to watch out for is scaring the child with the safety precautions he or she is taking and all the reassurances he or she is making.

Alert!

After divorce, parents can be unduly reassuring, take unusual measures to protect the child, and inflame the child's worries with their own. Instead of alleviating the child's anxiety over safety, this only makes it worse, and parents may become impatient with, critical toward, or angry at the child for being afraid. Act with acceptance, trust, and confidence, and your child will learn to do the same.

So the child is having some separation anxiety when going to school, fearful that when the day is done and he or she comes home, the remaining parent will not be there. "I don't understand why my daughter is so fearful," explains the concerned single parent. "I'm doing everything I can to help her feel safe. I repeat a whole list of promises before school about being at home when she gets home. I walk her to the classroom door each day to prevent her having to do that alone. I've gotten special permission from the counselor to let her call me at lunch. I've even given her a 'magic coin' to carry to stop the fear. What else can I do?"

The answer is, stop scaring the child with precautions. These well-intended efforts can end up just heightening the child's fear by testifying to how real the danger is that the child fears. If the parent is acting like there is something to be afraid of, the child is given cause to feel afraid. The parent is better advised to normalize the school separation, to accept the fear but treat the necessary adjustment with trust and confidence. By doing so, the parent encourages the child to do the same. It's a delicate compromise: how to give the child enough reassurance to feel supported, but not so much that extreme reassurance increases fear.

Signs of Trouble

The single parent is responsible for assessing the degree to which his or her child's adjustment to divorce is going okay. "Okay" does not mean without unhappiness or difficulty; but it does mean without creating additional hurt, thereby making a hard situation worse.

 **Question?**

What is worse than a child of divorce acting angry with others? The answer is, taking anger at parents out on herself. Fearful that expressing anger at parents over divorce might only drive them further away, the child may direct anger toward herself, becoming more self-critical, engaging in self-injury, or even developing physical symptoms that self-directed anger can create. So keep a weather eye out for self-destructive behaviors or the sudden onset of any chronic health problems.

Every child moves through this passage differently, so there is no "right" way for all children to follow. If you have multiple children, you will see variation among them depending on individuality and age. For example, as mentioned, there is a great range of emotional responses to divorce, and different children focus on different feelings. To the degree your child is willing to discuss those feelings, it is helpful for you to hear the child out.

Children must be told and told again: "Divorce means your parents have lost love for each other and do not want to live together anymore. However, divorce in no way changes our love for you."

Behaviors of Concern

When a child is severely emotionally impacted by divorce, that impact can be more than he or she can process in a productive way. Overwhelmed, the child may resort to behavior changes that can make matters worse, not better. Parents should attend to these behavior changes. A few of the more common trouble signs include:

- Physical behaviors such as headaches, stomach pains or nausea, allergic reactions, sleeplessness, nervous tics, compulsive overeating, extreme loss of appetite
- Regressive behaviors such as breaking toilet training, bedwetting, clinging, whining, loss of independent self-care skills
- Emotional disruptive behaviors such as nightmares, tantrums, separation anxieties, unexpected/uncontrollable crying
- Self-defeating behaviors such as giving up significant interests, giving up significant relationships, lack of effort at what traditionally mattered, school failure
- Self-destructive behaviors such as frequent accidents, injury proneness, cutting oneself, early substance use (like inhalants), suicidal talk or attempts
- Aggressive behaviors such as hitting and hurting others, getting into fights, breaking rules, resisting or challenging authority
- Asocial behaviors such as social withdrawal, isolation, electronic escape activities like excessive computer or video gaming or TV watching

What parents don't want is for their child to stay with any of these behavior changes too long (a month should give a parent pause), because the longer the child practices these behaviors, the more they can become habitual ways of coping.

Alert!

Don't be shy about relying on informants to get data about how your child seems to be adjusting to the family change. Whether it be the child's teacher, youth minister, coach, family friend, parent of the child's good friend, or scoutmaster, feel free to ask, "How do you think my child is doing since the divorce?" Outside observers often provide a valuable perspective.

Getting Help

Should any of these behavior changes continue for more than a couple of months, get your child some level of psychological help to guide him or her toward a more productive path through the adjustment to divorce. "Some level" refers to the spectrum of trained professional helpers available, including school counselor, licensed professional counselor, psychotherapist, social worker, pastoral counselor, psychologist, and psychiatrist. All these professionals can be of service, assuming they have had experience helping children your child's age better cope with the adjustment demands of divorce.

There are a number of questions to ask before you can determine if a helper is right for you and your family. First, does the helper have relevant experience? Second, do you feel comfortable with this helper after your initial screening interview? This session is a time not only for the helper to assess your family situation, but for you to assess the helper. Third, does your child feel comfortable with this helper? Remember, there is no universal helper. It doesn't matter what the professional designation, no helper (no matter how well trained or intentioned) can help everyone. If your child says the first few sessions weren't comfortable or helpful, then try another helper. The main thing is to get your child needed assistance.

Since it was your assessment of some trouble signs that indicated your child was experiencing adjustment difficulty with the divorce, it is reasonable for you to expect that those trouble signs will diminish over the course of help being given. So look for less frequent nightmares or episodes of separation anxiety at school or fights with other children, for example. It is the parent's job to hold the helper accountable, and if you feel the counseling is not being productive, talk about that with the helper.

 ## *Fact*

One of the most powerful sources of help for children going through divorce is the unbroken relationship with grandparents. These people, and their home, can come to represent constancy in a changing family world, a haven where children feel as securely accepted and anchored as they ever were. When parents divorce, it is important that grandparent connections are nourished and maintained.

"I Hate You!"

Although the exception and not the rule, some children can feel driven to make extreme emotional statements to which parents should attend. In extreme anger at the injustice of divorce, the child may say, "I hate you for divorcing!" That is grievance speaking. Parents should take this very seriously because of the degree of unhappiness being communicated and because of destructive behaviors such statements could possibly trigger.

What should you say when your child yells, "I hate you for divorcing!" In general, understand that you should take talk of hate, just like talk of suicide, very seriously. Ignore either statement and you risk the possibility of destructive consequences—of harm being done.

Sometimes, because the quality of communication is the quality of family life, parents may have prohibited the use of certain kinds of language in the family, hate statements among them. Thus, when the child uses "I hate you!" parents treat this as a violation of family rules and make a corrective response. "You have been told never to use that word between us. Now go to your room. We will discuss consequences later."

This is not a good decision. What is immediately needed is not punishment but communication.

 **Essential**

> One scary responsibility of parenting is trying to prevent a child's desperate words, driven by desperate feelings, from turning into desperate acts. Because divorce can wound children so deeply, parents need to give desperation statements the immediate attention that empathetic listening can provide.

At the same time, parents do need to understand that most statements of "I hate you!" don't really have much to do with actual hate at all. Actual hate is about abhorrence and enmity, a complete or irrecoverable absence of love. "I hate you" from your child is neither. It is usually spoken in the heat of the moment, in response to one or more of four upsetting issues.

- The child is feeling frustrated by parental demands, restraints, or lack of understanding. "I hate you!" really means, "I am at the extremity of my anger at you!"
- The child is in a hard emotional place because of unwise decisions made and wants to unload those feelings on someone else. "I hate you!" really means, "I feel like taking my bad feelings about myself out on you!"
- The child is feeling injured by what parents did or didn't do. "I hate you!" really means, "I feel really hurt from how you've treated me!"
- The child is using extreme language for extortionate effect. "I hate you!" really means, "If you don't want me to hate you, then let me have my way!"

What the young person needs at this point is not anger or punishment from the parent, but an empathetic response to talk extreme upset out. Rather than attacking back to defend themselves, parents need to show empathetic concern. "I care for how you feel, I want to know how you feel, and I will listen to how you feel."

To that end, when your child says, "I hate you!" respond with something like this: "Telling me you hate me tells me that you must be feeling extremely upset. Please talk to me about the unhappiness you feel or what you want." Then, after you talk things out, make a request: "Since unhappiness and not hate is what was really going on, maybe next time life gets so painful or frustrating, you can simply say to me, 'I feel extremely unhappy!' And we can talk. The problem with using the word 'hate' between us is that it can scare both of us. It can scare me because I wonder what you might do. And it can scare you because when you believe you hate me, you will feel unable to accept my love. Also, 'I hate you' can be dangerous to say. What we say in anger can motivate hateful actions. Bad words state beliefs that can be used to justify bad treatment. Say, 'I hate you!' and you may feel entitled to treat me in a hateful way that we both will have cause to regret."

Alert!

Parents should be particularly sensitive to the statement, "I just hate myself!" In service of self-loathing, children can allow the emotion of the moment to drive them in a self-defeating or self-destructive direction by acting to fulfill or punish the worthlessness they feel. Say to the child, "Beat up on yourself with bad names, and you will only feel worse. At hard times, loving ourselves is what we need to do."

Suicidal Statements

Have you heard your child say, "I could kill myself"? In extreme despondency over the losses created by divorce, the child may say,

"I feel like ending it all!" That is grief speaking. Sorrow is one thing; depression is another. Feeling sorrowful (depressed) and depression are not the same. Children often feel depressed and deeply saddened in response to the stress, adversity, and loss created by parental divorce. However, only some children become caught in depression, emotionally stuck in a mire of hurt, hopelessness, helplessness, anger, and worthlessness, bereft of energy and motivation to make any positive change. Give your depressed child emotional support. Get your child in depression psychological help.

When a child is emotionally devastated by divorce, parents must monitor the child's adjustment to make sure signs of depression do not indicate a child at risk. What signs? Here are a few:

- Withdrawal from friends
- Isolation within family
- Becoming significantly less communicative
- Acting sad, crying, expressing ongoing unhappiness
- No longer liking, even giving up, activities previously enjoyed
- Acting angrier, provoking more conflict in the family
- Making self-demeaning statements reflecting low self-esteem
- Having difficulty sleeping or sleeping all the time
- Loss of appetite or excessive eating
- Drop in school effort and achievement
- Appearance of psychosomatic complaints
- Suffering chronic fatigue and very low energy
- Increasingly pessimistic about life

Signs of depression can vary depending on the sex of the child because girls and boys may be socialized in our culture to manage pain in very different ways. Girls may be encouraged to acknowledge and express hurt feelings because being sensitive is feminine, whereas boys may be encouraged to deny and suppress hurt feelings because being tough is masculine. Thus, girls may more frequently express depression through tearfulness, dejection, guilt, discouragement, disinterest, social withdrawal, self-criticism, apathy, defeatism, resignation, or worry. Boys, however, may more frequently express depression through anger, hostility, blame, cynicism, antagonism, social aggression, sarcasm, irritability, defiance, disobedience, or explosiveness. Initially, depressed girls are more likely to be offered support, and depressed boys are more likely to be given punishment.

Alert!

A depressed child can be a danger to herself. When normal depressed feelings seem not to pass and signs of depression begin to appear, parents should seek a mental health evaluation of the child. It is better for all concerned to be safe rather than sorry.

Depression becomes dangerous when the despondent child considers ending pain by ending life. Despondency can give rise to suicidal thoughts, which can lead to self-destructive acts. Always take suicidal talk seriously.

Consider a possible suicide scenario. The child becomes subject to depression from the significant loss of family relationships created by divorce. (Therefore, parents need to treat divorce losses seriously and encourage the child to acknowledge and talk hurt feelings out.) The child withdraws into social isolation to conceal emotional pain. (Therefore, parents need to increase their support and ways to connect with the child.) The child allows distorted thinking to create an exaggerated picture of hopelessness and helplessness. (Therefore, parents need to provide a realistic perspective.) The child resorts to substance use to self-medicate pain, thereby increasing the likelihood that impulse may rule. (Therefore, parents need to keep a drug-free household.) The child has a ready means to end suffering by ending life. (Therefore, parents need to secure all household means for inflicting serious self-harm.)

CHAPTER 7

Adolescence and Divorce

Adolescence is that ten- to twelve-year period of growth that begins with the separation from childhood (roughly between the ages of nine and thirteen) and ends with the entry into young adulthood (somewhere around the early to mid twenties). Come adolescence, the hard part of parenting begins, as the boy or girl starts pushing for more personal freedom, social independence, and worldly experience to grow.

A New Challenge

Because it is so personally painful and so powerfully disruptive, parental divorce almost always makes for a more challenging adolescence. For the adolescent, divorce creates a degree of disconnection from parents, and instability in the home, at a time when the separation from family is developmentally ordained to begin. Feelings of loss, anxiety, and anger at divorce tend to emotionally intensify the adolescent experience and increase normal resistance to authority that is part of this more independent age.

For the single parent, there are now half as many parents in the home to cope with the adolescent push than there were before, and no partner to consult about parenting problems, with whom to share the parenting load. Now he or she must go it alone.

In light of both of these developments created by divorce, it is imperative that the single parent

understand what normal changes to expect as his or her child jour-
neys through adolescence, and how parental divorce can make
these changes more severe and difficult to cope with.

 *Fact*

> Adolescence takes courage for both child and parents. The courage
> of the adolescent is to pull away, get around, and push against par-
> ents for more independence, in the process daring to court parental
> disapproval and disagreement, creating more contention in the rela-
> tionship. The courage of the parents is to speak up about what the
> adolescent doesn't want to hear, to take unpopular stands the ado-
> lescent doesn't like, all in support of the adolescent's best interests,
> and be resented for their efforts.

How to Tell When Adolescence Has Begun

When most couples think about starting a family, they think of hav-
ing a child—of having a baby, a toddler, a little boy or girl, to look
after and happily attend. They think about the magical early years
of shared discovery, wonder, affection, and closeness that parent-
hood can bring. What they don't think about is parenting a teenager,
the "hard half of parenting," when adolescence begins that fractious
process of separation that causes them and their teenager to grow
increasingly apart. Although they will see their adolescent less than
when he or she was a child, they will spend more time thinking about
the young person because the risks of worldly freedom for which
their son or daughter now pushes are so high, and their authority is
more frequently contested.

Signs of Adolescent Change

What changes inform parents that their child's adolescence has
begun? Here are four categories to consider.

- **Characteristics change.** There is new social motivation to act older, and with the release of hormones at puberty, physical development causes the child to appear more adult. Consider growth spurts and becoming large enough to borrow parental clothes.
- **Values change.** To differentiate from the child that was and the way parents are, more counter cultural interests and tastes are developed. Consider graffiti covered T-shirts, psychedelic posters, and loud music that are often offensive to parents.
- **Habits change.** Patterns of behavior are now adopted that parents find more inconsiderate and harder to tolerate. Consider endless phone calls, littering the home, and the messy room.
- **Wants change.** Freedoms become more urgently demanded and harder to grant. Consider wanting to hang out at the mall and having a later curfew.

Alert!

It is not uncommon during adolescence for a discontented teenager, looking for a better family deal, to want to take up major residence with the noncustodial, good-time parent. Sometimes trying this switch out for six months or a year is not a bad idea. What the teenager discovers is that living with this "ideal" parent is not the same as visiting. Soon oppressive rules, restraints, and responsibilities become part of that household reality too, and conditions back "home" don't look so bad after all.

Changes in the Parent/Child Relationship

In addition, living with an adolescent feels different than living with a child. Old expectations of living with a child fit less well with the adolescent. Whereas the child may have been mostly loving, obedient, hardworking, and helpful, the adolescent is often more resistant, uncooperative, unmotivated, and moody.

Then there are changes in parents that the adolescent notices, but to which they themselves are often blind. Now the adolescent finds old expectations need to change to fit how parents have suddenly become. With the child they used to be understanding, patient, trustful, and fun loving, but with the adolescent they have now become more worrying, critical, questioning, and tense. And this adolescent observation is true because change in the child begets change in the parents, and the parent/child relationship itself becomes altered—with more discomfort and disharmony between them.

Adolescence is not just about a change that happens to a child on the way to adulthood. It is also about how parents change in response, and how parents and their adolescent struggle to keep their relationship together while these changes are causing them to grow apart.

Adolescence Defined

In the unfolding process of adolescence, parents encounter more uncertainty in their role based on three common changes in their developing child. First, there is more opposition over conflicting wants and interests than there was before—the child pressing for more freedom, the parent insisting on more responsibility. Second, there is more differentiation as the adolescent experiments with new beliefs, personal tastes, cultural identifications, and modes of dress to explore new images that fit an older age and cause friction when parents reach their limits on what differences they are willing to tolerate. Third, there is separation into a social world of friends for primary companionship, social reference, and emotional support. Parents often feel less important, left out, and left behind.

Opposition

On the adolescent side, healthy growth impels teenagers to press for all the freedom they can get as soon as they can get it. On the parental side, healthy fathers and mothers must undertake the thankless role of restraining that push for independence within the interests of safety and responsibility. Although this natural opposition makes for abrasive times in the parent/adolescent relationship, the intermittent conflict itself is serving a purpose. By wearing down mutual tolerance for dependence between them, this abrasion eventually leads teenagers to give up relying on their parents for support, and parents to relinquish managing their child's life.

 **Fact**

The transition into adolescence takes the child out of the age of command ("You can tell me what to do and I have to do it"), into the age of consent ("You can't make me or stop me unless I choose to go along"). During the age of command, parents felt more in control. During the age of consent, parents feel less in charge.

A natural antagonism arises between parents as perpetual rule makers, and adolescent as potential rule breaker. And now a mutual resentment can color the relationship. To the adolescent, parents can seem to turn mean: "They're always on my case, in the way, against what I like, against what I want, and down on how I am." To the parents, the adolescent can seem to turn exploitive: "She's always using us to get what she wants, is only nice when there's something she needs, acts unpleasant when we don't do what she wants, is always pushing for more, and never appreciates all we give."

 **Essential**

Adolescence is a functionally abrasive process. By creating ongoing opposition between them, it wears the dependence down between parents and child so that by the end of adolescence, each is willing to let the other go. The parents are willing to give up support and responsibility for the young person's care, and the adolescent is now willing to take them on.

Differentiation

Personal growth requires breaking old boundaries of definition to experiment with becoming different. Breaking boundaries and becoming different is what adolescence is about. Those parents who expect their child to stay "the same" while growing through this transformational process are setting themselves up for a surprise.

Alert!

The three engines that drive adolescence—opposition, differentiation, and separation—all converge on a common developmental objective: the achievement of more independence. Authority is contested to establish more autonomy. Experimentation serves the search for a new identity. And establishing membership with peers reduces social dependence on the company of parents.

They should be expecting differentiation on four levels. "I am different from how I was as a child," and the adolescent becomes more negative, dissatisfied, and critical. "I want to be treated differently than how I was as a child," and the adolescent demands less restraint and more freedom. "I am different from my parents," and the adolescent cultivates new interests and tastes that contrast with the parental identity. "I am going to act differently from how my parents would like me to behave," and the adolescent now questions rules, delays compliance, and argues more with authority.

One way to think about adolescence is a process through which the formerly compliant and cooperative child now starts to let the "bad side" out. "Bad" doesn't mean immoral or illegal or evil, just more difficult and abrasive to live with than was previously the case. Letting his bad side out serves a purpose. As parents find cause to increasingly set the adolescent straight, this increased tendency toward correction causes them to shift from "nice" to "mean" in his eyes, causing the adolescent to feel that becoming harder to live with is okay because now parents have become harder to live with too. One needs to have "bad" parents to justify letting one's own bad side out.

Essential

Receiving compliments from an adult friend about what a pleasure their adolescent is to be with, parents wonder if the friend is actually talking about their teenager, who is currently wearing and tearing relationships at home. Yes, this is the same adolescent, and she is exercising very good social sense by acting pleasant out in the world, only letting her bad side out at home with parents who she knows will love her no matter what.

Sometimes parents become so alarmed by the adolescent's differentiation that they fear a loss of moral compass and a complete rejection of childhood instruction. Judging by the young person's new behavior, they fear family values they instilled have been forever lost. This is not so. The differences that unfold during adolescence are more trial than terminal. Come the end of adolescence, the young person will end up more similar to parents, and to what parents taught, than different.

Fact

Come adolescence, parents often feel the popular culture has become a subverting influence in their family. The music, the advertising, the movies, the TV, the computer games can seem like media predators intent on corrupting the innocence out of their child by glamorizing beliefs and encouraging behaviors that create a cultural divide within the home. What interests and excites the adolescent often offends and alarms the parents.

Separation

When parents have been particularly close and companionable with a child, best buddies or intimate friends, that boy's or girl's separation from childhood into adolescence and preference for time with peers can be particularly painful. Parents may feel rejected and at a loss. "It feels like we don't matter to our child anymore!" Now parents will never have that old childhood connection with their son or daughter again, and they need to mourn childhood's passing—valuing the favored companionship they once were given, letting it go, and moving on to the next phase in their relationship.

Sometimes this parental letting go is hard to do without feeling hurt or acting angry. So the daughter who used to pour out her heart to her mother now has best friends in whom she'd rather confide her personal travails and secret longings. So the son who used to happily tag along after his father now prefers adventuring and just hanging out with friends. In each case, some separation from a beloved parent is the price of admission to the adolescent world of social belonging with peers. And the price of separation from parents is usually some degree of loneliness: "When I pull away from my parents, it feels like they are leaving me."

Does this adolescent separation mean parents should let go of all time together with their adolescent son or daughter? No! Parents need to keep up initiatives of wanting to talk with and wanting to do with the young person, always holding themselves in open readiness for a connection when the boy or girl feels able and wants to make it.

Alert!

Parents must not take natural adolescent separation as personal rejection, rejecting back in hurt or anger, thereby cutting off communication their son or daughter needs more than ever. Just because parents are no longer favored companions does not mean that they are not still important. By hanging in there, they provide the anchoring relationship the adolescent knows he or she can always depend on, a respite from the instability and uncertainty that rules relationships between friends.

How Divorce Affects Adolescence

From a global perspective, adolescence is about transformation. The young person separates from childhood. The young person differentiates from being a child. The young person tries out more grown-up behaviors. The young person assumes more responsibilities. The young person seeks more independence from family.

Through separating from childhood, the young person gives up some old dependency that went with being defined and treated as a child. Through differentiation, the young person begins to try on and cast off a host of images, seeking a fitting new identity. Through independence, the young person seeks to establish a social world outside of family.

Essential

When divorce disrupts family functioning during a child's adolescence, the young person often tends to push harder against authority for personal freedom (more conflict is created), to push for more dramatic differentiation (more extreme identities are sought), and to push for greater separation from family (peers become increasingly important).

The Power of Divorce

When divorce occurs during a child's adolescence, separation, differentiation, and separation are usually intensified. At a developmental time when the child is naturally growing more apart from family, family suddenly becomes much less secure. Stability the child could count on is to some degree lost. Family is less dependably "there" for the boy or girl than it was before, and in consequence, the adolescent's world is shaken at a very vulnerable time. He or she may now feel more abandoned, alone, and cast out on his or her own. He or she may feel less able to depend on family for security and social support. He or she may feel less attention from parents, who seem more wrapped up in themselves. He or she may experience the beginning of many family changes that make the normal changes of adolescent growth that much more challenging to meet.

One Less Parent to Cope with More Opposition

Even with two parents present, a hard-charging, highly intense teenager can be a handful. Fighting the battle for a teenager's responsible independence can be exhausting and lonely work for a single parent. This is why, during the "hard half of parenting" (adolescence), a single parent must find other adults with whom to share the perplexity and who can offer support, encouragement, and helpful ideas. A child's adolescence is no time for a single parent to go it alone.

 *Question?*

Come adolescence, what's the best kind of teacher at school for your child to have?
One who can honestly say to you, "I will risk students' disliking me in order to teach them knowledge and discipline, self-confidence and self-control, the value of effort and the rewards of hard work." It takes a tough teacher to earn an adolescent's respect.

This is not to say that a single parent is obligated to go through agony with each teenager, only that divorce is likely to make adolescence more intense. About a third of children seem to journey through adolescence pretty smoothly, finding adequate room to grow within parental tolerances and without much opposition to contain or correct. Another third may intermittently push hard and require occasional but firm reining in. A final third, however, seem to press all the parental buttons and test all the parental limits. In this third-degree adolescence, often the harder the single parent tries, the worse behavior seems to get—the child becomes more defiant, determined to go on more of an independent run. In this situation, getting parental support through an organization like Tough Love (see your local phone directory) to help you take meaningful stands with your more resistant adolescent, or seeking counseling for effective parenting strategies, can be helpful.

Holding the Adolescent Responsible for Behavior

The entire ten- to twelve-year process of adolescence is fraught with risks. More curious about the larger world than he or she was as a child, more interested in acting older and experimenting with the forbidden, more exposed to worldly dangers, more susceptible to pressures to do in a group what one would not do alone, the adolescent is trouble waiting to happen. To the degree that divorce has resulted in increased emotional upset, accelerated drive for independence, and more reliance on the company of friends, susceptibility to major kinds of trouble may be increased.

The Seven Dire Risks of Adolescence

There are seven risks that parents generally fear the most for their adolescent because of life-changing consequences that can occur: victimization from violence, accidental injury, school failure, illegal activities, sexual misadventures, suicidal despondency, and drug and alcohol involvement. Of the seven, the last is most serious of all, because substance use increases the likelihood of the other six. Alcohol and drug use affect judgment, perspective, attitude, and reactivity, all factors in how decisions are made.

Alert!

Make sure that your adolescent understands why you wish him a drug-free passage through adolescence. Adolescence is risky enough as is without increasing those risks through substance use. A sober passage is safest of all.

To varying degrees, divorce can elevate these risks by causing the adolescent to pursue freedom impulsively or unwisely. Only by metering freedom out very carefully, keeping the teenager on a "short leash," can a single parent encourage sound decision making to moderate these risks. To this end, the parent is well advised to hold the adolescent to performance account: "Freedom given must be freedom earned."

The Freedom Contract

Sometimes your adolescent, frustrated by your refusal to give permission, will complain, "You never let me do anything! Everyone else has more freedom than I do! You just don't want me to grow up!" Not so. What you want is for your son or daughter to grow up without falling casualty to dangerous exposures and damaging choices. This is why, at the outset of adolescence, you must make it very clear that you intend to contract with your son or daughter very carefully when it comes to granting freedom.

What do you want from your teenager when he or she wants more permission for freedom from you? You want evidence that your adolescent is trustworthy in six distinct ways, all six adding up to the freedom contract, which must be met before you agree to risk allowing more discretionary choice from which the teenager can grow.

 *Question?*

How do I know it's time to enter into a freedom contract with my child?
You know it's time to enter into a freedom contract with your child when he or she starts pushing for more independent choice and more social freedom of experience away from home.

The first provision has to do with honesty: "You will keep me reasonably informed by giving me adequate and accurate information about what is going on in your life and what you are planning to do."

The second provision has to do with mutuality: "You will live in a two-way relationship with me, doing for me in fair exchange for my doing for you, contributing to the family as the family contributes to your welfare."

The third provision has to do with sincerity: "You will honor your word, keeping agreements and following through on commitments you make with me."

The fourth provision has to do with responsibility: "Your conduct will be your passport to permission by showing me responsible behavior at home, at school, and out in the world."

The fifth provision has to do with availability: "You will be available for a free and open discussion of any concern I may have need to discuss."

The sixth provision has to do with civility: "You will communicate to me with respect, fulfilling agreements with a positive attitude, acting gladly and not madly in response to my requests and restraints."

Meeting these six provisions of the contract are what a young person brings to the negotiating table when wanting a parent to provide or allow further freedom. This means demonstrating actual performance, not making promises of performance (false currency which should have no bargaining value).

 **Essential**

If a single parent wants the child to live up to the freedom contract, then that parent needs to honor those six provisions as well. Live up to the standards of performance to which you hold your child.

At such negotiation points, if your teenager has shown evidence of being truthful, being helpful, keeping agreements, acting responsibly, being open to discussion, and talking respectfully, then you will tend to be more inclined to consent to his or her request.

If, however, your teenager is in breach of contract (lying to you, taking but not giving, breaking agreements, acting irresponsibly, refusing to discuss concerns with you, or communicating disrespectfully), then you may be inclined to deny the request. You may even reduce existing freedom for a while until the provisions of the freedom contract begin to be honored once again.

CHAPTER 8

Divorce and Stages of Adolescence

There are four different stages of adolescence, and how your child reacts to your divorce will depend greatly on which stage he is in when the divorce occurs. It's important to understand the differences among the stages to know what your child is experiencing and what the best way is to help him deal with your divorce.

Four Stages of Adolescence

At four different stages of adolescence, different growth goals come into focus that should be of concern to the single parent. In early adolescence (ages 9–13), there is the separation from childhood, and the desire to rebel against old demands and constraints. In mid adolescence (ages 13–15), there is the desire to explore worldly freedom in the company of peers. In late adolescence (ages 15–18), there is the desire to act more grown-up, and more intolerance of parental directions and rules. And in trial independence (ages 18–23), there is the desire to experience living more on one's own and grappling with more freedom than one has ever had before.

Pursuing these goals, the adolescent poses normal problems and conflicts for parents to cope with. However, what is "normal" is not necessarily okay. For example, in mid adolescence, more lying to get more worldly freedom is normal (i.e., to be expected), but parents have a responsibility to take a stand against lying and hold that young person accountable for honesty. It is important that a

single parent know what normal adolescent changes to expect so
that appropriate, and not over-reactive, responses are made.

> *Expect* does not mean *accept*. *Expect* means that as a single parent,
> you know enough about adolescence not to be blindsided by nor-
> mal changes, and in surprise, disappointment, or betrayal undercut
> the effectiveness of your response by overreacting. So, while you do
> not accept mid adolescent lying, you did expect it, and so are able to
> respond in an appropriate disciplinary way.

What follows is a stage-by-stage description of what changes to
expect, how divorce can make them more challenging, and parental
choices that can help a young person stay on a healthy adolescent path.

Early Adolescence

Somewhere between the ages of nine and thirteen, the entry into ado-
lescence usually begins. What parents typically notice is a change in
their son or daughter's energy, attitude, and behavior.

This was the child who used to be extremely active, interested in
many things, always on the go. Suddenly, it is as if someone pulled
the plug and all the positive energy has been drained away. Now
all the child seems up for doing is lying around, complaining about
being bored, about being at loose ends with nothing to do. Unhappy
being passive but unwilling to be active, he or she does not appre-
ciate helpful suggestions from the parent, shooting all these ideas
down to prove that a parent can no longer be of any helpful use. "No,
I don't want to do that! You don't understand! Just leave me alone!"

Then, as positive energy is lost, negative energy begins to build.
Discontent with everything, critical of everyone, the early adolescent
communicates complaints that begin to irritate the single parent, who

sometimes criticizes back, only increasing the boy's or girl's negativity in return. Now the parent who could previously do little wrong in the child's eyes can apparently do little right.

Essential

Sometimes a parent will become concerned about the early adolescent's low self-esteem. But low self-esteem is not a problem to be changed at this age; it is a reality to be accepted. Having cast off esteem-building interests, activities, and relationships he enjoyed as a child but now dismisses as "kid stuff" he has outgrown, the early adolescent's self-worth is riding on empty, with nothing positive yet established to take their place.

What's going on? The answer is, the separation from childhood has begun. Rejecting the identity of "being just a child," the boy or girl knows how he or she doesn't want to be defined and treated, but does not yet have a clear positive alternative in mind to replace the definition that has been given up. As for the parent, that person is now considered more of a hindrance than a help, part of the problem, often blamed for the early adolescent's discontent.

Fact

For most children, early adolescence brings a host of personal insecurities and worldly fears. Bodily changes feel out of control as hormones begin to do their transformational work, and specters of all the bad things that can afflict oneself and parents out in the world begin to haunt the young person's anxious imagination. Divorce at this stage only makes anxiety worse. "Suppose something else bad happened to my parents?"

How Divorce Intensifies Early Adolescence

For the early adolescent, parental divorce can come at a particularly bad time. Just beginning the separation from childhood, daring to pull away from parents and family and experiment with becoming different, she suddenly loses the stability of family. Now less secure at a more anxious time, less connected during a separation time, the early adolescent may experience a significant loss of trust.

When parental divorce coincides with early adolescence, certain development changes typically become intensified: the negative attitude, rebellion, and early experimentation.

The Negative Attitude

The opening shot of adolescence is the birth of the bad attitude—a pervasive negativity in the child that the parent did not see before. Where is this negativity from? People don't initiate change in themselves unless they are dissatisfied with who and how they are, and now the early adolescent is dissatisfied with being defined and treated as a child. He or she wants to relinquish this old identity and find another—older, more grown-up, more adult. This self-dissatisfaction provides the motivation to change, propelling the adolescent out of childhood by rejecting the old definition of child, this rejection the source of all the negativity the young person is feeling. "Don't treat me like a child!"

Rebellion

Part of this negativity is a sense of grievance about the rules and restraints the parent places in the way of new freedom for growth that the early adolescent wants: "What right do you have to tell me what I can and cannot do!" As a child, this authority was okay. As an adolescent, it is not. And it is this sense of grievance about the unfairness of parental (and other adult) authority that sets the stage for the second phase of early adolescence: rebellion.

Now the young person becomes more actively and passively resistant. Actively, she argues more about demands the parent makes and limits the parent sets, sometimes up for an argument about anything just for argument's sake—to test assertive power against established authority. Passively, she delays compliance with parental requests, making the new compromise between them clear: "You can tell me what, I'll tell you when, and when I get enough 'when,' I'll do what you want—partly." (And so, after being reminded five times, she finally washes the dishes. But she doesn't use soap. And the parent feels like he or she is back to square one.)

Alert!

Self-rejection with the old definition and treatment that went with being a child is what begins the process of adolescence. This rejection can coincide with puberty, but it does not have to. When it does, this rejection tends to be accompanied by more intense emotionality and dramatic mood swings.

Early Experimentation

And rebellion works. Through stubborn debate and relentless procrastination, the adolescent is able to create more freedom because sometimes parents are unsteady on their stands or too tired to follow through at the time. And with this new measure of freedom, the third phase of early adolescence begins: early experimentation.

Experiment with what? With a host of new experiences that were beyond the boundaries of childhood but are now temptingly within the reach of adolescence, experiences that the parent often disapproves of. Now begin different styles of dressing, alternative tastes in popular music, underground interests, outlaw identifications, countercultural beliefs and attitudes, and daringly different friends. In addition, substance experimentation often begins at this age, particularly with tobacco, alcohol, and inhalants.

Then there is early experimentation to test behaviors that rules have forbidden. Vandalizing, prank calls, and shoplifting all occur at this age, usually in the company of adventurous friends who all share an interest in risk taking and seeing what can be gotten away with.

 **Fact**

The three phases of early adolescence each serve a developmental purpose. The negative attitude creates the motivation to change. Rebellion creates the power to change. Early experimentation creates the experience to change.

Reducing the Intensity

To help reduce early adolescent intensity created by divorce, know what not to do—don't pour gasoline on the fire.

Don't criticize or argue with the negative attitude, because your negative attention will only make it worse. Your job is to get the early adolescent to mind, not to change his mind. Simply disagree with negative pronouncements. "I understand you think doing homework is a waste of time, and you are certainly entitled to your opinion. However, like it or not, homework will be done."

Don't punish a child for passive resistance like delayed accomplishment of chores. Repeatedly pursue your objective with supervision (nagging), until your insistence wears her resistance down. "I intend to keep after you and after you until you get it done." As for active resistance like arguing, don't cooperate in disagreement for disagreement's sake. "This is all I have to say on the subject. I'm not going to change my mind, so I have nothing further to discuss."

 **Alert!**

When divorce occurs during early adolescence, the parenting challenge is to expect the young person's negative attitude, resistance, and limit testing. Don't take these behaviors personally but that will put you at risk of emotionally overreacting. Instead, hold the boy or girl to responsible account, keeping a positive parental attitude during a more negative time.

Don't let the early experimentation with limit testing go, dismissing it as "innocent mischief" of the age. Let minor testing of limits go now, and major testing of limits (of rules and laws) is more likely to occur later on. So close the loop of responsibility. "You will confront the victim of your misbehavior, hear how the victim felt, and make restitution for what you did."

Mid Adolescence

Somewhere between the ages of thirteen and fifteen, the entry into mid adolescence usually begins. Contrasted to early adolescence, when the parental right to restrict social freedom was a theoretical issue to argue about, in mid adolescence, the reality of parental restriction becomes a source of significant conflict. As social freedom to grow becomes more important, as peers create more pressure to go out and explore the larger world, the young person can quickly become combative when that freedom is denied.

Increasingly self-preoccupied and more focused on peers, the teenager becomes less considerate of, and more impatient with, parents. Delay of gratification becomes painful because immediacy of want becomes so urgent. Frustration and its companion anger are easily aroused. The teenager feels he or she must have what is wanted, as soon as it is wanted, which means "now!"

This is the age where parents must beware the end run, exploiting of loopholes, and social extortion. An end run is spending the night with a friend who has less parental supervision (hence more freedom) than you provide at home. Exploiting a loophole is doing what the parent neglected to specifically forbid, the teenager then claiming innocence: "You never said I couldn't!" (Because the parent never thought he would.) Social extortion is last-minute asking to go out in the presence of impatient friends who apparently have been given parental permission. Don't play these illicit freedom games.

Mid adolescence can speed up family interaction with the teenager's increase and urgency of demands. The single parent needs to slow the rate of decision making down to "all deliberate speed" (taking sufficient time for due discussion and deliberation). Don't let the teenager set the speed of family life. If the teenager creates immediate deadline pressure by saying, "I need to know now!" then your answer is no.

How Divorce Intensifies Mid Adolescence

For the mid adolescent, parental divorce can come at a particularly bad time. Now daring to adventure out into the perilous world in the company of peers, having a solid family to rely upon provides much-needed security. A solid home is a safe base to return to after an adventure or exploration is done, a sanctuary in which to recover from the pressures of pretense and conformity that are part of peer pressure (of going along to belong). Divide and weaken this base, as parental divorce usually does, and the young person becomes more detached from family and more dependent on peers, more vulnerable to the pressures of impulse and conformity they can exert.

The task for the single parent is to assert a stable and consistent set of demands and limits, and impose a clear structure of expectations and prohibitions, that protect the young person by providing guidelines for making constructive choices. Don't worry about your popularity with your teenager at this age. Be more concerned with your child's safety. To that end, when in doubt about how to respond to what your impetuous teenager is doing or wanting to do:

- Delay and think,
- Question and find out,
- Check and verify,
- Search and discover,

- Push for what's right,
- Feel free to say no.

What do you have to lose?

Two kinds of behavior often intensify when divorce coincides with a young person's mid adolescence: conflict and lying. They are both used to get social freedom with peers, freedom that has now become more urgent in consequence of family loss at home. As parents become less dependable because of divorce, the young person comes to depend more on his or her family of friends. Ten common mid adolescent lies are: "I already did it," "I didn't do it," "I don't know," "I forgot," "I promise I will later," "I didn't think you'd mind," "I didn't know that's what you meant," "I didn't think you were serious," "It wasn't my fault," "It was an accident."

Conflict can be used to coerce or exhaust a parent into submission, particularly one who hates, or is too tired, to fight. Lying is used to cover up the truth of what was done or what is intended. In each case, the single parent must rise to the challenge of giving conflict no extortionate power, and of confronting dishonesty when it occurs.

Reducing the Intensity

To help reduce mid adolescent intensity created by divorce, meet conflict and lying head-on.

Let your mid adolescent know that continued argument after a full discussion is over and a decision is made (request or permission denied) will make you less, not more, inclined to grant the next freedom he or she desires. "You don't have to like my decision, but you do need to stop contesting it once it is made."

Let your mid adolescent know that lying will be treated as a serious offense and explain why: "Without honesty, there is no trust, no safety, no intimacy. Lies do emotional damage. I feel mistreated and hurt, I feel betrayed and angry, I feel misinformed and anxious." Then apply some act of reparation: "As a function of lying to me, you will have some task to do around here to work it off. Afterward, I intend to trust you again and expect you to tell me the truth."

Essential

Sometimes a parent will become concerned about the early adolescent's low self-esteem. But low self-esteem is not a problem to be changed at this age; it is a reality to be accepted. Having cast off esteem-building interests, activities, and relationships he enjoyed as a child but now dismisses as "kid stuff" he has outgrown, the early adolescent's self-worth is riding on empty, with nothing positive yet established to take their place.

Late Adolescence

Somewhere between the ages of fifteen and eighteen, the entry into late adolescence usually begins. For the young man or woman now in high school, the world begins to open up as older and more experienced students, by encouragement and example, stimulate the desire to act more adult. Now more grown-up behaviors—such as attending parties, recreational substance use, driving a car, getting a job, significant dating, having sexual relations—can become rites of passage that certify one's progress and affirm one's older status.

Alert!

To moderate the risks that go with acting more grown-up in high school, hold your late adolescent to responsible account. Don't give permission for any of those four rockets to independence—going to parties, dating, holding a part-time job, driving a car—unless he or she is behaving responsibly at home, at school, and out in the world.

Yet, with the freedom of acting older comes more anxiety. Now the twin luxuries of not having to think beyond present gratification and depending on parental support are coming to an end as the reality of the next step into more independence comes into view. In a couple of years, whether in school or not, the age of high school graduation brings with it more expectations of autonomy, more serious thought about one's future, and the inevitability of leaving home. Troubling worries about readiness for this next step can create a lot of doubt at the departure point as fear contends with excitement to anxious effect.

How Divorce Intensifies Late Adolescence

For the late adolescent, parental divorce can come at a particularly bad time. Soon he or she will be leaving home, and now parents are splitting apart. Family unity is broken and family stability is shaken. Independence feels safest to try when a strong family foundation is there to rely on, to push off from, and to return to should need arise.

The security of home now to some degree weakened, the teenager may accelerate her separation from family in response to parents' separating the marriage. Going on a run against rules to escape feelings of loss and to express anger, some teenagers may feel driven to act more grown-up because, deserted by the unified family they could once count on, they now feel more impelled to grow up quickly and operate on their own. In the impulse and confusion of their response, teenagers can resort more to older, self-destructive activities like substance use and sexual activity—the first to forget pain, the second to forge physical connections to feel close.

 **Fact**

Sometimes there can be regression in late adolescence as the teenager sees the next step into more independence looming ahead. He or she may start backpedaling, failing classes to put off graduation. Preparations like filling out job or college applications may become stalled. A parent can give the support of his or her insistence to help the teenager overcome reluctance to face this next hurdle in growing up.

Reducing the Intensity

To help reduce the run against rules, which is often self-defeating, the single parent needs to keep a firm structure of healthy expectations around the teenager, with which he or she can comply when the run is done. Also, the parent, directly or through counseling, can empathetically respond to the emotional turmoil beneath the rule-breaking activity by helping the teenager talk out hurt feelings that are driving this behavior.

To shore up the teenager's confidence at this point, the single parent needs to assign more grown-up responsibilities. What helps reduce fear of unreadiness in late adolescence is evidence of preparedness the young person cannot deny—mastery of those exit competencies and responsibilities that a strong independence depends on. To that end, the single parent systematically transfers more responsibility for self-regulation, self-care, and self-support over the several years leading up to graduation. Thus, even when parental divorce occurs, such preparation has given the late adolescent cause to believe, "I know how to take care of myself."

Alert!

Sometimes, when divorce occurs during late adolescence, parents will try to compensate for family loss by doing more for the teenager than he could be doing for himself. This is a mistake. Transfer more responsibility. Do not create less.

Don't discuss your worry about your teenager with your teenager because that will be sending a vote of no confidence when he or she has enough doubts of his or her own. Instead, give the opposite communication—an expression of unwavering faith that your son or daughter has what it takes to take the next step toward more independence. "Not only do you know how to make good choices, but you have what it takes to learn and recover from bad ones." If you have worries, confide them to a friend instead.

Essential

When divorce occurs in late adolescence, the parenting challenge is to insist on commensurate responsibilities to accompany the accelerated push for more complete independence—voicing confidence, not worry, that the young person can learn to master the freedoms that come with this next level of self-management successfully.

Trial Independence

Somewhere between the ages of eighteen and twenty-three, the entry into trial independence usually begins. Living away from home usually for the first time, sharing an apartment or room in a dormitory, holding a job or going to college, the young person typically finds so much freedom and responsibility more than he or she can successfully handle right away.

Consequently, there is much slipping and sliding, lack of direction, and many responsibilities that prove too hard to keep. This is the age of breakage—of leases, bank account and credit card agreements, laws and legal obligations, educational requirements, job commitments, promises to self and others, to name a few. This is also the age of maximum alcohol and drug use, twenty-four-hour-a-day partying, and the companionship of peers who are also losing their footing on the slippery slope of independence. No wonder young people at this challenging age, without sufficient discipline, a clear sense of purpose, and self-restraint, have moments of feeling developmentally incompetent.

Just think about the seemingly simple challenge of living with a roommate—a lesson in interdependent living. Now young people have to learn to share joint use of space, cooperate with each other's needs, depend on mutual commitments, tolerate differences, communicate about disagreements, resolve conflicts, and get along with someone whose behaviors one does not always like. And all this is only one challenge among many at this more independent age.

 **Fact**

There is a major self-esteem drop in trial independence, a painful sense of developmental incompetence. "I'm old enough to be adult but I keep messing up!" Tell your son or daughter, "Most young people don't find their independent footing without first making some slips because there are so many new responsibilities to learn."

How Divorce Intensifies Trial Independence

For the young person in trial independence, parental divorce can come at a particularly bad time, creating two extremely complicated problems: the problem of the divided future and the problem of commitment.

Overwhelmed with all they have to manage and often feeling, with good cause, not up to the task, suddenly a bombshell explodes in their life. Mom and Dad are going to divorce! Now the home left behind, which represented stability not only in the past and present, but in the years ahead, is split. In the process, divorce creates a divided family future for the child. On the threshold of adulthood, beyond the age when custody agreements determine visitation, now the young person is going to have to take responsibility for deciding how to divide time out with parents, apportioning time with each so attention given will be fair.

In addition, older now and more inclined to form a serious relationship of lasting and loving value, parental divorce clearly communicates that love does not last. Given this harsh reality, the young person's trust in loving commitment is shaken. It violates faith in commitment on at least five levels:

- Commitment to love
- Commitment to marriage
- Commitment to family
- Commitment to children
- Commitment to commitment

Now the young person faces a crisis of commitment when it comes to love relationships that can be resolved only by daring to commit to commitment again.

 **Essential**

Perhaps it is because of lack of faith or fear of hurt that children of divorce are less committed to commitment when they grow up. Deciding to marry, they are more likely to divorce than adult children of parents between whom the commitment to stay married was kept. Divorce can teach that it is easier to walk away from hard times than to stay and work through them. Most children of divorce have issues about trust in commitment to resolve in their adult caring relationships.

Reducing the Intensity

To ease the complexity of the young person's managing a divided future, it helps if parents do not hold the child to some strict accounting of equal time with each parent, or compete with each other for the child's time. When parents vie and compete for contact with the child in trial independence, the son or daughter only becomes loyalty conflicted and less eager to spend time with either parent.

As for the problem of distrusting commitment in caring relationships, common short-term solutions the young person may choose include the following:

- Becoming very cautious in caring relationships, delaying commitment for a long time
- Becoming very casual in relationships, refusing to get deeply attached, keeping relationships on a superficial level
- Becoming very conflicted in caring relationships, one moment ready to commit, ready to break it off the next
- Becoming very controlling in caring relationships, working to ensure the other person will act compliantly and so not leave

What can help is for the parent to discuss the issue of commitment that parental divorce can create for children, particularly in trial independence. "Just because we got divorced does not mean that you cannot keep a commitment in love." And then, without blaming the other parent, you can describe some of the mutual sources of disagreement and estrangement that contributed to your decision to divorce. You can even frame your explanation in the model given in Chapter 1 if you so choose. In trial independence, young people are often able to learn about creating their own caring relationship by understanding how parents were unable to keep marital caring alive.

CHAPTER 9

The Only Child and Divorce

W hy a separate chapter devoted to the only child in a book about children and divorce? Because an only child, being the recipient of all the affection, attention, and attachment that parents have to offer, often has more to lose in divorce than do children who are used to sharing what parents have to give and can depend on siblings for companionship and support. The only child must go through divorce alone. In addition, there are dynamics built into only-child family functioning that create special complications when parents divorce.

The Two-Parent/Only-Child Family

There is a luxury that comes with having an only child. Parents don't have to worry about providing for one child at the expense of another, having to fairly divide resources between competing demands, or having to figure out which sibling started a fight and how to settle it. They never have to go through "second-child transition," that painful realization that now they can no longer provide child number one the undivided attention that was given before, and they can never provide child number two as much attention as they first gave child number one.

There are two myths about having an only child. Myth number one: having an only child is less demanding than having multiple children. This is not true. Since "only" is first and last child in one, having an only child is high-pressure parenting. Because this is the only chance at parenting they get, parents want to do the job right. Myth number two: having an only child is less complicated than having multiple children. On the contrary, extreme attachment and sensitivity make having an only child interpersonally complex.

Unity of the Family

Parents can devote themselves entirely to the welfare and happiness of an only child who has brought them together in a new way. Before the child, they were just married as partners, as wife and husband. Now they have become additionally married as parents, as mother and father. The only child has birthed them into parenthood, and in the process has created a threesome of undivided love where mother and father treat the child more as "one of us" than as "one of them," as happens when a second child is born.

At the center of an adoring parental world, the child soon instinctively and intentionally imitates adult characteristics, becoming verbally and social precocious, peering with parents and their grown-up friends, becoming "adultized" in this way, coming to presume grown-up standing in the family. "I get to have my say in what we do."

Part of the Parental Marriage

In effect, as the only child grows, he or she feels like an integral part of the marriage, gathering strength from belonging in four common ways.

- There is an enormous sense of security that comes from being so deeply anchored in the parental relationship.
- There is a satisfying sense of intimacy that allows the child to deeply know parents and to feel deeply known in return.
- There is a sense of equity with parents that encourages the child to assume comparable standing with parents, to be outspoken, and to claim rights of full participation in family decision making.

- There is ongoing inclusion in parental conversations, parental social relationships, and parental activities outside of the home, which creates a powerful sense of togetherness.

Being treated as a primary focus of parental concern causes position in the family to become central to the only child's world. "My parents always take me into account." When parental divorce occurs, that unified world is divided, and now parents put their own happiness above that of their only child, who must accept a decision over which she was not consulted, which she does not support, and which she cannot change.

Fact

Parental divorce is disillusioning to any only child: how can parents who love her so much bear to cause her such pain? Parents who were once trusted completely are now trusted less. "Now my family is broken and I'm going to have to look out for myself."

When the Parental Marriage Splits Apart

When divorce occurs, an only child feels caught in the middle between two loved and loving parents who no longer love each other, an excruciating place to be. Now the downside of the child's intimacy with parents can be strongly felt.

The Pain of Parental Divorce

"It was the worst part of my growing up. Although my parents both loved me, they lost love for each other. At the end, I was the only family happiness they had. The pain they felt with each other became my pain. Sometimes I wondered if it was my fault. Were they just staying together for me? I did everything I knew to help make their marriage work. Then, when my efforts came to nothing and they divorced, I felt I had failed the two people I loved. And when there was pressure to take one parent's side against the other, their fighting just tore me up."

Parents cannot divorce each other without also divorcing the only child, who loses the secure sense of feeling embedded in the parental relationship. The threesome in which she played such a central role is no more.

Competing for the Only Child's Affections

Because parents of an only child so strongly want to do right by their son or daughter, divorce can feel like an act of doing that child wrong. Instead of creating security and happiness, parents are inflicting insecurity and pain. Instead of putting the child's well-being first, they are giving priority to their own. No wonder each parent wonders what effect divorce will have on his or her relationship with the child. No wonder single parents want to make that relationship okay. No wonder, out of their own insecurity, they may feel threatened by the child's relationship with the other parent.

It is very common for divorcing parents to vie for loyalty of their only child, lobbying to maintain the primary attachment. Often the parent who was divorce reactor ("I never wanted divorce") will claim sympathy and support for feeling victim and experiencing rejection. Often the parent who was divorce initiator ("I wanted out of an unhappy marriage") will petition for understanding and to be forgiven.

Divorced parents who insist on competing with each other to be "most valued parent" in their only child's life create a losing contest all the way around. The child is enlisted in playing a game of favorites, a losing game because to appear to like one parent better creates the appearance of valuing the other less. In addition, now the boy or girl feels like a prize to be won rather than just a child to be loved.

The parents create a contest between each other that gets in the way of collaboration for the sake of the child, neither willing to cooperate if that might give the other some competitive edge. To support the other parent creates the risk of undercutting one's advantage with the child.

Alert!

An only child cannot be pulled into alliance with one divorcing parent without feeling painfully estranged from the other. "How can you bear to see your mother after how she has mistreated me, and you, by leaving the family?" Don't play the politics of loyalty with your only child. Don't try to get the child to take your side.

Stopping the Competition

What helps absolve the problem of parental competition is realizing that there really is none. The child is still going to have a mother parent and a father parent, and neither parent can usurp the other's role. At most, the parents can continue to complement each other, creating an ongoing partnership for the sake of the child, in which each parent wants the child to have the benefit of two solid parental relationships. "Despite what's happened, I want you and your mother to enjoy a close and loving relationship, because I want you to have your mother in your life, and because I can be your father, but I cannot be her." "Despite what's happened, I want you and your father to enjoy a close and loving relationship, because I want you to have your father in your life, and because I can be your mother, but I cannot be him."

Essential

When it comes to the only child's affections, divorced parents can declare that there is no competition, "no contest," between them because the two parental relationships are simply valuable in different ways, and always will be (see Chapters 16 and 17). In addition, each parent wants the child to have the full benefit of both, not just the partial benefit of one.

Discomfort with Conflict

It is not uncommon for an only child to intervene when parents argue. "Stop fighting! I hate it when you fight!" The child wants to make the conflict go away because parental argument creates discord in the family, and the child wants unity, not division. Conflict is seen as the enemy of closeness, as a threat to everyone's getting along.

Most only children are uncomfortable in conflict because they are unpracticed in the process of confronting, contesting, and resolving differences in relationships. This is one price they pay for the consideration of sensitive parents, the absence of competing siblings, and membership in the parental marriage.

Parents tend to be considerate and protective of their only child's feelings. They want to handle any friction gently and with care. Thus when conflict with the child arises, parents tend to be very sensitive in what they say and how they say it. "When we have a disagreement, we do our best to be calm and diplomatic so our child doesn't get upset."

Alert!

The more preciously parents treat their only child, particularly in conflict, the more their solicitude can risk preventing robust emotional growth by reinforcing the notion that he or she is easily bruised or damaged by the expression of opposition. In consequence, the only child may develop a sense of emotional fragility that causes him or her to become conflict-averse.

From being an only child, the boy or girl is spared the daily social contest and emotional abrasion that tends to characterize normal sibling rivalry. Unlike conflict between parents and their only child, siblings typically do not feel obliged to act so considerate or careful with each other when differences arise. Intermittent conflict is usual, hurt feelings happen, people get angry, differences are dealt with directly, and the young combatants usually find a way to reconcile and become good companions again. When it comes to feeling comfortable in conflict, an only child has a lot to learn. Fighting does not mean siblings can't get along. It is a normal part of how they get along—contesting differences, competing for resources, venting emotion, testing power, and vying for dominance. So in multiple-child families, the push and shove of conflict is a normal part of daily life. In an only-child family, it is not.

When parents fight, an only child will experience the opposition as an emotional distance between parents, particularly if there is anger from fixing blame, and momentary estrangement from needing separation and time apart. Parental conflict can threaten the only child by creating disunity in the family threesome. "I want us all to get along!"

Keep the Child out of Parental Conflict

Like most children, an only child has divorce fears since divorce is so common today. Because it leads up to divorce, parental conflict carries the threat of divorce, particularly if that conflict is frequent or intense. So divorce itself actualizes the only child's worst fear of conflict. And that fear is made worse when, either pre- or post divorce, the child becomes embroiled in this conflict by parental design.

 **Fact**

> The only child is so strongly identified with parents and family that when divorce occurs, the boy or girl feels literally torn apart. Gone is the family unit, gone is the loving threesome, gone is the sense of "me equals we" upon which the child based so much personal definition. Now the worlds of self and family must be redefined.

In each of the following three ploys, the only child is enlisted in parental conflict in an extremely painful way.

- Don't use the child as a weapon. One parent can claim the only child's sympathy against the other: "We don't know how you can call yourself a responsible father when you act this way."
- Don't use the child as a pawn. A parent can enlist the only child in a manipulation "to get" the other parent: "Talk to you mother if you want to know why we don't get along!"
- Don't use the child as a mediator. Parents can enlist the only child in solving their marital problems: "See if you can get your mother (or father) to forgive me."

Avoid Making It Worse

Divorcing parents can, and should, avoid certain actions that make the only child's predicament more painful.

- Don't use the child as an emotional refuge or support when not getting along with each other. ("Well, at least my child loves me, even if you don't.")
- Don't blame the child for marital conflict. ("We are arguing about you.")
- Don't ask the child to take sides. ("Who do you think is right?")
- Don't complain about the other parent to the child. ("He never does what he promises." "She never gets things right.")
- Don't compare the child to the other parent in negative ways. ("You're stubborn just like your mother." "You have a temper just like your father.")

Alert!

Beware a highly responsible only child who becomes unduly preoccupied with emotionally supporting parents after divorce. The anxious child may be ignoring his or her own needs in order to take care of parents so that the relationship to each is secured, and so that the relationship between parents doesn't get any worse. No child should be cast in the caretaker-of-parents role when parents divorce.

When divorcing with an only child, as in providing professional help, the injunction for parents to follow is, "First, do no harm."

Parental Guilt

The last thing most parents want to do is hurt their beloved only child, but when they divorce, deeply hurt is how their son or daughter is going to feel. In response, it is normal for parents to experience guilt. Guilt is blame and punishment directed at oneself for injuring others. It is most strongly felt when injured others are well loved, and it requires forgiveness from self and others to create absolution.

Divorced parents of an only child need to distinguish between responsible guilt and compensatory guilt. The first they should assume; the second they should not.

Responsible Guilt

Responsible guilt means that each divorced parent, particularly the one who initiated the divorce, accepts that one consequence of separating the marriage is to cause profound hurt to the only child. By this adult decision, the boy's or girl's secure world of family is torn apart. In recognition of this emotional cost, it is normal and healthy for parents to experience responsible guilt: "By our self-serving actions, we are causing suffering to our child." Healthy parents admit this culpability.

They also then forgive themselves so ongoing guilt does not exact continuing emotional cost. They must normalize the relationship and move on because parenting from guilt can do two kinds of harm.

First, for parents who cannot forgive themselves for the hurt divorce has done their only child, self-punishment after divorce only creates unhappiness divorce was supposed to ease. It is no mercy for a child to have a parent who is as unhappy after divorce as he or she was before. If parents are going to make themselves miserable with guilt after divorce, they may have been better served staying married.

And second, few children can resist manipulating a guilty parent when it comes to escaping responsibility for wrongdoing. "I wouldn't be failing in school now if you hadn't divorced!" No. It is the child's choice not to do schoolwork. If they accept the child's blame with their divorce guilt, parents are at risk of letting the child cast off responsibility for the poor choices he or she has made.

Fact

By claiming responsible guilt, parents also make it clear that the only child (who often feels part of marital functioning) bears no responsibility for the divorce, thus preventing the child from engaging in any self-blame.

Compensatory Guilt

Compensatory guilt exacts ongoing tribute from divorced parents who feel they must not only continue to punish themselves for hurting their child, but they must make reparation to the child for injury received. "We will atone for the hurt we have done." Unhappily, compensatory guilt is self-perpetuating. Each payment parents make only confirms the guilt they bear, and the burden of guilt gets heavier, not lighter, with every act of compensation made.

To end compensatory guilt, parents must forgive themselves and normalize their treatment of the child. If they do not, compensatory guilt can drive parents into making it up to their child by saying yes too often (excessive indulgence) and no not enough (inadequate restraints). "I have caused my child suffering enough. I can't stand to see her suffer any more." As for forgiveness from the child, that tends to be delayed when parents cannot forgive themselves.

CHAPTER 10

Establishing the Single-Parent Family

There is a kind of nuclear reaction that needs to follow divorce. The custodial mother or father, in an effort to establish the new single-parent family unit and adjust the children to it, pulls them close, expands his or her parenting role, redefines family rules and routines, and pushes the ex-spouse away (and pulls away) to create autonomous space for this redefinition to occur.

Detaching from the Ex-Spouse

During this period, the custodial parent often wants separation and privacy from the noncustodial parent, to accomplish three tasks:

- To reexamine and reaffirm their own parenting values and adjust to new circumstances, often altering parenting priorities and practices from how they were before divorce, as the separation of households creates more freedom for independence
- To reassess the goals and roles that direct the growth of themselves, their children, and the family as a whole to reflect new freedoms and necessities
- To set and defend new rules, asserting sole authority against the demands of children who may contest these limits before accepting and respecting them

To attain these objectives, the custodial parent may need to push away the noncustodial parent (and pull away from old dependencies upon that person), no matter how well meaning and temptingly useful his or her continual involvement in their new family may be. The sooner everyone adjusts to the reality of two parents in separate homes, the better.

Fact

Usually, a noncustodial parent has possession of the children no more than one-third of the time, so most parenting responsibility is vested in the custodial parent, who maintains the major domicile and is responsible for most continuity of care.

For the noncustodial parent, however, this adjustment is not easy. Living apart, this parent must watch family grow close and develop into a new unit without his or her presence. He or she must stand by as the custodial parent expands the role of major parent, in many cases taking over activities for which the noncustodial parent was once responsible. Feeling replaced can be scary. Being excluded can make the noncustodial parent feel insecure and lonely.

Alert!

Not only do custodial parents need adequate separation to establish their single-parent family, but so do the children whose reunion fantasies are fed by divorced parents who are continually seen together in the same home. "If Daddy spends so much time over here, maybe he and Mommy will get back together after all."

Unlike the custodial mother or father, whose role as daily parent continues unbroken, the noncustodial parent must give up this continuity for more occasional contact with children, agreeing to live apart from the family. Until this new role is established, the noncustodial parent may cling to what is missed, trying to maintain his or her old place, not as husband or wife, but as parent. Calling up, checking up, dropping in, offering advice, fixing things, and helping out are some of the means a noncustodial parent can use to maintain family attachment. In response, a custodial parent may find this ongoing presence intrusive. He or she may want sufficient distance for separation to take place and independence to become established.

What to do when the noncustodial parent still clings to the family? The custodial parent needs to give a double message: "I appreciate and want your continued involvement in the children's lives. However, I need you to base that involvement on their visitation with you, not by your coming by to visit us."

Separation, Not Rejection

It is essential that the noncustodial parent not take the custodial parent's desire for independence as a rejection of the noncustodial parent's presence in the children's lives. A noncustodial parent who feels rejected and dispensable in this way is at risk of deciding to withdraw from the children's lives, rarely or even never seeing them. "I won't be missed. They don't need me anymore." This decision hurts everyone. Therefore, during the nuclear reaction following divorce, the noncustodial parent needs to keep contact with his or her children, keep faith in the importance of his or her enduring parental contribution and role, and understand that the custodial parent needs time and space to set up family on his or her new terms.

The challenge of divorcing well is to emotionally reconcile the marriage between husband and wife (freeing it from lingering attachment, anxiety, or animosity) while keeping the former partners working together as father and mother in support of the children's growing needs.

What enables this collaboration is the capacity of each partner to create a satisfying life separate from the other. Living happily apart, they are better able to cooperatively unite when a joint parental stand is required, as it often is during children's adolescence when the teenager challenges and breaks disciplinary boundaries that must now be firmly reinstated in both homes. "Lying about homework means that when you are staying with either of us, there will be increased supervisory contact with the school to see your assignments are brought home, completed, and turned in."

Alert!

When a custodial parent remarries, the noncustodial parent may fear that the stepparent will now take over the noncustodial parent's role, rendering that parent unimportant to the children. This is not the case. A stepparent's role is never "instead of" or "in place of" the same-sex parent. A stepparent is only an addition, not a replacement.

Divorce is a declaration of independence. Ending marriage, the partners agree to live apart. Pushing the ex-spouse away, and pulling away from the ex-spouse, is a necessity for this separation to become established. Without adequate separation and independence, it is difficult for ex-partners to come together for their children's sake, authentically able to communicate this message: "Although we cannot live happily in marriage as partners, we can work together cooperatively as parents, and we shall."

Essential

Particularly during adolescence, a boy or girl may exploit ignorance and differences between two households, playing one situation against the other to gain freedoms that would be prohibited by both, if only both knew. Ex-partners must be able to communicate directly in order to get the straight story about what is really happening. Depend on the teenager's self-serving account and they are liable to be led astray.

Creating Stakeholders in the New Family

A single parent creating a new family not only needs to clarify how he or she wants it to operate on similar and different terms from the old married-parent family, but the single parent also has to bring children into the new family fold. How this is most effectively done is by expanding children's role in the new family, and the name of that expansion is responsibility. The more children feel a stake of responsibility in the definition and operation of the new family, the more supportive of that family they are likely to be.

Question?

What is the most important statement the single parent can make to children about the formation of the new family?
"We are all in this together, and it will take the efforts of all of us to make it work."

Creating a New Sense of Belonging

The single parent can ask five questions, the answers to which can increase children's sense of responsibility in the new family.

The provision question is, "What have I historically done for my children that they could learn to do for themselves?" Example: help prepare meals.

The protection question is, "What am I keeping my children from doing that they could safely learn to do for themselves?" Example: use the car to do family errands.

The preparation question is, "Looking ahead, what responsibilities will they need in order to master later independence that I could start teaching them now?" Example: share family budgeting to teach how to budget when on their own.

The participation question is, "What service contributions to the operation and maintenance of the family could each child make?" Example: teaming on the weekends to get housework done.

The possibility question is, "What good ideas for working and playing together might the children have to offer that would create a more enjoyable and effectively functioning family?" Example: planning an inexpensive family vacation.

Alert!

Establishing a schedule of unifying activities for single parent and children is very important. Each gathering point affirms the new togetherness that has been created—preparing and eating meals together, going to church together, doing housework together, going on vacations together, celebrating special occasions together. The more activities the single-parent family can do together, the more unified that family will feel.

Holding Family Meetings

For the first year of single parenting, it can be worthwhile to hold family meetings at a regular weekly time during which the operation of family can be discussed by all, and ideas for improvement can be shared. The overall agenda question you are asking is, "How can we all work and play together more enjoyably and effectively?" In addition to identifying what is working well that is worth continuing as is, you could use the four categories of change (see Chapter 3) to structure additional discussion. "What could we stop doing (end), what could we start doing (begin), what could we increase (do more of), what could we decrease (do less of) that would help the family run better?" Everyone can make suggestions, but final decisions on implementing any change must be up to you, since you are the adult in charge. The more responsibility children can take, the more ideas they can suggest, the more contributions they can make, the more involvement they can feel, the more committed they will be to supporting the new family unit.

In addition to helping everyone stay on the same page, the role of family meetings is to provide children with a mechanism for creating and investing in the definition and operation of family. Children feel most invested in, and committed to, supporting that which they help create.

Coping with Sibling Conflict

For a while, divorce often increases conflict between children, who jockey to establish position and standing with each other in the new family situation, and to use abrasion with each other to act out hard feelings from divorce. Unwelcome as this change may feel for the resident mother or father, since an increase in sibling conflict immediately following divorce is so common, it behooves the single parent to understand the nature of that conflict and how to keep it within healthy bounds.

"Why can't the kids just get along? Why must they always fight?" The parent gets tired of the persistent bickering, teasing, competing, and ongoing provocation between the children. The parent can't understand why the children won't stay off each other's case, get out of each other's way, leave each other alone, and just be friends. Sibling conflict seems like an additional and unnecessary source of family stress. "Who needs it?" the parent asks.

The answer is, "the children do." Fighting is not a sign of children's not getting along. It is how they get along—using conflict to test their power, establish differences, and vent emotion with a familiar family adversary. Conflict from sibling rivalry is built into family life as children compete for dominance, parental attention, parental support, and household resources. Who gets what? Who does what? Who goes first? Who gets most? Who's right? Who's best? Unless children are eight to ten years apart in age, there will be sibling rivalry between them. Even then, an older child will probably resent a younger for getting away with more, being given more, and being allowed to do more than the older child was at the younger child's age. And the much younger child will resent the older for acting like another parent and for getting freedom the younger is forbidden.

 *Fact*

With an only child, parents don't have to listen to sibling arguments, break up fights, or divide parental attention and resources. Of course, the downside of being an only child is often manifest later on. By missing out on the rough and tumble of sibling rivalry, the young adult only child may be woefully inexperienced with the complexity of sharing, and may have a low tolerance for and limited experience in dealing with conflict.

The more similarity there is between children (same sex, close in age, similar interests), the more sibling conflict over the 3 Ds—dominance, differentiation, and distribution of resources—there is likely to be. The major exception to this is in the case of identical twins, for whom similarity can create a valued intimacy.

For other siblings, however, similarity only increases conflict by increasing the need to win in competition and to establish individuality. To reduce some of this need for conflict from similarity, a parent can encourage more diversity by establishing separate social circles for siblings, separate interests and activities, separate goals and future directions, separate times with each parent, even attendance at separate schools. At the same time, also encourage joint activities that both siblings enjoy doing together. The more diversity between siblings, the less they have to fight to differentiate from one another and contest dominance between them.

Fairness

The issue of parental "fairness," however, remains a divisive one. Charges the fourteen-year-old, "Since I'm older, you should treat me differently and give me a later bedtime. That's only fair!" Charges the twelve-year-old, "Since we're both your children, you should treat us the same and give us the same bedtime. That's only fair!" And both siblings are right. Fairness is treating people differently to honor their individuality and the same to honor their equal standing. Fairness is a double standard—siblings demanding to be the same and different at the same time. A single parent can't win. Fair to one child often seems unfair to the other. What's a parent to do? Maybe treating them equally unfairly is the answer. That way, both children can agree: "Mom and Dad are just not fair!" To which the parent can reply, "I am going to treat you each according to what I believe are your individual needs."

 **Fact**

Age differences create conflict. Younger child provokes conflict to get the older child's attention, often using imitation to prove, "I am your equal!" "Stop copying me!" complains the older child. Then older child puts the younger down to assert supremacy, teasing to show, "You are my inferior." "Stop making fun of me!" complains the younger child. Putting the older child in charge can add fuel to the competitive fire.

Managing Sibling Conflict

Just because conflict is built into sibling relationships, and just because divorce can increase the incidence and intensity of that conflict, doesn't mean the parent should passively accept that reality, play hands-off, and let it go. Sometimes, tired of the bickering, a parent may want to separate the combatants to get a little peace and quiet. And that can be wise. It is also important, however, for the parent to maintain a watchful eye on the conflict so it doesn't get out of hand and do either child emotional or physical harm. To this end, a parent must act as governor of the conflict in four ways.

First, hold both children responsible for whatever conflict arises between them. It always takes a joint effort to create a conflict (conflict is cooperative), and only one to stop it (conflict stops when one refuses to play the game of opposition, to fight or argue back). If you try to determine "who started it," you will only go back to year one. They both started it.

Second, separate, don't mediate. Say you expect them to work out their difference without continuing to fight about it. Instruct them to use separation time to think about how this peaceful resolution can be accomplished. Remember, "Blessed be the mediator because he/she will be hated by both sides."

Third, monitor safety of the conflict. Conflict between siblings should never be used by either sibling as an excuse to do physical or emotional harm. In family conflict, the rule of safety must prevail. To let one child continue to injure the other only encourages the hitting child to think it's okay to abuse and the hit child that it's okay to be abused (and the frequently hit child will grow very angry at the parent for allowing this mistreatment to go on).

Fourth, hold both children accountable for any conflict cooperatively created between them, but hold them each separately accountable for conduct in that conflict. Anytime either child violates the rule of safety, that child will have family business to discuss with you.

Managing Television

Frequently, marital tensions leading up to divorce can cause families to depend on television to escape from conflict by reducing interpersonal communication. Whoever got home first turned on the television, and whoever went to bed last turned it off. When parents didn't want to argue, one or both would watch television. When they did argue, children watched television to escape the conflict. When they all had to assemble as a family, television kept them apart while they were together. They could focus on the program, not on each other. When the painful reality of family life became hard to take, the desire to seek electronic refuge from that reality increased. The more unhappy everyone felt, the more isolated they became, relying on television to create the barrier for separation that was needed.

The Power of Television

Because television commands more attention than anyone else in the household, the single parent may as well consider it another member of the family and treat it accordingly. Make sure what it says is within bounds of what is considered appropriate for children to see and hear, and don't let it interfere with everyone else's communication. Sometimes television, like a spoiled child refusing to relinquish center stage, can monopolize conversation and get in the way of other family members' attending to each other and speaking up.

This intervention is easier said than done because there is no one in the family who can communicate as entertainingly as the television. Try eating supper together with the television on, and conversation with each other becomes turned off. Try to get an answer to a question, and the other person doesn't seem to hear. Try to speak up about something important, and the best available attention is the side of the other person's head. Try to interrupt and get some help or remind the children about a chore, and they plead for delay: "Wait 'til this program's over!" Then, after the parent has waited as requested, by the time he or she asks again, another program has begun. "Not now!" the children object.

Alert!

Once divorce is final, the single parent may need to restructure the role of television to put it back in its proper place—as a servant, not as a master—as something that enhances and does not interfere with the quality of family life.

A Mixed Blessing

Like all technology, television is a mixed blessing. On the positive side, it is a pipeline to popular culture, a window on current events in an ever-changing world, an education in every imaginable facet of human experience, a source of infinite information, a marketplace to sell and shop for new products, a teller of endless stories, a constantly available escape from drudgery and the trials of daily life, a family of familiar characters that can provide a sense of social company, a baby-sitter to distract and enthrall restless children, a stimulant to wake up with, and a soporific to put one to sleep. It's hard to imagine modern life without it.

The Downside

On the downside, however, there are some costs that a parent must consider and some questions he or she must ask. As an activity, does watching television interfere with meaningful communication, needed cooperation, or engaging in other constructive family activities? As an influence, does it import into the home content that violates a parent's family values by encouraging children to believe certain unacceptable behaviors are okay? As an escape, does it allow children to avoid hard responsibilities or healthy pursuits?

What to Do

If the answer to any of these questions is yes, then the parent may want to limit viewing, monitor what is being watched, and take the time to editorialize with children about the implications of what they see. For starters, what can a parent do?

Against the protests of children who have gotten out of the habits of conversing, helping, cooperating, and entertaining themselves, parents can lock the television away for a couple of weeks. "Until we can function well without it, we're not going to watch television. And when we do start watching it again, we shall continue to do so only as long as our family is communicating and relating the way it should."

Unplug the television, and children may feel disconnected. Like people suffering the loss of something they are dependent on, they may feel anxious, bored, or irritated for a while, which can be a lesson in itself.

CHAPTER 11

Establishing
Discipline

D iscipline is part of a parent's training responsibility. Adequately defined, discipline is the combination of parental instruction and parental correction that teaches children to live according to family values and within family rules. It is about how parents can influence their child's decision making by the choices they make. It is how parents behave to get their children to behave.

How Divorce Changes Discipline

In a dual-parent home, mother and father, out of their separate backgrounds and traditions, create common rules and values both agree upon and are willing to support. Part of the process that partners go through when they have a child is marrying as parents, coming to compromises over how they agree to discipline the child and divide up parental roles.

The first responsibility of a single parent is to put a system of discipline (of similar and different family rules and values) firmly in place into which children can safely and securely fit. Children need to know what is expected of them, confident that the resident parent has what authority it takes to be in charge.

Come divorce, the focus and administration of discipline become redefined, challenging the single parent's role in several ways.

Instead of two parents articulating and enforcing family rules and values with their authority, now there is only one. If, in the old family unit, the single parent was a secondary or backup authority to a more commanding partner, now the single parent must learn to be more assertive and influential. If the children are adolescent—pushing against, pulling away, and trying to get around parental authority for more independence—then there will be less power of parental authority to cope with more testing of limits and resistance to demands.

Alert!

Parents often become complicit in their child's behavior problems when they refuse to factor in behavior of their own, often modeling the very conduct they want the child to stop—yelling to stop yelling, for example. If you want to help your child change his actions, take the time to check out your own reactions in response. To change your child's choices, change your own.

Instead of two parents being able to consult about discipline and cope with infractions, now there is only a single parent to think through these decisions and take these stands. "What should I do when my child is home fifteen minutes after the agreed-upon time?" There is no partner to talk to. The single parent has to come to his or her own disciplinary decision. Parenting alone can be a lonely business, with more uncertainty because of less adult support. Now there is no one to switch off with when it comes to taking unpopular stands, with whom to take joint stands, or to back you up.

Instead of continuing the joint rules and values that have supported discipline in the past, now the single parent is free (and obligated) to redefine and assert his or her own rules and values that he or she now wants to teach the children to live by. So the priority of single-parent values may shift. For example, now talking together at supper becomes more important than enforcing table manners. Rules may also change, becoming stricter in some ways ("You won't be allowed out on Saturday until chores are done") and more lax in others ("Picking up your room once a week instead of every day is good enough for me").

 **Fact**

The longer parents are divorced, the more their lifestyle differences create a contrast in discipline between the homes. "When we're at the other house, we don't have to do this!" The children's complaint is correct. Divorce creates two codes of family discipline for them to live by, resulting in differences that increase when parents remarry and the influence of stepparents changes discipline even more.

Inconsistency of Rules and Values

So what is the single parent to do when rules and values in his or her home are not observed in the home of the ex-spouse? First, understand that freedom to live apart increases diversity of family functioning between ex-partners, diversity that requires mutual tolerance if both, for the sake of the children, are going to get along. These lifestyle differences, and the differences in discipline that result, unless clearly harmful to children (causing danger, neglect, or abuse), need to be respected, not contested.

Personal dissimilarities will create inconsistency of rules and values between two households, and that's okay. What is not okay is for parents to criticize these differences, because that presumes more influence than either one has the right to claim. Neither parent has to govern his or her life out of consideration for the other anymore. If the children's bedtimes in the two homes are not exactly the same, if chores are not the same, if TV watching is not the same, if social freedoms are not the same, so be it. Commitment to care for and support their children is what ex-partners share.

It is definitely not beneficial for one parent to complain about the other to children ("You are not being fed right over there"), because children only feel conflicted when this criticism occurs. It is better to acknowledge and explain the increased divorce diversity to children. "You will live somewhat differently with each of us, because now we live more differently from each other than when we were married. What we each believe is important, what rules we have will not all be the same. This doesn't mean that one way is right and the other way is wrong. However, you will have to learn to adjust to these differences as you go back and forth between households, and I will try to remember that this adjustment is not ever easy. I have to live only one way; but now you have to live two."

 **Question?**

Where is parental consistency between households helpful?
Where regular regimens or medication are required for educational growth or effective treatment, or where similar expectations are needed to encourage appropriate behavior in both homes, consistency of discipline between households can be essential, and parents need to discuss to what degree this can be practically accomplished.

The Power of the Positive

Divorce is a negative event in the lives of children. It causes hurt feelings and does not, as a rule, engender more confidence in parental judgment or respect for their authority. Out of injury and anger, children can become more difficult to manage, at least until the separate families get organized and the two-household routine gets established.

It is easy for the single parent, now under more stress from increased family demand than before (see Chapter 13), to let fatigue have its discouraging way. When fatigue causes the single mother or father to become more impatient and negative to deal with, parental discipline becomes its own worst enemy—more critical and punitive than positive and praising, inspiring less cooperation, not more.

 **Fact**

> A frustrated parent who declares to the resistant child, "I will keep criticizing you until your attitude gets better and I will keep punishing you until your behavior improves," risks making a hard situation worse. The child thinks or responds defiantly, "Why should I do what you want if all I ever get is criticism and punishment?"

Four Principles for Effective Discipline

Consider four principles for effective discipline (instruction plus correction).

The first principle for effective discipline is about proportion: keep discipline 90 percent instruction and no more than 10 percent correction. Reverse this ratio, and a child may develop a more sullen attitude and resistant behavior. Why? Because all correction is critical in nature, overemphasis on correction can yield a negative response.

The second principle of effective discipline is, never give correction without instruction. Telling a child to "Stop that!" has no reforming power because you have suggested no alternative behavior. You have not positively instructed the child in what to do instead. "Carry it with both hands, and that way you will be less likely to spill." Don't correct behaving badly without also giving instruction for behaving well.

The third principle of discipline is, keep correction nonevaluative to reduce its negative impact. Rather than finding fault and laying blame, "You made a stupid choice and did wrong, and now you'll have to make it right," say instead, "I disagree with the choice you have made, this is why, and this is what needs to happen in consequence of what you did."

The fourth principle of effective discipline is, keep discipline 90 percent positive and no more than 10 percent negative. Animal trainers have practiced this mix for years. They know that the trick to teaching tricks is creating a rewarding relationship with the trainer that keeps the animal interested in working to learn behaviors for rewards the trainer has to give. Punishment reduces value of the relationship for the animal or child punished. With a child, parents seem to keep this principle in mind, but come that child's adolescence, they seem to forget it, becoming overly negative with their teenager, at the cost of diminishing cooperation.

Essential

Remember: positive parental responses tend to lift the child's spirits whereas negative parental responses tend to drive them down. Positive feelings toward parents engender more cooperation; negative feelings can arouse more resistance.

Whenever you find yourself facing repetitive resistance from a child over a matter of conduct, take your own inventory: "How am I treating my child?" Make one list of the positive responses you have been making to the child (at first patiently asking), and another list of the negative responses you have been making (acting irritated, complaining, criticizing, threatening punishment). If the negative list is longer than the positive, you may be contributing to your child's resistance. A child who feels positively valued by you is much more likely to cooperate than one who feels negatively perceived.

Alert!

Since positive responses encourage a cooperative return, keep corrective discipline from having undue negative effect by following the rule of 2-for-1. For every corrective response you make to your child, make two other positive responses within the next few hours.

The Choice/Consequence Connection

It is through respecting your child's power of choice and holding the child accountable for dealing with both positive and negative consequences of those choices, that responsibility is learned. Owning choice plus facing consequences creates the learning from experience that builds responsibility. And responsibility is a major objective that discipline has to teach, because it is the major protector upon which the child can rely. Being mindful of lessons from past choice/consequence connections can teach responsibility. "I don't play with matches anymore." And taking the time to consider possible choice/consequence connections can teach responsibility. "Maybe I won't spend my money now in case saving it could get me something better later on." Thinking back (reflecting on lessons from the past) and thinking ahead (delaying to consider future outcomes) are skills a parent wants to teach.

In the immediate emotional wake of divorce, children can be prone to think with their feelings and not their heads, following impulse and ignoring judgment. Returned by the police, your child explains, "I just figured if you can run off and leave the family, then why shouldn't I?" Parental divorce must never be accepted as a valid excuse for making an unwise, disobedient, or unlawful choice. "Before we talk about your running off," replies the parent, "I'd like to hear your thoughts and feelings about my decision to divorce."

 **Fact**

Rescue your child from the consequences of a wayward choice and you risk depriving the child of a vital lesson that hard experience has to teach. When parents pay the consequences for the child, the child ultimately picks up the cost: he or she didn't get the instructional benefit of the choice/consequence connection. One unhappy role for parents is allowing or applying negative consequences when a misguided or misbehaving choice is made.

Teaching Two-Step Thinking

To be an effective disciplinarian, a single parent must understand the difference between one-step and two-step thinking. Children begin life as one-step thinkers and must be taught to become two-step thinkers. It is the job of parents to provide this education.

One-Step Thinking

One-step thinking is what children are born with—relying on want, impulse, feeling, and instant gratification to make decisions. By fussing, crying, or grabbing, the infant is making step-one attempts to get his or her needs met. Then, as crying repeatedly results in being held, the little child learns a choice/consequence connection: one possible outcome of choosing to cry is getting picked up. So step-one thinking works.

Alert!

A parent can't just let a child grow up managing her likes and dis-likes with step-one thinking, resorting to thoughtless impulse and demanding immediate gratification when any feeling or want arises. Sooner or later, self-defeating outcomes will occur, and other people will not gladly accommodate the young person's impatient demand.

Two-Step Thinking

So, as the child grows up, a parent begins to encourage two-step thinking. Two-step thinking is taught by delaying impulsive action and immediate gratification to consult reason, values, judgment, and past and possible experience. "Before you decide right now, stop and think twice," advises the parent, "about what happened when you did this before and about what might happen if you do it again."

Teach your children to think twice. Teach them to delay, think, consider past and possible consequences, and use second-step judg-ment to moderate a tendency to indulge first-step impulsive choice.

"I know what you want to do, but stop and think and ask yourself what is wise and right to do."

A single parent must be prepared for children to regress under stress of family change. It is quite common for those who were accomplished two-step thinkers in the married family to lapse into more one-step thinking immediately after divorce. Explain to the child: "I want you to think with your head, not your feelings, but I want to listen to what those feelings are."

Sometimes out of duress from divorce, sometimes out of anger at divorce, sometimes out of feelings of entitlement from the injustice of divorce, a child who has been a reliable two-step thinker will act out in step-one ways. The ten-year-old whines for what he wants, the twelve-year-old acts without thinking, the fourteen-year-old throws a tantrum when denied. What's a single parent to do? The answer is, hold each child to two-step thinking account. To the ten-year-old: "In a reasonable voice, tell me what it is you want or do not want me to do." To the twelve-year-old: "If you had used your judgment, how would you have acted differently?" To the fourteen-year-old: "Yelling will not cause me to change my mind, but if you want to calmly discuss your frustration with my decision, I will be glad to listen."

The Single Parent and One-Step Thinking

Children model behavior from parental example, imitating much of what they see. Overtired and easily frustrated, when a single parent lapses into step-one thinking—relying on impulse, emotion, and the demand for immediate gratification in his or her treatment of children—then that parent may encourage by example behavior he or she doesn't want the children to adopt.

Losing your temper over a child's refusal to immediately comply only primes her to get angry when someone won't do what she wants. Interrupting a child to stop interrupting only encourages him or her to interrupt some more. Hitting a child to stop him or her from hitting a younger sibling only teaches him or her that, if you're bigger, hitting is okay.

Essential

Although growing up is hard to do for children, acting grown up can be even harder for a single parent to do. Acting grown up means having the maturity to be a second-step thinker most of the time. It means not allowing a one-step behavior by the child ("You can't make me!") to trigger a one-step response from the parent ("I'll show you who's boss!"). The most powerful way to teach a child to become a two-step thinker is to model two-step thinking yourself.

Establishing Authority

Discipline expresses the rules and values a single parent expects children to live by. Authority is how a parent backs up those rules and values. Parental authority is the foundation upon which discipline must rest. Discipline says what the parent means. Authority shows the parent means what he or she has said.

Authority is partly conveyed by an attitude of parental confidence: "I expect you to do as you're told." And it is partly conveyed by the certainty of positive consequences when compliance is given (appreciation: "Thank you for doing what I asked") and negative consequences when it is not (correction: "Since you chose not to do what I asked, this is what is going to happen").

Alert!

Assuming and asserting authority is part of a single parent's family leadership job. A parent must direct much of the children's lives with discipline, encouraging adherence to that direction with authority, and gradually turning over increased power of authority to children as they grow older and learn to direct themselves in more responsible ways. "I discipline you until you learn to discipline yourself."

When divorce occurs and two new single-parent families are created from a unified one, it is only natural that children will test the rules and the authority behind them. "Will one parent be as firm as two?" "Will one parent be easier to get around than two?" "Will I still have to play by old demands and limits in this new family situation?" When parents choose to break a family apart, one consequence is opening up the possibility of new freedoms in each single-parent household that children will try to exploit.

Five Pillars of Parental Authority

A family system is defined by the rules and values, norms and expectations, that parents set and children are taught to live by. Parental example is one key to this education; the other is discipline—that mix of continual instruction and occasional correction that convinces children to go along with what the parent wants and does not want to have happen. So when a twelve-year-old friend asks your child why he clears the supper table and helps with the dishes, your son can answer without thinking, "Because I always have." Practice makes well-disciplined behavior automatic. Parental discipline has become self-discipline.

However, suppose in the wake of divorce, in service of testing new household requirements, your children resist doing what they are told, to see what happens when they refuse your request. At this point, you invoke one or more of the five pillars of your social authority, to see if this additional influence can encourage their consent to go along with what you want.

- Making demands. "I'm no longer asking you; I'm telling you to get it done now."
- Setting limits. "The TV stays off until you do what I say."
- Asking questions. "I want to know what's causing you to refuse to do what I have asked."
- Confronting to discuss. "We need to discuss your refusal to cooperate until we can work out my getting the help I need."

- Applying consequences. "Unless you do as I ask now, I may refuse to do what you want of me later on."

Question?

"Why do I have to do more chores, do more for myself, and give you more help now that you're divorced?"
Directly or indirectly, that is a question most children of divorce will ask of the single parent, who needs to be prepared with an answer. "With only one parent in the family, who now has twice as much to do, I need more contributions from everyone to make this family work."

Asserting authority does not usually earn a single parent immediate favor in the children's eyes. Adolescents particularly can respond with considerable displeasure when being told to do what they don't want to get done, the power of parental authority having both specific and symbolic value. Specifically, it backs up a particular parental request. But symbolically, it represents that when it comes to running the family, the single parent, not the teenager, is in charge. "So long as you live with me, you have to live on a lot of my terms."

For a single parent who may not have been used to dealing with a lot of resistance or asserting a lot of authority in the dual-parent family, who may have had another parent for backup, asserting authority as a single parent can be an act of courage. He or she must act for the best of the family, and children will not be appreciative of the stand. The children don't like the parent's pulling rank, and the parent doesn't like being unpopular. Assuming the single parent is not threatening or abusive in the exercise of authority, however, he or she needs to assert the rules and values that define the new family, insisting on compliance and conformity to get everyone aboard.

Although children may resent the imposition of this authority at the moment, treating the parent more as adversary than friend, over time, a firm and well-intentioned authority, consistently applied, creates security and conveys love. Children know that the parent cares enough to sometimes oppose their wants for the sake of their best interest and that of the family.

Alert!

Respect for your authority can be based on love (children give consent to what you want because of valuing you), or it can be based on fear (children give consent to what you want because of dreading you). Fear-based authority is very costly because children become distrustful of the scary parent, relying for safety on distance and deception to "manage" the dangerous mother or father, eroding love from the relationship.

Empathy Before Authority

Before a single parent goes overboard asserting authority every time resistance arises, however, that parent should take the time to make an empathetic response first. Rather than reflexively confronting opposition with your authority, see if you can reach beneath the resistance and connect with what emotionally may be going on instead. A lot of the time, the child is acting out frustration, hurt, or anger from other causes that, given the chance, he or she would welcome talking out.

So next time your child defiantly declares, "I'm not going to do that," instead of replying, "You better do what you're told!" try and connect with whatever may be going on emotionally.

- "Have you had a hard day?"
- "Is something wrong?"
- "How are you feeling?"
- "Are you hungry?" (Feeling hungry can feed resistance.)

Once those feelings are talked out, and the child has received a good listen, he or she is likely to be in a more appreciative, compliant, and cooperative place, and you will know more about your child than you did before. So, before you allow the child's resistance and your authority to harden opposition between you, try an empathetic response. You have nothing to lose and much to gain. Concern-based authority elicits far more cooperation and consent from children than does control-based authority, which often just incites unnecessary conflict.

CHAPTER 12

Strategies for Discipline

Becuase a child's behavior ultimately depends on his or her own decisions, a single parent cannot "make" his or her son or daughter behave. A parent can inform the child's choice, can influence the child's choice, but cannot control the child's choice. Conforming to parental values and complying with parental rules (the twin goals of discipline) mean that the child has chosen to cooperate with what the parent wants or does not want to have happen. The name of this cooperation is consent.

The Principle of Consent

When the early adolescent defiantly declares, "You can't make me and you can't stop me!" he or she is telling the truth. Rather than feel intimated by this declaration, however, the single parent immediately needs to take the issue of control off the table of argument. Declare in return, "Of course I can't control your decisions. They are always up to you. But what I can control are my choices in consequence of the decisions you choose to make. Cooperate with me, and the consequences will feel good. Refuse to work with me, and they will not. As you say, your choices are entirely up to you."

Working for Consent

It seems like the only time a parent is aware of the principle of consent is when he or she is not getting it. "You never do what I ask!" "You always give me an

argument!" If that's what you truly believe and continually broadcast, your child will become a negative believer too, giving you more resistance and less consent. "All I ever do is give my parent a hard time."

You must, you must, *you must* affirm your children's cooperation whenever it occurs if you want to encourage its continuation. Otherwise, your child, with justification, will complain, "You don't appreciate what I do!" No child is always resistant and never cooperative. That is just the tired, discouraged, frustrated, or angry single parent's perspective, which has become so fixated on the problem that he or she has lost sight of the bigger picture, which is that sometimes the child does cooperate and sometimes not. To work for consent, reward it with appreciation, approval, or affection whenever it occurs.

Giving children choices within a larger parental choice can go a long way in getting compliance. Receiving some measure of choice can make it easier for that child to give you consent. So the parent couples a requirement with latitude for child choice. "This is what I need to have from you. Here are some times it can be done. Which one would you like to choose?"

The Relationship Between Child and Parental Choice

Rather than tell the child he or she has no choice, remind the child that he or she always has a choice to cooperate with you or not, and that for every choice the child makes, there will be consequences—for good or ill.

"If you really want freedom, like you say—freedom from my keeping after you to get tasks done, freedom from worry about getting caught for wrongdoing, freedom from my correction, freedom from my questioning and checking—then work within the system of limits and demands I have created for the family. Compliance will set you free. You can determine my choices with choices of your own."

To encourage the child's consent to act within parental rules and values, parents tend to rely on four major approaches to disciplinary influence: guidance, supervision, structure, and the exchange points. The first and most powerful of the four is guidance, most powerful because it has the most instructional power.

Guidance: Good Parents Don't Shut Up

Guidance is the power of persuasion—through explanation, feedback, and providing a moral compass. Guidance means the parent explains what is wanted and why, how to get it to happen, as well as providing practical information the child needs to know. It means giving children a steady stream of feedback about their conduct, a running commentary about which of their decisions are working well and which are not and why. It means constantly informing children about what they need to know. And it means providing a constant value reference for what is appropriate behavior and what is not, what is wise and what is not, and what is right and what is wrong.

The Power of Communication

The most effective single parents are constant communicators, unafraid to tell a child what he or she may not want to hear, willing to take the heat of the child's disapproval or disagreement. They know they can't control a child's choice (change the child's mind), but they also know they can inform that choice (by adding their own perspective). To that end, they offer information, evaluate risk, consult on problems, editorialize about realities in their child's world, and help the child keep a positive self-perception.

Question?

What should I do when my child acts like she is tuning out what I have to say?
Although parents may not always listen to their child, the child usually listens to her parents, entering that information into her awareness, even when not liking, agreeing with, or acting on it at the time. Give up giving guidance and the more your child will be at risk of relying on misguidance from peers.

Creating Talking Points

When a willful child gets into difficulty or commits an infraction, the primary consequence needs to be communication and instruction, extracting guidance from an unhappy situation by turning what happened into a talking point so the child can learn from hard experience. "I will let you know later about what restitution you need to make for what you did. First off, however, you and I will discuss how you got into that situation, what led you to make that decision, and how you can avoid getting into that kind of trouble again. Although I wish this hadn't happened, since it did, I want you to be able to learn all you can from the experience so you'll be better informed and better advised from now on."

Supervision: Good Parents Don't Give Up

Supervision is the power of pursuit. It takes commitment. Harnessing the power of persistence, the parent keeps after children to take care of business at home, at school, and out in the world, overcoming their delay and objections to doing what they're told by using repetition and insistence to wear that resistance down.

Supervision is nagging, and nagging is honorable work. The problem, however, is that it is also the drudgework of parenting. It needs to be shared, because wearing down a child's resistance can wear down a parent's resilience. Come divorce, though, instead of two parents shouldering this unrewarding responsibility, now there is only one.

Essential

Nagging is part of supervision and it is not enjoyable to give or to receive. And it is very labor intensive. Nagging essentially says, "I will keep after you and after you and after you until you get what I wanted done." It finally wears down the child's resistance. "I finally did my chores because I got tired of being hassled. My mom just refuses to give up." (Sounds like a good mom to me.)

Children know nagging works, because they become dedicated naggers in their own right. When they want something that is initially refused, they will nag and nag and nag to see if they can wear down the parent into giving in, and sometimes they can.

Nothing supports continuation of undesirable behavior in children like inconsistent enforcement of limits and demands by a parent. In behavioral psychology, inconsistency is intermittent reinforcement. Sometimes patrolling misconduct, sometimes letting it go makes children's misbehavior almost impossible to extinguish. A parent who doesn't consistently enforce a household rule sends a double message: sometimes it's important to the parent, and sometimes not. Given this double message from inconsistency, most adolescents will at first ignore the rule to see if today the parent will ignore it too.

Keeping Supervision Unemotional

When supervising a procrastinating child, a parent must beware of unwittingly encouraging the child's resistance by becoming impatient, frustrated, and emotionally upset. Effective supervision requires emotionally sober insistence. Keep emotions out of it. When a parent gets frustrated and angry in this pursuit, the child learns that delay has the power to get the parent emotionally worked up. Therefore, when you feel yourself emotionally heating up in the process of supervision, take a break, cool down, and then take up the pursuit again. The issue isn't going anywhere. Then re-engage in a determined and rational manner. Part of being an effective parent is being a persistent nagger.

Never Punish Reluctance to Do Chores or Homework

The most common supervisory issues that parents pursue are those in which repeat, ongoing performance of basic responsibilities is required—like doing chores and homework. Sometimes a parent will punish a child for not discharging one of these responsibilities. This is a mistake because it seems like the parent is making doing chores or homework optional. Choose not to do them, and the child receives a negative consequence. "If you don't do your homework, no allowance this weekend!" No. Not discharging an ongoing responsibility must not be treated as a matter of choice. The child cannot choose to get out of doing chores or homework. He can only delay the inevitable. When it comes to discharging these tasks, there is no escape. Supervision says, "Chores and homework are not up for choice. They will be done. And I will keep after you until they are accomplished."

Question?

What are enough chores to give children?
Assign enough to get some help you need, but don't assign more than you have energy to supervise. If you commit to more chores than you can afford to pursue, you risk appearing inconsistent when lapses in your attention allow children to get out of the required work.

Structure: Good Parents Don't Back Off

Structure is the application of a punitive consequence when some major rule (some fundamental "do" or "don't" of family life) is violated. When parents divorce, traditional family rules are often modified as mother and father create a new family definition that fits their individual beliefs and needs.

If parents are going to change the rules, they must give the children due notice or else grievances about unfairness will be aroused. "You never told us that we can't watch TV on school nights anymore! We're still allowed to at the other house. So what gives you the right to change the rules?"

All rules limit freedom by prescribing or prohibiting choice. As children enter adolescence and demand more freedom and the single parent imposes restrictions for responsibility's and safety's sake, more conflict is created between the parent as constant rule maker and the teenager as occasional rule breaker. In the course of this contest, sometimes the adolescent will decide the punishment is worth the crime (taking some illicit freedom).

The Purpose of Punishment

Punishment is reserved for major rule violations where boundaries of prescribed behavior are deliberately broken. Breach these boundaries (lie about whereabouts or sneak out after hours) and a consequence is applied (now there is work to do this weekend that would not ordinarily be required). Punishment is not for recurrent minor irritations (playing music too loud) or neglected household membership requirements (timely completion of chores). These are supervisory issues.

Sometimes, natural consequences can occur that are "punitive" in their own right. Choosing forbidden freedom and getting personally injured or into legal trouble can teach more powerfully than parental punishment can instruct. Other times, however, a parent must devise a consequence where no natural ones exist. The purpose of punishment is to catch the errant child's attention with a symbolic consequence, discourage repetition of the infraction, and encourage living within the structure of rules again.

Alert!

In frustration or anger, a parent may choose to inflict physical hurt as a punishment—spanking, slapping, belting, for example, to teach the child "a lesson not to act that way again." But the lesson taught is often not what the parent meant to teach. "I learned that if you're bigger and not getting what you want, beating up on someone weaker is okay." Spanking teaches hitting. It teaches might is right. It teaches using force to get your way. It can arouse fear in the young child and extreme resentment in the adolescent.

Beware the use of extreme punishment. "You are grounded for three months!" Extreme consequences can cause extreme anger, particularly in an adolescent, who may take unforgiving resentment and turn it into revenge, self-sabotaging to get back at an excessively severe parent. "I'll show you how bad I can be!" To be effective, punishment must be moderate. Excessive punishment does more harm than good.

Deprivation and Reparation

The most common punishment parents seem to use is deprivation—restricting the child's freedom of movement or use of resources in consequence of major wrongdoing. "Because of what you did, you get to do without." A time-out for a younger child or short-term grounding for the adolescent can catch the young person's attention, particularly if before freedom is normalized the boy or girl has to talk with you about what happened that shouldn't have happened, why it happened, and what he or she is going to do differently so it won't happen again.

Beware excessive deprivation where a parent mistakenly believes that the more opportunity for choice is taken from a misbehaving child, the more obedient behavior will be encouraged. Not so. Strip a young person of every freedom and you have effectively set that person free. He or she has nothing left to lose. "Now you've got nothing left to take away!"

The problem with deprivation as a punishment is the passivity of the demand. All you have done is gotten the child to do without. This is why reparation is the more effective consequence. "As a consequence of breaking the rule, you're going to have to work the violation off to my satisfaction before you get to do anything else you want to do." Now the parent gets some work done around the place that needs doing, and now the child must actively make restitution for doing wrong, in the process staying mindful of the infraction he or she committed. A parent asserts far more authority with reparation than with deprivation because now the child has to actively do something instead of just passively having to do without.

Exchange Points: Good Parents Don't Do All the Giving

Children are dependent on their parents for a great variety of supports—for permissions, services, and resources that mother or father controls. "Can I go over to my friend's house?" "Will you drive me?" "Can I have some money if we go to the arcade?" It takes a parent's agreeing to do what children request for children to get a lot of what they want. And it is useful for the parent to keep children mindful of this dependency.

When a Child Is Uncooperative

Suppose a child is so filled with self-interest that he ignores the household needs of the parent. He acts like what he wants is important and should be provided *now*, but what the parent wants is unimportant and can be put off until later (in the hopes that "later" never comes). How might the parent address this resistance?

Well, asking, explaining, and directing (using guidance) didn't seem to do any good. She has nagged (using supervision) multiple times to no apparent effect, and is exhausted by the effort. And she doesn't want to resort to structure (using punishment) because wasting a significant consequence on a minor offense only lessens the effect of punishment when a major violation occurs.

Invoking the Exchange

So what the parent decides to do is to say something like this: "Before you can have anything you want from me, I want to get what I want from you—the chore I asked you to accomplish." Now the parent is invoking the principle of exchange. The child is being told that to receive benefits from the parent, he or she has to be of benefit to the parent as well. "I will be happy to drive you over to your friend's, but before I do, you need to put away the dishes like I asked."

 *Fact*

> When a parent exploits the child's dependency to encourage cooperation by withholding daily services, resources, or permissions until the child fulfills a parental request, that is neither a threat nor a punishment. If anything, it is an object lesson that teaches the child that in a healthy family relationship, giving is required if getting is desired.

When a child starts refusing to perform routine household responsibilities, becoming more self-serving as some children do after divorce, the parent can simply wait for the child's next request for a permission, service, or resource. Then delay what the parent would normally provide, withholding what the child wants until the parent gets what he or she wants. As for the child's pledge to deliver what the parent wants later (after getting the parent to give), explain that you bargain with performance and not promises, which have not been kept in the past. To be an effective parent, insist on an adequate exchange.

CHAPTER 13

Stress and the Single Parent

C hange can trigger the response of stress because the transition adjustments, losses from change, and additional changes from divorce can create overtaxing demands for both parents and children. Feeling overwhelmed by excessive change is one common source of stress. "There is so much going on, I can't keep up with it all!" When striving to meet over demand becomes a daily challenge, stress becomes a way of life. Because the single parent is family leader, he or she must not only strive to keep the pace of change within tolerable limits, but must also cope with inevitable stress in ways that do not make a hard problem worse. Thus, being able to recognize common signs, major sources, and damaging consequences of stress is prerequisite to understanding what decisions can help keep the single-parent family relatively stress-free.

Understanding Stress

Over demand from current changes, new challenges, and clamoring children is a constant problem for single parents. There always seems to be more that needs doing than they can get done. By electing to overdo in response to over demand, however, they risk depleting their energy to the point where stress from continuing pressure to keep up and keep going and get everything done becomes an unhappy and unhealthy part of daily life.

Stress as a Survival Response

Stress is an invaluable and endangering response. On the positive side, it can be lifesaving, enabling people to focus, exert themselves, and cope with emergencies in ways they ordinarily could not. On the negative side, however, if it is of long duration, it can be life threatening, running people down into a state of exhaustion and causing them, in this weakened state, to act destructively from ongoing duress. Because stress is such a mixed experience, single parents need to rely on it selectively. They must guard against its negative consequences for themselves and their children.

Alert!

What you primarily give your children is who and how you are. What you model, the example that you set, is the primary instructional power you possess. So when it comes to stress, limit it where you can so children learn to limit it as well. And when under stress, manage it in nondestructive ways so your children can learn to do the same.

How Stress Can Arise

Consider how stress can arise. For every demand placed upon human beings by themselves and by the world, people must spend some unit of energy in response. Energy is one's potential for doing or action, and it is limited. People do not possess an infinite supply of this precious life resource.

In the case of single parents, as long as the demands upon them remain equivalent to or less than their readily available response energy, they will feel okay. When the demands exceed what they can readily give, however, then they feel not okay. Now the opportunity for stress has been created in the form of two threatening questions: "Can I meet this over demand?" and "If I can't, what will happen to me?"

In consequence, single parents find themselves confronting a personal energy crisis. To meet what feels like an over demand, they will have to put themselves into emergency energy production. Using force of will (determination and discipline) and perhaps the assistance of chemicals (sugar, caffeine, or other stimulants) to impel themselves into action, they decide to force or stress their system to produce additional energy to cope or survive.

For example, motivated by urgency, fortified by resolve, stimulated by a cup of strong coffee, and energized by a candy snack, the single parent gives up the first moment of relaxation he or she has had since getting home from work, in order to meet a child's emergency. Driving across town at 9:30 P.M., the tired mother or father borrows the resources for a project that the child forgot, just now remembered, and must hand in tomorrow, which will require parental help to complete. And so begins a long night of supervision after a long day on the job.

 **Fact**

To some degree men and women have different vulnerabilities to stress. Often a woman, because she has been socialized to value relationships most of all, will enter stress through self-sacrifice for others. Often a man, because he has been socialized to value performance most of all, will enter stress through overachieving. Then a woman may relieve stress by seeking social support by confiding in friends, while a man may relieve stress through social companionship doing some relaxing activity.

To rely on stress occasionally like this creates a short-term cost. To meet demands at the office the next day will require forcing more energy than feeling tired will naturally allow, energy having been depleted the night before. But what happens if reliance on stress becomes constant, not just occasional? Then, predictably, more serious costs begin to be sustained. These costs can mount over time because the effects of protracted stress are additive—they accumulate, the next level overlying the last.

Four Levels of Stress

Consider four levels of stress. The first level of stress is experienced as continuing fatigue. "I feel worn-out most of the time." Now one's view of the world becomes consistently negative. Beyond fatigue, the second level of stress is chronic pain. "I experience physical hurt or mental suffering most of the time." Now aches and tensions and worries become chronic. Beyond pain, the third level of stress is burnout. "I just don't care as much as I used to." Now what used to matter seems not to matter much anymore. Beyond burnout, the fourth level of stress is breakdown. "I just can't get myself to function." Now even normal coping feels overwhelming or impossible to do.

Alert!

It is tempting for a single parent to cut back on sleep to get everything done. This is a bad trade-off to make. Fatigue from lack of sleep is like a drug that has a negative effect on the mind and the mood. (Sleep deprivation is a common form of torture.) Pessimism and irritability rise, and sense of well-being and content are diminished. Make it a number-one priority for everyone in the family to get adequate sleep.

Stress Is Contagious

Lest you believe the costs of stress felt by the single parent are confined to the single parent, think again. Stress is contagious. Children often feel the impact of the stress their single parent undergoes as that mother or father becomes more difficult to relate to.

- Fatigue can make the single parent more negative and critical to live with. "Can't you do better than that?" And the child feels unappreciated and disapproved of by the parent.
- Pain can make the single parent irritable and oversensitive to small problems. "When you don't do what I want when I

ask, I get really angry!" And the child feels tense and nervous around the parent.

- Burnout can make the single parent insensitive and nonresponsive. "I wasn't listening to what you said." And the child feels ignored and discounted by the parent.
- Breakdown can make the single parent nonfunctional and unavailable. "Don't bother me, I want to be alone." And the child feels rejected and abandoned by the parent.

 **Fact**

If a single parent pays the costs of constant stress, so shall the children. More important, what goes around comes around. Upset by their parent's negativity, irritability, nonresponsiveness, or unavailability, children will likely increase their clamor, only creating more opportunity for parental stress through over demand.

Moderating Start-Up Demands

A trap is set for some parents who have recently divorced, and its name is freedom. Recently liberated from a marriage in which happiness felt sorely lacking and much hardship was endured, they may resolve to make up for what they missed now that they are single. Feeling deprived in the past, they want to compensate in the present. In doing so, they run a risk. Satisfying just some of their longings may feel insufficient. Only excess seems enough for making up for what had been denied. They want it all, and they want it now. Only extremes will do.

Deprivation and Compensation

Wanting to make up for lost time, they may want to socialize to compensate for years of isolation. They may want to exercise in the extreme to compensate for years of being sedentary and physically inactive, in order to "get back in shape." They may want to enroll in many self-improvement activities to compensate for years of self-neglect. Although all of these activities may be affirming, in excess they can become too much of a good thing, adding personal change to family change at the expense of meeting basic family commitments. Now this additional change can result in stress.

Essential

Single parents must beware the trap of compensation—rushing to make up for what was lacking when unhappily married. Family demands have already increased with single-parent responsibility. If, in addition to this adjustment, the single parent invests in excessive personal change, energy can be overtaxed, and stress may result. Start doing good things for yourself, but do so in a moderate fashion.

Speed of Life

It is hard to moderate one's appetite after feeling starved because the pangs of hunger and dreams of satiation are so strong. However, moderation is the key for stabilizing the single parent who feels liberated from a restrictive marriage. It takes restraint to go slow when the temptations of new possibilities are urging full speed ahead. "After the divorce, I wanted more than was good for me. I had to learn not to go too fast."

Speed of a single parent's life can roughly be calculated by resorting to that formula he or she probably learned back in elementary school: rate of speed = distance/time. Change the distance variable into demand, and the speed with which a single parent is living can be estimated by assessing the number of demands to be satisfied in relation to the amount of time available to satisfy them in.

Speed of life = demand/time. The more demands, the less time, the faster and harder the single parent must push himself or herself to get everything done. To slow down, he or she must reduce the number of demands, increase the time allotted, or do a combination of both. More specifically, to regulate his or her speed of life, the single parent must learn to manage three important self-controls: goals, standards, and limits.

Goals

Goals have to do with achievement. *How much* does the single parent want to accomplish and *how soon* does that parent want to get it all done? If, within the first year after divorce, he or she wants to lose substantial weight, train back into good physical condition, find a meaningful relationship, and go back to school a few nights a week to get a better job, the single parent has committed to a high speed of life. That's a lot to want very soon. High ambition can create a high speed of life. (Speed of life = how much/how soon.)

Standards

Standards have to do with excellence. *How well* does the single parent want to do *all the time*? If the parent decides to apply standards of perfection to everything he or she does, whether keeping the home immaculate, keeping the children exemplary at school, or exceeding job requirements at work, an impossible ideal becomes the measure for what is good enough. There is no room for inconsistency, error, or ordinary achievement. Less than impeccability is considered failure to adequately perform. One has to lead a high speed of life to keep from falling short of the high criteria one has set. Extreme standards can create a high speed of life. (Speed of life = how well/all the time.)

Limits

Limits have to do with tolerance. *How much* can the single parent do (tolerate) *at one time*? If the single parent strives to satisfy every demand that children make to ensure their happiness, or (in guilt) to make up for unhappiness caused by divorce, he or she is likely to encourage even more demands. The more the single parent tries to satisfy their demands, the more the children's demands increase and the more exhausted the single parent becomes. Letting children set parental limits is a taxing way to go, and a high speed of life results. Incapacity or unwillingness to set limits encourages excess demands.

Incapacity to set limits can create a high speed of life. (Speed of life = how much/at one time.)

Moderating Speed of Life

Starting up a single-parent family, a mother or father is advised to go slow, both for her or his own sake and for the sake of the children. Discipline yourself to think about how much demand is enough for a given amount of time. One helpful exercise is to make three lists.

- Specify maximum goals, standards, and limits you would love to live by.
- Itemize the minimum goals, standards, and limits that would allow you to barely get by.
- Chart a middle course, describing a moderate set of goals, standards, and limits that would provide sufficiency without going to excess.

Alert!

Instead of going full speed ahead, leading a high speed of life, unmindful of the stressful costs, a single parent is best advised to go at all deliberate speed—where some is enough, imperfection is human, and failing to satisfy every want is okay.

Limiting Stress

So are single parents doomed to labor under constant stress, their children doomed to catch the sad results? Not if parents are clear on the limiting choices they have to make, and have the courage to take the stands required. Like all difficult human problems, managing stress has no easy solutions, only hard ones. In this case, the solutions are two little words: saying "no" to regulate demands, and saying "yes" to ensure renewal.

Saying No

By saying no to themselves, single parents can resist the temptation of positive possibilities. There is a multitude of ways in which they could enhance their lives, yet each way creates one more source of demands to meet. Sometimes invitations must be refused and some opportunities forgone because single parents have too much demand going on already. They would love to do more, but they physically can't afford the additional expenditure of energy.

 **Fact**

Parenting, particularly single parenting, is not a popularity contest. There are times when single mothers and fathers must deny their child to preserve themselves, to the displeasure of their son or daughter. To have no limits, or to let other people set one's limits, is to court constant stress.

Resisting others can be even more difficult. By saying no to a demanding child, parents can face a negative response. The frustrated son or daughter may well express disappointment, argue, or get angry. "You never let me!" "You have no good reason!" "That's not fair!" "You don't love me!" Against the emotional costs of receiving these complaints, single parents have to weigh the stress of giving in and doing more than they can physically afford. Saying no is how people set limits on demands from themselves and others.

Single parents who can't bear to disappoint their child, who can't endure their child's disapproval, who will actually say, "I can't say no," have given that child open access to their energy account and are at risk of feeling overdrawn. Then, feeling overdrawn by unending requests, they end up feeling angry at the child for taking too much, when that is not the problem. The problem is single parents who cannot restrict their giving.

Saying Yes

Saying yes to oneself to gratify a sustaining need or pleasurable want can feel selfish because, in fact, it is. Without responsible selfishness, however, single parents will not adequately attend their own health and well-being, putting their capacity to adequately care for their children at risk. Whether from sacrifice or guilt, parental self-neglect is in nobody's best interest. Without investing in his or her own upkeep and renewal, any mother or father will eventually run down.

There is another kind of "yes" that needs to be said to children, one that some single parents, who believe they should go it alone and do it all themselves, have a hard time declaring: enlisting and accepting help from children to service special and ongoing family demands. "Yes, I really need you to give me a hand." "Yes, thank you, I would really appreciate your help." For a single-parent family to work well, everybody has to share in the work. When the parent does it all, a stressed parent results; but when a single parent shares the load with children, stress is reduced because the demands of family work are spread around.

The Importance of Self-Maintenance

Self-maintenance is self-care. On the one hand, for most single parents, it seems logical to credit the importance of those personal and family activities that must be repeated each day for basic support needs to be met. And yet, in the crush of new challenges to be met and initiatives to be accomplished, it is easy to overlook the importance of ongoing basic needs. To keep stress from ruling your life, you must learn to limit demands, enlist and accept the aid of children, and give a high priority to your own self-maintenance and renewal.

Maintenance Activities

What are maintenance activities? They are any activities that must be done on a regular basis for the parent and family to function well. For example, here is a partial list: provisioning the home; making money; health care; hygiene; eating; sleeping; cleaning; cooking; paying bills; family transportation; running household errands;

relaxation; exercise; and basic supervising of, communicating with, care of, and affection toward children. The list of basics goes on and on.

This list is so long that on a daily basis, it probably consumes somewhere around 90 percent of a single parent's time and energy just to get it mostly carried out. And when the list is accomplished, the single parent is best positioned to get from one day to the next feeling good about himself or herself, with a full supply of energy at his or her disposal, ready to face another day's recurrent and new demands.

Alert!

It is easy for a single parent to place care of the children before care of herself, and at times of special need, setting her own well-being aside to attend to them is appropriate. In general, however, children need to be treated as a second-order priority, with the single parent's maintaining herself at number one because the welfare of the family all depends upon her. The watchword is, "maintain yourself first to take care of your children best."

Why Maintenance Is Discounted

Given this reality, you might think that a single parent would place a high priority on maintenance activities. After all, most single parents know from occasional sad experience that when maintenance activities are neglected (sleep deprivation or irregular eating or bills overdue or health care ignored or attention to children neglected, for example), stress is the result. Demand pressure builds and available energy declines and a sense of crisis is easily created. And yet, asked about what she accomplished over the weekend, a single parent honestly replies, "Nothing, I just kept up with my regular chores," not recognizing that keeping up is prerequisite to keeping on.

Maintenance activities are just taken for granted. Unglamorous, they are discounted because of being just what a person is "supposed to do"—doing the same old daily basics over and over again. After all, how often does someone say to a parent, single or otherwise, "Congratulations, you just made it through another day!" The answer is, not very frequently, because our society doesn't recognize faithful maintenance as an accomplishment to be recognized or rewarded.

Maintenance and Change

Instead, because of the culture that we live in, another kind of activity is valued more: change—doing new and different and more and better and faster. Given this bias, there is a distinction that a single parent is well advised to keep in mind—the difference between spending energy on maintenance and spending energy on change. A powerful reward system in our culture teaches people to recognize the importance of change and to discount the basic utility of maintenance.

 **Essential**

Because divorce creates so much change in the lives of all concerned, stabilizing the family so that it is properly maintained needs to be a primary goal of the single parent. He or she must recognize, establish, and ensure that the basic operations that support family functioning are regularly and reliably accomplished, one day to the next.

Why Change Is Valued over Maintenance

Why are the values of change activities recognized and the contributions of maintenance activities ignored? Maintenance activities just allow you to keep up, while change activities enable you to get ahead. Maintenance activities offer only the dull routine of repetition, while change activities provide the excitement of variety and innovation.

Consider several common comparisons. Maintenance activities are often boring, while change activities can be interesting. So the child hates having to do regular chores but enjoys helping the parent assemble a new appliance. Maintenance activities are taken for granted, while change activities are rewarded with social notice. So the single parent just expects his or her child to keep up with homework but praises the child for making an athletic team. Maintenance activities support the status quo, while change activities lead to improvement and success. So holding a job is treated as a usual responsibility, but finding a better-paying job is considered worthy of notice.

Change at the Expense of Maintenance Means Stress

Both maintenance and change activities are important to an individual's well-being. Maintenance activities create stability and provide support. Change activities create innovation and allow adjustment. The single parent engages in both, but must keep them in healthy balance. If about 90 percent of a person's energy is required for daily maintenance, that leaves only about 10 percent available for change. Because people are culturally encouraged to favor change and to not credit maintenance, this can be a hard balance to strike. Give in to the temptation to invest in change at the expense of maintenance, and sooner or later, the single parent will end up under stress.

For example, consider a single father with two elementary school children in his primary care. After a year of reorganization and adjustment since divorce, the household is well maintained—the basic needs of parent, children, and family are regularly being met. Then he receives an offer for a promotion at work. His immediate response is to treat this opportunity as a positive change, which in many ways it is. It's a new position, more money, different responsibilities, a better opportunity, and will move him up the career ladder faster. The rewards of change are tangible and real; however, so are the costs.

To accept the promotion, he will have to invest in change at the expense of maintenance. In doing so, he risks inviting stress into his family life. Accepting the new position, change begins to take its toll. Now there are longer hours at the job, earlier and later meetings, take-home work, additional worries, less time for self-care, and more irritability with children. As they become anxious at the changes in their father, they increase demands on their parent, and family stress begins in earnest.

Alert!

Think before you commit to a good idea for change—adding something new, doing something different, doing something more, doing something better or faster. All good ideas are partly bad because of trade-offs and unintended consequences they bring. So until you have assessed the bad (the additional caretaking demands of getting a puppy for the kids), don't commit to the good (how your children will love having such a pet).

Investing in a major life change, like divorce, is usually at the expense of maintenance, at least for a while. This is why early divorce creates so much stress for all concerned. The maintenance requirements in the new family situation have yet to be determined and regularly observed. This is also why it is important for single parents to establish new family-maintenance routines as soon as possible, to secure and support their children. Investing in change at the continued expense of maintenance leads to stress. (Change > maintenance = stress.)

One of the hardest choices a single parent has to make is resisting change that offers some improvement, in order to protect the integrity of maintenance. If the choice is made to go forward into change at the expense of maintenance, then this needs to be talked about with the children. The single parent has to explain the long-term gain, discuss the extent and duration of short-term costs, and devise strategies with the children to make these costs sufficiently bearable so that stress does not become an ongoing and harmful fact of all their daily lives.

CHAPTER 14

The Importance of Support

T wo great enemies of single parenthood are fatigue and iso-
lation. Together they can make any problem immeasurably
worse. To lessen the likelihood of fatigue from stress, setting
limits on demands and ensuring self-maintenance are important. To
lessen isolation, the single parent needs adequate social and emo-
tional support.

Don't Go It Alone

Single parenthood is no good excuse for being solitary: "I've gotten
so used to living with children and without another adult, I don't
need any friends." And it is misplaced pride that claims a virtue of
going it alone: "I can handle everything by myself."

Creating Adequate Social Support

One of the first tasks of single parenthood is creating adequate
social support. If as a consequence of divorce, for example, the
extended family has been diminished as in-laws pulled away, and
former friends have socially allied with your ex-spouse, then
the task becomes more difficult and all the more important.

If you have never been a "joiner," then making an effort
to form a circle of friends or to affiliate with a church, a
self-help group, or some social-activity group organized
around a common interest may feel daunting, but it is

worth the challenge. The psychological risks of isolation are not worth taking. Consider four of the worst consequences:

- Exhaustion from refusing to arrange or ask for help. "I'm worn out from doing everything myself."
- Distortion from a limited perception. "With only my way of seeing what is happening, I overlook the good and exaggerate the bad."
- Overreaction from blowing up small problems into major crises. "I explode at small stuff all the time."
- Loneliness from being socially disconnected. "I have no one but the kids to be with or to talk to."

 **Essential**

The more a single parent chooses to isolate, the more vulnerable he or she becomes to exhaustion, distortion, overreaction, and loneliness, to the whole family's cost.

Four Kinds of Support

Four kinds of support are needed, some (not all) of which can be contributed by the children: sharing the care, emergency help, social companionship, and compassionate listening.

Sharing the Care

Sharing the care of children can partly be accomplished by training children to take more care of themselves. The single parent can ask the question, "What am I routinely doing for my children that they can learn to do for themselves?" Then teach them—how to do their own laundry, for example. Education in responsibility is preparation for independence. A child is just an adult in training needing instruction and experience to grow. As a single parent, you can train your child to assume more responsibility.

If the ex-spouse is still cooperatively in the picture, then visitation provides a mechanism for sharing the care. Having people in other places who are happy to receive the children, like friends, parents of the child's friends, neighbors, extended family and in-laws, creates security for children and provides relief for the single parent.

This support allows for flexibility as plans change and unexpected needs inevitably arise. When a single parent has created a community of caring, children become surrounded by a group of adults with whom they feel at home, and this social circle strengthens the child's sense of belonging and safety.

Emergency Help

Emergency help needs to be discussed with children. Suppose they have a crisis and the single parent is not immediately available? Whom can they call? Where can they safely go? Both the single parent and the children need to know what these provisions are. Post a list of adult friends who have agreed to be available should there be a problem for the children when you are not around. Include addresses, phone numbers, and the location of emergency money for transportation, should the children ever have need.

Social Companionship

Social companionship of children, no matter how enjoyable, is no substitute for the adult company of friends with whom the single parent can relax and relate, independent of the parental role. Conversely, by becoming the major social friend for his or her child, as happens not infrequently where there's an only child, the single parent can limit the child's desire for same-age companionship. "I like hanging out with my parent more than with anyone else." By setting an example of social independence, the single mother or father can encourage social independence in the child.

Compassionate Listening

Compassionate listening from children is important because it helps them learn that emotional understanding is a two-way street.

"Just like I want you to tell me when you have had a hard day so I can be sensitive to your needs, I also want to be able to tell you when I have had a hard day, so you can be sensitive to mine. I want us each to keep the other emotionally informed." Beyond this family sensitivity, however, it is important to have adult friends with whom to share the personal problems and pressures of single-parent family life. The single father or mother needs some other adult to call when the weight of responsibility, the uncertainty about what to do, or personal unhappiness threatens to create emotional interference in his or her effective conduct in the home.

The outside supporter can be a problem solver or advisor or just a safe and caring person who, through nonjudgmental listening, will allow the single parent to express whatever perplexity, hurt, or frustration is being felt. Without the availability of someone to talk this out with, the single parent is at risk of emotionally closing off. Then, he or she will be at risk of acting out suppressed and stored-up feelings, most likely with the children, in ways they all will have later cause to regret.

Alert!

Social support is like a combination safety net, social companionship, sane counsel, and safety valve. It allows the single parent to reach out, connect with caring others, feel understood, get good advice, sometimes receive assistance, and know that he or she is not alone.

Self-Respect for the Single-Parent Role

The most important support a single parent needs is not from others, but from himself or herself, and its name is self-respect. Why is this important? Because there is at work in our society common beliefs about divorced single-parent families that compare them unfavorably to two-parent households. Social beliefs tend to support the reputation of the dual-parent family as healthy, but suspect the health of the other.

Social Stigma

There is a lingering social stigma with which single parents must contend, either because they believe it themselves or because others insist on communicating that belief. This belief is a stereotype, a negative generalization about how a single parent presides over a broken home that provides inadequate care and so produces troubled children that provoke trouble for other people—at home, at school, and out in society.

This social prejudice is as wrong as it is real. However, unless single mothers and fathers disbelieve this popular prejudice, they are in danger of undercutting their confidence with doubt, attacking their self-esteem with guilt, and ending up indicting themselves for inadequacy no matter how much they care, how hard they try, or how well they do. Not only is this self-recrimination for no good cause, it can actually reduce the effectiveness of their parenting.

It's not the number of parents in a family but the quality of parenting a child receives that matters most. A home is only "broken" when healthy family interactions break down—when people stop communicating adequately, betray trust, or conduct conflict destructively, for example. As for troubled children, from the vantage point of private practice, they are no more likely to come from single-parent homes than from dual-parent families.

What is true is that single parents, because they have no parent partner with whom to share the daily child-raising load, must absorb additional family demand. However, by rising to this challenge, custodial single parents develop significant strengths that merit recognition. It is the continued recognition and appreciation of these strengths that are key to a single parent's self-respect and self-support.

Strengths of the Single Parent

Consider just a few of the common strengths single parents often seem to possess.

Single parents are highly committed. Taking their family responsibilities very seriously, single parents vote with their actions, doing more caretaking now that they are parenting alone, thereby increasing dedication to the welfare of their children.

Single parents are clear communicators. With much to talk about and less time to talk, busyness causes single parents to talk directly and to the point, not hesitating to speak up when difficult issues need to be addressed.

Single parents are firm decision makers. Accepting that parenting often requires taking a stand against what children want for their best interest, single parents are not afraid to make tough and unpopular rules stick.

Single parents are well organized. With so much to do and one parent to do it, single parents create efficient systems to manage so much responsibility.

Single parents manage diverse family functions. Parenting alone, single parents expand their range of responsibilities to include family tasks the absent parent used to do, often breaking out of sex-role stereotypes to do so.

Single parents create a network of social support. Knowing parenting alone does not mean going it alone, single parents are willing to admit problems and reach out for social support, something dual-parent households are often reluctant to do, disinclined as they are to let the world know when all is not going well at home.

Single parents have clear priorities—single-parent welfare first, family welfare second, and child welfare third. Single parents know that unless they take care of themselves and the needs of their family, the welfare of their children will not be secure.

Single parents value family values. Because there is no marriage partner in the home, single parents focus a lot of attention on the children, on the quality of that relationship, and on what values matter most to keep the family functioning well.

Single parents are good at making ends meet. For most single parents, learning how to stretch a dollar seems to come with the territory, a skill that children in these homes often learn to their later benefit.

Single parents give children clear expectations. In order to be able to count on each other, single parents create a family system in which children know what to expect of their parent and what the parent expects of them.

Single parents give children family responsibility. Knowing they cannot do every routine task that needs to be done, single parents are good at delegating household responsibilities to children, who draw self-esteem from contributing to the family, from being of significant family use.

Single parents are realistic about setting limits. Because single parenting is an over demand situation, single parents tend to be realistic about the limits of what they can do, saying no to themselves and children when doing more would drive them into doing too much.

 ## Essential

Single parents rise to the challenge of parenting alone, and in the process, they come to parent extremely well. They develop significant strengths that become self-supportive when they are recognized and respected. "I have learned to do a hard job well!"

Support from Friends

Because the journey through divorce into single parenthood is so demanding, many fathers and mothers sensibly seek social support along the way. However, support can be risky. By asking for or demanding too much help from friends, a single parent can end up driving those friends away.

To understand these risks, consider four common kinds of support that are often sought.

- **Listening.** Most common of all is the single parent's desire to be listened to, to be able to talk about problems with another person who will take the time to attend to what he or she has to say. "Hear me," asks the single parent. And having been heard, he or she feels known by someone else, no longer all alone.

- **Empathy.** Sometimes simple listening is not enough. There is a desire to be emotionally understood, to have another person register the single parent's experience. "Feel with me," asks the single parent. And receiving that response, he or she feels that someone else can relate to what the single parent's situation is emotionally like.

- **Service.** There are certain support needs that listening and empathy cannot provide, like helping with over demand in the mother or father's early transition into single parenthood. Now there is a need for service support from other people to help bear the burden of daily tasks. "Do for me," asks the single parent. And receiving this assistance, temporary respite is provided.

- **Responsibility.** Finally there are those overwhelming times when the single parent simply doesn't know what to do. Either the will to choose has been weakened by exhaustion or a problem cannot be figured out. "Help me decide," asks the single parent. And by relying on someone else's judgment or resourcefulness, relief at least from sole responsibility is given.

The Costs of Giving Support

Listening, empathy, service, and responsibility: there are times when most single parents are in need of these kinds of support. And usually, the people approached for these kinds of responses are people who care—family and friends. Because they care, they want to be of help. Overburden them by calling on them too frequently or urgently, however, and the availability of care may fall away.

So the friend whom the single parent has called daily about current difficulties and concerns suddenly becomes harder to reach. What has happened? The support the friend has been regularly giving has become too much. As the single parent has unloaded, the friend has loaded up until calls from the single parent feel less like welcome opportunities to give than threats to be avoided. "I've reached the limit of my listening and don't feel like I can do it anymore."

Alert!

Examine the extent and type of support demands you are making. If your friend is continually giving listening, empathy, service, and responsibility, he or she may be in danger of giving too much. Now help from a friend may be in danger of hurting the friendship. Support is expensive because it takes energy to give and it can encourage dependency that is hard for the supporter to bear.

In the extremity of need, a single parent may not consider the costs upon others of the calls for support that he or she continually makes. The weight of dependency can threaten to become too much for the friend to bear. To help keep support within healthy limits for the friendship, follow these guidelines.

- Don't rely on a single friend for all four kinds of support. Work through multiple relationships to get the broad support you need.
- When good friends refuse your appeals for support, it is important for you to know that it is not because they do not care, but because they simply do not have the energy at that time to give in response to your need and are setting healthy limits for themselves. Let your friends know that it is okay to say no.
- Don't allow your needs for support to dominate communication with your friends. Talk about other topics, focus some attention on your friends, and do fun things together where concerns and problems are not discussed.
- Don't let friends do everything they can for you, lest in their goodwill and caring they over give and then feel trapped by, and resentful of, unrealistic commitments they have made.
- Avail yourself of existing single-parent support groups, which are available through many churches and from national

organizations like Parents Without Partners (local chapter listed in your phone book).

Support from Children

Divorce often increases closeness between child and single parent as they come together to create a new family structure and rely more upon each other than before to make that structure work. A kind of re-bonding between parent and child is required to form a firm basis for the single-parent family. In addition, there is an increase in companionship—the children focusing companionship needs that were previously given to two resident parents upon one, and the parent relying more for companionship on children in the absence of an adult partner. "We really circled the wagons after the divorce, the kids and I. It felt like us against the world."

Because of all the new changes and attendant demands, adults do not accomplish the transition into single parenthood without experiencing some duress. So there are times when the single parent will experience some unhappiness, times when new closeness with a child may cause the boy or girl to want to be emotionally supportive, and times when the single parent wants to accept the gift of that support. Gratefully, the parent declares, "Last night, when you listened and cried with me and gave me a hug, I felt a lot better. You really fixed me up!" And the child feels good for being able to help.

On an occasional basis, this kind of emotional support can work well for both parties concerned, but on a continuing basis, it can cause problems of emotional enmeshment and emotional responsibility.

Emotional Enmeshment

Unhealthy closeness can be fostered when the child becomes so instrumental in managing the single parent's emotional well-being that the boy or girl comes to link his or her emotional well-being to the parent's. "For me to feel okay, my parent has to feel okay. When my parent feels sad, then I do too." Now the boy's or girl's emotional focus is primarily on the parent's feelings, and not on his or her own.

And there may be cause for the child to keep it that way. Having lost one parent from the home, the child wants to be sure he or she doesn't lose the other and so keeps close emotional surveillance on the remaining parent. "I want to be sure that my single parent is okay."

 *Fact*

When a child is treated as the emotional confidante of a divorced single parent, it is hard for the child to refuse what feels like too much responsibility, to set limits without abandoning a parent in need, to risk refusal and appear not to care.

Emotional Responsibility

Now comes a feeling of responsibility. Giving emotional support to a distraught parent to keep that person "feeling okay" can create feelings of caretaking responsibility in the child. As for the parent, having a sympathetic listener in the family does feel genuinely supportive. "It's like having another sensitive adult to talk to who will understand." And now the child becomes "adultized" to meet the parent's emotional need. In this way, the child is parenting the parent as roles become reversed, the child inappropriately bearing the weight of an adult dependency that he or she does not feel free to moderate or to give up. In addition, now both child and parent can neglect emotional hardship the child may be going through, while the child resents being cast in a supportive role he or she doesn't want but dares not refuse.

Keeping Emotional Support Within Healthy Limits

So how is the single parent going to keep his or her emotional support needs within healthy limits? Should the parent just keep all feelings regarding the divorce locked away from the children? No. By recognizing and sharing some feelings with his or her child, the single parent encourages, by example, the child to do the same. But do so in a declarative way ("I am just feeling sad that the marriage is over") rather than in a demanding way ("I need to tell you how unhappy I feel about the divorce"). In the first case, the child is informed about the parent's emotional state; in the second case, he or she is enlisted as an emotional support.

Fact

Siblings can be uniquely supportive of one another because they understand the turmoil each is going through in ways parents cannot. So long as an older child does not feel obliged to emotionally take care of a younger, thereby assuming a "parental" responsibility, this sharing of the divorce experience can be invaluable—a quality of support that an only child, or siblings who are consigned to separate homes, must do without.

The single parent needs to make clear a separation of emotional responsibility. "I appreciate your wanting to take care of me when I am feeling unhappy, but that is not your job. After divorce, I will have my downs just like you. You need to know, unless I tell you otherwise, that those downs have nothing to do with you. My feelings are not yours to fix. Yes, I will tell you when I am going through a hard time so you can know, and understand my quietness is just my feeling sad. However, I will manage those feelings myself, and if I need someone to talk about them, I will talk to a friend or family member, or even a helper if that feels like what I need. When you are feeling down, however, I want to be there for you, to listen to you, because that is part of my responsibility. My job is to parent you. Your job is not to parent me. Of course, if you want someone safe outside of family to privately talk to about how you are feeling, that can be arranged."

CHAPTER 15

Managing Education

Demands can be supportive. When divorce creates unhappiness at home, the demands and distraction and distance created by school can provide a welcome escape. School creates a world apart from family where those changes and tensions are not in play, and where socializing with friends and performing well academically both can buttress a child's spirits. So, as a supportive single parent, your job is to help the child maintain good contact with friends and achieve grades that affirm his or her capacity. When school goes socially and academically badly, the child has no sanctuary from emotional turmoil at home and so may have an even harder time adjusting to divorce. Therefore, parents need to do what they can to support a positive school experience, and this takes knowing what educational and social pitfalls to beware.

Keeping Performance in Perspective

No question, school achievement is important. It supports present self-esteem, is evidence of learning, and enables future mobility. Academic performance, however, is only one part of a child's development, a small part of a large person. It is the parent's responsibility to always keep that larger perspective in mind. There are many other important areas of growth: social, emotional, moral, spiritual, physical, artistic, expressive, and relational to name a few.

Alert!

If, in the wake of divorce, a teacher discloses to you that your child is acting more socially withdrawn or aggressive or emotional than other children she has taught, treat this data very seriously. Because teachers work with so many children, they can provide a valuable normative reference for your child's behavior. If a teacher expresses concern about your son's or daughter's adjustment, get a counseling evaluation of the child.

The Dangerous Equation

There is a dangerous equation the single parent should beware: parent = child. This equivalence can imply that the conduct of the child depends on the parenting received, and that parenting is evaluated by the performance of the child. Thus, if the child does well, the parent should be credited for doing a good job, and if the child does poorly, the parent should be criticized for falling down on the job. To use the child's school performance to measure the parent's performance creates two unhappy outcomes. Either the child is burdened with responsibility for making the parent look good, or is blamed for making the parent look bad.

Essential

To avoid enmeshment in the child's achievement, the single parent needs to make a strong declaration of independence about school performance, a statement that might sound like this. "No matter how you perform at school, I feel good about myself as your parent and you as my child. When you perform well, I do not take the credit. When you perform badly, I do not take the blame. My responsibility is to guide and support you the best I can, to help you make good choices while understanding that your choices are your responsibility to make."

Because the single parent has no partner with whom to share daily child raising, it is easy to assume too much responsibility for how children are doing at school. Often conscientious to a fault, the single parent can ask himself or herself evaluative questions. "Am I doing enough? Am I doing right? Am I doing wrong?"

Two Statements to Avoid

There are two statements that are usually not helpful to your child in response to his or her performance: "I'm proud of you" and "I'm disappointed in you."

Fact

Don't read too much into superior academic performance. It does not mean that your child is necessarily highly responsible, hardworking, extremely motivated, healthily adjusted, happy, well behaved, interested in learning, destined for a successful life, or drug-free. It just means the child, through aptitude or effort or both, is able to make good grades.

Although intended as a statement of approval, "I'm proud of you" can invoke the parent = child linkage in a damaging way. When interpreted by the child to signify that the parent now feels good about himself ("proud") because of how the child did, the child can feel pressure to do well to support parental self-esteem. Better for the parent to simply say, "Good for you." That places credit for performance where it belongs.

The statement "I am disappointed in you" can have devastating effect. Not only must the child now recover from some degree of failure, but he or she usually feels the need to somehow recover loving standing in the parent's eyes that less than acceptable performance has lost. Better for the parent to simply say, "I'm glad you gave it a try —keep on trying!" That keeps the focus on effort, not outcome.

Setting Grade Expectations

When communicating to your child about your expectations for adequate school performance, be specific, not abstract. General statements such as "Just do your best," "Try your hardest," and "Work up to your potential" do not provide meaningful guidelines that the child can follow because they are not sufficiently objective. How can the child know for sure if she is doing her best, trying her hardest, or working up to her potential? She can't. Nobody can.

It is best for the parent, based on intimate knowledge of the child's ability, to specify a level of performance that, with reasonable effort, is realistic for the boy or girl to attain. "I think the maximum grades you could probably achieve would be a mix of As and Bs or better. The minimum grades I consider acceptable are all Bs and maybe an occasional C. Should you fall below this minimum, I will step in with my support to help you rise above it." Treat the report card seriously. Use it like a mirror that should provide an adequate reflection of the child's capacity to perform.

Alert!

Get an academic benchmark on your child to get an accurate reading of his or her operating capacity at school. For an entire marking period, make sure your child does all homework and projects in a complete and timely fashion, finishes all class work, and studies for all tests. Use the grade outcome of this consistent effort to create a realistic set of performance expectations, an academic benchmark, for your child.

Keeping Family Safe for Learning

Most single parents support their child's education because they believe that learning can increase sense of competence. and self-esteem. This conviction is true except when the experience of education is conducted in a manner that inhibits the desire to learn. A lot depends upon the teacher, and the most powerful teachers of all are parents who shape a lot of the child's willingness to learn from others, including from classroom teachers at school.

The Risks of Learning

The willingness to try and learn is easily discouraged because learning can feel risky. What risks? To acquire a new skill or understanding one does not possess, one must dare to

- Admit ignorance
- Feel stupid
- Look foolish
- Get evaluated for one's efforts

If the risks feel too scary, the child can decide it is safer not to try. A disapproving parent or an intimidating teacher can cause the child to feel reluctant to learn. The risks get in the way when elevated by an impatient or critical adult who

- Puts down ignorance ("You should know this already!")
- Is frustrated by mistakes ("Why can't you do it right the first time?")
- Criticizes by implying stupidity ("How can you be so dumb?")
- Ridicules to encourage feelings of foolishness ("Even a three-year-old could learn this faster than you!")
- Gives a punitive evaluation ("This just shows you'll never learn to do this right!")

If out of fatigue or from other stress you are in danger of making any of these kinds of responses to your child (who may be struggling to understand homework that you are impatiently trying to coach), disengage from the child's project and declare a break. Do not try to help educate the child when you feel emotionally unprepared to patiently encourage.

Instructional Amnesia

Parents as teachers are often insensitive to the child's difficulty learning because they suffer from instructional amnesia. This is a common problem that afflicts many adults. Long after they have practiced a skill or mastered an understanding, they forget how difficult it was to learn. So when sitting down with their elementary school–age child who is slow to comprehend homework, parents may have a hard time understanding, and being patient with, the child's slowness to learn what seems like a very simple assignment to them. Whatever is the matter with the child? Nothing. The parents have just forgotten what their own initial learning experience was like. And they have also grown out of touch with fears of learning that may be retarding the child's efforts now.

After divorce, there is often more competition among children for standing in the new family. To assert dominance, they can put each other down: "Is that the best you can do?" Let one child tease another's efforts to perform, and the target child may decide it's safer not to try. Keep the family safe for learning: "No ridicule of learning is allowed."

How to Encourage Learning

To encourage your child to take the risks of learning:

- Give ignorance permission by declaring, "It's okay not to know because all learning starts with ignorance."
- Treat mistakes as efforts: "Good for you for trying—try again."
- Be sensitive to feelings of stupidity: "It's scary doing what you've never done before."
- Admire the willingness to look foolish: "You're brave to let others watch you struggle to learn."
- Always give a positive evaluation independent of outcome: "You made an effort and now you know more than you did before!"

Fact

Modeling matters. If you get impatient and angry with yourself for making mistakes or being slow to learn, you are showing the child that if one can't learn quickly and easily, then something must be wrong with the learner.

Social Cruelty at School

When parents divorce, children feel hurt by many of the losses divorce creates (see Chapter 2). In order for other unhappiness not to make a hard time worse, it helps if life outside of family feels safe and rewarding, particularly life with friends at school. Unfortunately, come early adolescence (around ages nine to thirteen), from grade three until grades six or seven, relationships among children at school can become very harsh and hurtful. Why? Because, suffering from loss created by the separation from childhood and from anxiety about uncertain growth ahead, early adolescent students jockey for personal and social security at each other's expense, engaging in social cruelty to survive. (For a fuller discussion of the hardships of early adolescence, see Chapter 8.)

Essential

When talking about the social cruelty at school that starts around grade three and continues through grades six or seven, we are not talking about "bad" kids. We are talking about "good" kids treating each other badly to cope with the developmental insecurity, social instability, emotional vulnerability, and frail self-esteem created by early adolescent change. In a world where everyone is easily hurt, hurting others first becomes a way to prevent getting hurt yourself.

When parents divorce with a child in early adolescence, they should pay particular attention to the boy's or girl's life at school—not just academically, but socially and emotionally. If the child is experiencing a significant amount of social cruelty from other students, the parent must provide emotional support, social strategizing, and, if the cruelty is excessive, with the child's permission, adult intervention at the school.

Social Cruelty Behaviors

At a time when children feel personally insecure, social security through being popular seems like the Holy Grail. "If only I could be really popular, then school would be okay." But the problem is, popularity is an exclusive club, membership usually limited to a classroom few (the popular crowd), who use niceness to cement relationships with each other, and meanness to keep others out. To make matters worse, popularity is often not the sanctuary it seems, because the more popular you are, the more social envy there is, resulting in gossip and rumors attacking your reputation to bring you down. Popularity can be lost in a hurry when, for reasons usually to do with rivalry, supposed friends turn suddenly against you and cast you out.

Students at this age can fall victim to social cruelty from intimidation (bullying, threatening, vandalizing), from exclusion (being ignored, not selected, rejected), from embarrassment (nicknamed, teased, put down), and from having reputation attacked (rumor, gossip, slander).

For many parents, reading this portrait of social hardship at such a young age will clash with their image of childhood innocence and fun. Social cruelty is neither innocent nor fun in early adolescence. It is real. And parents need to stand by with support and coaching should their child of divorce face this additional unhappiness to a significant degree.

Here are a few pieces of helpful advice parents can sometimes give.

About teasing, explain, "Teasing is not about anything wrong with you. It is about another person wanting to be mean to you. Because people usually tease about what they fear being teased about themselves, you can truly say that teasing shows a whole lot more about the teaser than it does about you. Then just ignore what they have said."

About bullying, explain, "Usually it's not bullying that's so much the problem, as fear of being bullied. So be brave and ask yourself, 'How would I act if I were not afraid?' Consider how the bully predicts you will respond, and then act to violate that prediction. There is no such thing as a self-made bully, so don't act in ways that invite bullying, and don't react in ways that encourage bullying."

Alert!

At this age that is so complicated for friendship at school, it is helpful to have other social circles outside of school to which the child can belong—extended family, neighborhood, sports, church, special interest, for example. That way, when social relationships get hard at school, the child has other social outlets to enjoy.

About gossip and rumor, explain, "You don't control your own reputation. No one does. Gossip has more bad to say than good, and the more popular you are, the more reputation you have to lose. Secrets are the most powerful gossip to tell, and slander is the most destructive—lies that are told as truth. Remember, anyone who gossips to you will gossip about you."

About ganging up, explain, "There are three roles in ganging up—bully, follower, and victim. The bully has power, but also is personally disliked. The follower escapes mistreatment, but also loses self-respect. The victim gets attention, but believes mistreatment is deserved or unavoidable. I don't want you to act in any of these three roles."

Assessing Amount of Social Cruelty at School

You can roughly assess the degree and nature of social cruelty your child is experiencing at school by asking your child if he or she is regularly experiencing any of the common social or personal hardships listed below.

- People gossiping about you
- People laughing at you
- People spreading rumors about you
- People teasing you
- People calling you a hurtful nickname
- People not wanting to sit with you at lunch
- People ganging up on you
- People cutting you down with an insult
- Quarrelling with a good friend
- Growing apart from a good friend
- Having a good friend turn against you
- Having a good friend share a secret you confided
- Feeling jealous when a good friend wants to be with someone else
- Seeing a friend change into a different person
- Being bullied
- Having possessions stolen
- Having belongings vandalized
- Receiving prank calls that hurt your feelings
- Having to go along with a dominating friend
- Having someone threaten "to get" you
- Feeling scared to go to school some days
- Having to fight to prove how tough you are
- Having to hide feeling hurt and pretend you don't care
- Worrying if people will like you
- Feeling bad about your appearance
- Being excluded from a party when your friends were invited
- Having people write notes about you
- Having people say things about you that are not true
- Feeling shy at a party and wishing you were outgoing
- Having someone break up your best friendship
- Wishing you had a best friend

- Wishing you had as much as other people
- Having a good friend compete with you
- Having people want to be your friend only because you're popular
- Having people not want to be your friend because you're not popular
- Being spoken to one day and ignored the next
- Feeling trapped by a friend who is too possessive
- Feeling you don't have the "right" thing to wear

Alert!

When social cruelty reduces social safety at school, studies usually suffer because the victim of social cruelty becomes far more preoccupied with daily survival than concerned with accomplishing daily work. Social cruelty reduces academic focus.

Most of these feelings and experiences are subsurface—not observed by teachers or reported to parents. The code of the school yard ("You shouldn't tell on other people") keeps children from telling adults what is going on, and adolescent pride ("I should handle hard stuff by myself") keeps the young person from disclosing a lot of school suffering at home. Although no child escapes all these hardships, most children navigate this complicated social passage okay, without major injury or lasting hurt. However, because you have an adolescent who is already hurting from divorce, part of your job is to monitor what level of social cruelty occurs.

So, in light of this information, what should a single parent do? If you ask your child to check which behaviors and feelings on this list square with his or her experience at school, you both may be surprised. You child may be surprised that you actually know what is going on, and you may be surprised to hear how much social cruelty your child is coping with. The goal of this exercise is to normalize discussion of this hard experience, get you and your child on the same page, give your child an empathetic listener to count on, and help your child strategize to alleviate what is going on. So long as you arm your child with fresh choices to help cope, he or she will feel empowered and not act like a helpless victim in the face of social cruelty at school.

Alert!

The list of social cruelties given here is, of course, very incomplete. Use it to prime the pump of discussion with your child. If so inclined, he or she will be able to add other kinds of bad feelings and mean treatment that can happen at school—some directly experienced, some only witnessed. Because they are not usually told, parents and teachers are woefully ignorant of how hard student relationships can be during the early adolescent age.

The Early Adolescent Achievement Drop

Early adolescence (around age nine to thirteen) can be the enemy of school achievement. Rebelling against being defined and treated as a "child" can cause early adolescents to resist the educational system at their own expense, the price of this newfound independence being failing effort and falling grades. A child of divorce, with more grievance to energize rebellion and more determination to self-direct, can have a higher vulnerability to this common disaffection. Unhappily, since divorce is already contributing to some bad feelings for the child, a loss of achievement will only add more.

Common expressions of this disaffected attitude include:

- "It's dumb to ask questions."
- "It's smart to act stupid."
- "It's stupid to work hard."
- "It's cool not to care."
- "It's good to act bad."
- "It's right to buck the system."
- "It's good enough to just get by."

This change in motivation can catch a parent off guard when the conscientious child who took pride in doing well becomes the apathetic adolescent who seems not to care about doing poorly. The old academic priority of working hard to achieve gives way to a more urgent priority, to socially connect with friends and be popular. Energy that used to be invested in doing homework is now diverted to talking long hours on the telephone and to instant messaging over the Internet.

The Common Problem

In most cases, this performance drop doesn't really mean the adolescent no longer values doing well academically, it just means he or she doesn't want to do the work to do well—class work, homework, reports, projects, papers, and studying for tests. So it is at this juncture that parents find themselves confronted by a number of anti-achievement behaviors. The most common ones are not delivering deficiency notes sent home to parents, "forgetting" or lying about homework assignments, not turning completed homework in, not finishing class work, and being disruptive by talking and acting out in class.

All these behaviors contribute to the early adolescent achievement drop, and they are all easily remedied by the parent who is willing to take stands for the adolescent's best interest against what he or she wants.

What Not to Do

Two tacks not to take in addressing these behaviors are (1) becoming emotionally upset, and (2) resorting to rewards or punishments to encourage different choices. Although both stands can work with a young child who wants to please and values material incentives, they tend to be counterproductive with the adolescent, who often courts parental disapproval and may resent a show of parental control over desirable resources.

Grades are too important to become emotionally upset about. Growth is just a gathering of power, from dependence to independence, the parents' job being to help their adolescent gather that power in appropriate ways. It is not appropriate for the parent to give the adolescent power to upset him or her over grades, because then the academic focus is lost and the young person wins influence over parental feelings. "I can really push my parent's buttons by doing poorly in school." When parents get upset over grades, they only turn a performance issue into an emotional encounter with their adolescent.

Grades are too important to reward or punish about. Parents often mistakenly believe that offering an adolescent some significant payoff for good grades will be seen as a reward, when it is not. In fact, most adolescents will see it as a threat that they resent. "If you say you're going to give me five dollars for an A, that just means that if I don't get an A, I don't get the five dollars." As for punishment if certain grades are not maintained, taking away some resource or freedom "until grades improve" usually engenders more resistance than cooperation. "I don't care what you take away, you can't make me do my work!" And the adolescent will go down in flames to prove to parents that such power tactics are doomed to fail. When parents reward or punish grades, they only turn a performance issue into a power struggle with their adolescent.

The Solution to the Achievement Drop

What, then, is a parent supposed to do? Just stand by and watch his or her early adolescent fail by failing to work? Sometimes that's the advice middle school teachers give to parents. "Don't be overprotective. Let your child fail and learn responsibility from the consequences." This is usually bad advice because unless the adolescent manages to self-correct in consequence of failing, deciding to bear down to bring grades up, he or she will only learn to adjust to failure, treating failure as okay when it is not.

After all, a report card is meant to act like a mirror, the adolescent seeing in that evaluation an adequate reflection of his or her capacities. Parents' saying to an unmotivated adolescent who is capable of As and Bs "All we want you to do is pass" is tantamount to giving up on their child, abandoning their responsibility to influence school behavior. But if emotional upset and rewards and punishments tend to be ineffective with the early adolescent achievement drop, then what is the parent to do?

 **Fact**

Although underachievement of many children has to do with setting standards that are too low, with an only child, underachievement often arises from setting standards too high. Putting himself on equal standing with parents, the only child can then apply adult standards of performance for himself: "If I'm their equal, I should do equally well." Then when these standards prove unreachable, the only child can give up trying and achievement can fall from failing effort. Realistic goals need to be set.

The answer is supervision. Remember that the early adolescent, unlike the child, does not want parents showing up in his or her world at school. Desire for independence means keeping parents out of his or her society of peers. Now the company of a parent at school feels like a public embarrassment because the young person should be able to handle school without parental interference. To which the parent replies, "I have no desire to interfere at school so long as you are taking care of business. However, if you do not do schoolwork and if you are acting inappropriately, I will extend my supervision into your school to help you make better choices."

If deficiency notices are not delivered home, a parent may want to say something like this: "Since information for me that the school entrusted to you was not delivered, you and I will meet with the teacher *together*, and you will have the opportunity to explain why the notice failed to reach me, and what you are going to do differently next time so it does."

If a parent is told there is no homework when it turns out there was, they may want to say something like this: "Since you said you had no homework, but you did, you and I will meet *together* with the teacher. At that time, you will have the opportunity to explain why you said there was no homework when there was, and what you will do differently the next time so I will be told the truth. And this weekend, before you get to do anything you want to do, you will have to complete the missed assignments, turning them in for zero credit because they are now late."

If the adolescent still fails to bring assignments home, a parent may want to say something like this: "Since you can't manage to bring homework home, I will meet you after your last class and *together* we will walk the halls and make the rounds of all your teachers to pick up your assignments."

Essential

If an early adolescent achievement drop occurs and self-correction by the child in response to consequences (failing) does not follow, a parent must commit to steadfast supervision in support of responsible behaviors at school. Why? Because improved school performance will ultimately cause the adolescent to feel better about himself or herself, and advance his or her future as well.

If the adolescent does the homework but chooses not to turn it in, a parent may want to say something like this: "Since you can't manage to turn your work in, I will go up to school with you and *together* walk the halls and make the rounds of all your teachers to make sure your homework gets turned in."

If the adolescent is talking out or acting out disruptively in class, not completing teacher assignments, a parent may want to say something like this: "Although this is not something I want to do, I am willing to take time off from work and sit *together* with you in class to help you behave appropriately as the teacher asks."

Usually, an early adolescent will not welcome any of these options, considering them outrageously invasive, preferring to correct self-defeating conduct instead.

CHAPTER 16

Sex-Role Influence of the Single Parent

This chapter is about tendencies, not certainties. It describes how the sex role of the single parent (whether mother or father) can raise somewhat different relational issues in parenting based on the sex role of the child (whether son or daughter).

This difference comes into sharpest focus during the adolescent passage when a boy starts wanting to act and be treated more like a young man, and a girl starts wanting to act and be treated more like a woman. At issue is not whether it is more appropriate for mother or father to become the major single parent, only that sex role of the single parent can play out into a somewhat different set of parenting issues with a son and with a daughter.

Origin of the Parent/Child Relationship

Think about the origin of the parent/child relationship. It is different for a mother and a father. The mother, through bearing, birthing, and breastfeeding, begins the relationship with a physical connection to the infant that the father can never know. He begins the relationship with the child from a position of separation, as a person apart with whom a sense of connection must be created. It is only through caretaking, companionship, and communication that the father can begin building attachment to and from the child.

 **Fact**

More primary attachment to the mother does not mean that the father cannot become equally loved. He can. But with the mother, a basis for attachment to and from the child is built in from the beginning, while attachment to and from the father must be learned and earned.

Mother and Father Roles Are Not the Same

The mother literally sacrifices her body, putting herself at physical risk and through physical pain in carrying and eventually birthing the child. During this time, the most the father can do for the child is be supportive of the mother. From conception, the father can start taking more care of the mother so the mother can take care of the child. "Traditional" parenting roles often build on this difference, mothers tending more toward personal sacrifice for children and fathers tending more toward working for family support (although fathers can certainly sacrifice for children, and mothers can certainly earn a family living).

The "Go To" Parent; the "Get From" Parent

Because she begins the relationship with her children physically connected to them, the mother usually becomes the primary source of nurturing in their lives, the parent to whom children are most inclined to go for sustenance and comfort. In this sense, the mother is often the "go to" parent.

Because he begins the relationship with his children clearly separated from them, to become connected requires pleasing him to bring him close. So the father usually becomes the primary source of approval, which children seek to become more emotionally attached to him, any experience of his disapproval often amplifying power of the father's authority. He is often the parent they are most inclined to look to for validation and respect. In this sense, the father is often the "get from" parent.

Approval and authority are often more strongly vested in the father, while comfort and support are often more strongly vested in the mother. Again, we are talking about tendencies, not certainties.

When divorce occurs, a custodial single parent usually expands sex-role activities to cover what the missing parent is no longer there to do. Often this includes the mother's now becoming more of a "get from" parent, becoming the major adult authority and source of approval, and the father's now becoming more of a "go to" parent, becoming the major adult support and source of comfort.

In a very simple sense, the mother's relationship to the child begins with a physical connection, and the father's relationship to the child begins with a social distance, in each case these characteristics contributing to the definition and development of their respective parenting roles.

Early Influence of Parents

Unawares, children learn a lot about the sex role they "should" fill during the daily experience of growing up. They learn it from parents and they learn it from peers and they learn it without ever knowing they are receiving this formative education.

 **Fact**

As a single parent, you give your child not one example to follow, but two—how to be and how not to be, both models influencing how your child chooses to develop. "My dad was very responsible, taking care of all of us the way he did, and so I have always tried to be responsible too. But he was also very uncommunicative about himself, kind of a mystery to us kids, so I have always tried to be more talkative about myself."

During childhood, children tend to learn how to identify with the same-sex parent and complement the other-sex parent. Sexual similarity exerts modeling effect as daughters identify with their mother as woman, imitating some of her ways, and sons identify with their father as man, imitating some of his ways.

At the same time, daughters get more sense of differentiation from their father, their sense of "girl-ness" complementing the male role of the father. At the same time, sons get more sense of differentiation from their mother, their sense of "boy-ness" complementing the female role of the mother. So boys may come to especially value compliments about their male prowess from their mother, and girls may come to especially value compliments about their female appeal from their fathers. Again, this is only tendency, not certainty.

Early Influence of Peers

Peer groups also have a powerful socializing effect of sex-role development in childhood, particularly around intimacy with friends. Growing up primarily in same-sex peer groups as children soon tend to do, boys primarily affiliating with boys and girls primarily affiliating with girls, establishes "male" and "female" role definitions in addition to those created by identifying with and complementing parents.

 **Essential**

Sex-role stereotypes are often built into early peer-group play, acting "tough and aggressive" to be considered "male," and acting "sensitive and supportive" to be considered "female," as boys play at conquest and girls play at caretaking. To some single parents, this kind of division can seem offensive. After all, women can act tough and aggressive, and men can act sensitive and supportive. Best to be patient with the sexism of the age and encourage growth of other traits as well.

In same-sex peer groups, building friendships with each other, girls tend to rely more on confiding in each other, while boys tend to rely more on companionship with each other. Girls tend to establish closeness through giving support and personal disclosure, and often draw primary self-esteem from the power of these relationships. Relational traits can include emotional sensitivity, sharing of inner experience, and affectionate touch.

Boys tend to establish closeness through sharing exploits and competition, and often draw primary self-esteem from the power of performance. Performance traits can include physical aggressiveness, competition, and risk taking. Because their parents were often socialized in similar ways, the mother may be more of a "talking to" parent and the father may be more of a "doing things with" parent.

Come adolescence, definition of sex role becomes developmentally more important for your son or daughter, the boy child now wanting to grow into a young man, the girl child now wanting to grow into a young woman. From this point on, the single-parent mother or single-parent father no longer has a child to raise; he or she has a young person in active training to become an adult.

 *Fact*

Because she is the most deeply connected parent, the mother is usually the most deeply committed parent. In addition, socialized around performance, it is easier for fathers to put work and career ahead of family, while for mothers, socialized around relationships, it is easier to put family first. This doesn't mean that there are not many deeply committed dads, only that they are fewer in number than deeply committed moms.

Sex-Role Expansion of the Single-Parent Role

After divorce, each single parent often expands her or his role in the other's direction—the mother becoming more of a companion to do things with, the father becoming more of a support to confide in.

 **Fact**

Because many a gay single parent has already broken with sexual stereotype, children are often offered a very inclusive sex-role model from which they can benefit, developing a broader sense of human self-definition for themselves.

Broadening the Parental Model

When children say, "My parents have really changed after the divorce," they are often responding to the expansion of traditional sex roles that has occurred. "Now my mom does more fixing and repairing, and my dad does more housework and cooking." "Mom things" and "Dad things" often get reassigned. Seeing these changes can often cause the child to expand his or her sex-role definition in response.

This is not to recommend divorce, but one positive effect of children's seeing a single parent expand his or her sex role is often that they feel permission to expand their own, in the process broadening self-definition to include more traits typically assigned to the opposite sex role. So a son, seeing his single-parent dad act in more nurturing ways, receives permission to become more nurturing in response. And a daughter, seeing her single-parent mom assert more leadership in the world of work, receives permission to assert more leadership herself.

 **Essential**

One outcome of differences in sex-role socializing between male and female can be a mother who feels her son (just like her ex-husband) doesn't do enough talking, and a son who feels his mother wants to talk too much. And yet, he may often find his mother easier to talk to than his father, who is more inclined to silent companionship than to personal sharing.

When the Parental Model Causes Complaint

As children grow through adolescence, they often struggle with each parent around opposing issues. With the mother, teenage children can pull away for more separation, sometimes complaining about too much closeness: "My mother is overprotective; she won't let me go." With the father, children can long for more connection, sometimes complaining about too much distance: "My father is so removed, I can't really talk to him." When a mother or father becomes a single parent, sometimes the mother has to learn to separate from children to give them room to grow, to allow more independence, while the father has to attach to children more closely, to provide more communication, to give them adequate emotional support.

If you passively accepted mistreatment from, or actively gave mistreatment to, your partner when married, you must correct the error of your ways as a single parent. For example, if you are a single-parent mother, use your relationship with the children to teach your son how to treat a woman well and be treated well by a woman. And if you are a single-parent father, use your relationship to teach your daughter how to treat a man well and be treated well by a man.

The Problem of the Absent Father

When a custodial single parent is all the parental presence there is, and in the vast majority of these instances the single parent is the mother, the effects of the absent parent, in this case the father, must be addressed. Sons or daughters growing up with little or no contact with their fathers can be at risk of some damaging effects.

In the absence of a father to provide the primary male model or complement, children (particularly in adolescence) can become more susceptible to competing models idealized by peers and popular culture. Thus, an adolescent son without a father may come to rely on influential teenage boys to example male definition. Adopting their manly posturing in order to be accepted by his group of peers, he comes to identify with a set of immature stereotypes that may include using girls to prove his masculinity. Meanwhile, an adolescent daughter without a father may turn to opposite-sex peers to provide missing male attention and primary male attachment, and end up being exploited.

 **Question?**

What can I say to my children about the father who has abandoned them?

Say this: "Don't take your father's actions personally. He is not rejecting you. He is rejecting the rewards and responsibilities of being a father. It is not about something wrong with you. It is about something wrong with him. Unhappily, his refusal to be part of your life creates a loss in yours—not having a father to love who will love you in return."

A teenage boy who has lost contact with his father can be easily led astray by a dominant male peer who provides example and leadership the missing dad does not. A teenage girl without a father may seek from older boys the salient male presence she is missing, and end up having her longing and trust taken advantage of in the relationship.

What a Single Mother Can Do

The single-parent mother without an active father presence for her children has the power to counter these negative sex-role influences from peers and popular culture that have now become so influential. How she treats her son as a man has formative effect (male = responsible), as does declaring how she expects him to treat her and other women (male = respectful). With a daughter, what the single-parent mother models with other men and expects her daughter to follow has formative effect (female = assertive and independent). What she teaches that daughter about acceptable and unacceptable treatment from men also counts for a lot (female = not being used or abused).

Parental Loss and the Need for Substitution

When parental divorce occurs in childhood and a noncustodial parent becomes significantly less present in the child's life or, at worst, abandons the child, the opportunity for modeling after the same-sex parent or complementing the other-sex parent is lessened or lost. Should this turn of events occur, it helps if the single parent can arrange for another adult, the same sex as the absent parent, to provide a significant substitute presence whom the child can identify with or complement. Sometimes such a stand-in can be found in the single parent's extended family (an aunt or uncle, a grandparent, for example); sometimes in an adult friend of the family; sometimes in an instructor of some kind, a youth leader, or a coach.

Essential

One risk created by a missing parent is that an adolescent will not have that mother or father figure to identify with, model after, or complement, and so feel inclined to seek from peers what the absent parent does not provide. Therefore, find a salient adult substitute for the missing parent if you can. Even a few hours a week of this companionship can have a positive modeling effect for the child.

It's important to find such a substitute if you can. Why? Because in the absence of a real salient sex-role model to imitate or complement, the child will gravitate toward cultural stereotypes in the media, or even depend on influential friends to fill the absent parent's role, friends whose immature and sometimes damaging influence may become extremely hard to deny.

CHAPTER 17

Sex-Role Influence Traps to Beware

A s a custodial single mother or father, your sex-role influence is amplified because you are the only parent in the home. For this reason, you must be aware of the pitfalls that await a parent/child relationship when sex-role influence with your son or daughter goes awry, as it is more at risk of doing in adolescence. Remember, that injunction that holds true for helpers also holds true for parents: "First, do no harm."

Simple Psychology of Sex-Role Influence

Recall two attributes of the parent/child relationship that affect the degree of natural connection mentioned in the last chapter. There is the physical attachment of mother to child through bearing, birthing, and breastfeeding, which a father and child lack. And there is sexual similarity between parent and child that a mother can have with a daughter, but not a son, and a father can have with a son, but not a daughter. Taken together, these two attributes, by their absence or presence, can contribute to predictable tensions and conflicts between parent and child during adolescence, when the teenager's need for separation (versus attachment) and differentiation (versus similarity) dictate much of his or her own growth toward more independence.

It is because of lack of physical attachment that physical similarity in appearance often becomes so important to a father. "He looks like me." "She looks like me." These appearance similarities can help a father begin to feel connected with a little infant he has yet to grow to know. For the mother, already physically attached, similarity of appearance with her infant often seems to matter less.

Question?

What is the long-term lesson about male/female relationships that a single parent has to teach a daughter and a son?
By how they act, single mothers and single fathers should teach their sons how to respectfully treat and be treated by women, and should teach their daughters how to respectfully treat and be treated by men.

To begin to appreciate the parenting challenge a single mother or father can face with an adolescent son or daughter, consider how these attributes can create different tensions depending on sex role of the parent and sex role of the child and the degree of natural connection between them.

Mother/Daughter Conflicts

Because mother and daughter are connected both by physical attachment and sexual similarity, it often requires a lot of intense conflict initiated by the teenage daughter to get adequate separation and differentiation to occur. "It doesn't matter what I say, it's always wrong!" complains the mother, who is as worn down by the conflict as the daughter is determined to have it. One challenge for the mother is to keep the conduct of this conflict safe and constructive, so no harm to either party is done. Typically, because there is a double dose of closeness from attachment and similarity to be resolved, mother/daughter conflicts are about separation. Of parent/child conflicts during adolescence, mother/daughter conflicts are often the most intense.

 **Fact**

During adolescence, a boy or girl may express the desire to spend more time or even live with the same-sex noncustodial parent. This desire is not a matter of preferring or loving that father or mother more than the custodial parent. Developing and defining emerging manhood or womanhood, the young person simply wants more exposure to the same-sex model to help define how the teenager wants and does not want to be.

Mother/Son Conflicts

Because mother and son are connected by physical attachment but not by sexual similarity, it usually requires establishing distance from, and less communication with, his mother for the son to get space for the male differentiation he needs during adolescence. "I can't get my son to talk to me anymore!" complains the mother, who is as discouraged by the distance between them as the son is determined to keep it. One challenge for the mother is to keep communicating without insisting on a similar return, treating the distance as an effort to detach and grow sexually apart. Typically, because the son needs more distance to claim male distinction, mother/son conflicts are over the lack of adequate communication.

Father/Son Conflicts

Because father and son are connected by sexual similarity but not by physical attachment, it requires asserting personal differences for the son to break down resemblance to his father in order to claim individuality and independence. "No matter how I try to explain my way to lead life, he wants to go the other!" complains the father, who is as frustrated by his son's opposition as the son is determined to follow an alternative path and grow on his own terms. One challenge for the father is to bridge the differences between himself and his son with interest, and not discredit those differences by making unfavorable comparisons to himself. Typically, because the son needs to be his own man, father/son conflicts are characterized by a power struggle that the son ultimately wins, because children more often defeat their parents than the reverse.

Father/Daughter Conflicts

Because father and daughter are not connected by physical attachment or sexual similarity, it often requires overcoming a certain distance to establish a relationship both can value and respect. "I don't know my daughter that well because we don't have that much in common," complains the father, who feels as out of personal touch with his daughter as she often feels with him. One challenge for the father is to find common human ground with his daughter on which a meaningful relationship can be conducted, and to be there when she has need. Typically, because there is a double disconnection from lack of physical attachment and lack of sexual similarity to be overcome, father/daughter conflicts are about estrangement. They can feel extremely frustrating as both parties often inadequately communicate with each other, making honest differences particularly hard to resolve.

A single parent needs to manage the interplay of sex-role issues in the parent/child relationship with sensitivity lest common conflicts lead to hurt, particularly during adolescence. For mothers and daughters, there can be tensions from separation versus similarity. For mothers and sons, there can be tensions from distinction versus closeness. For fathers and sons, there can be tensions from acceptance versus comparison. For fathers and daughters, there can be tensions from affirmation versus devaluation.

Mother and Daughter: Similarity Versus Separation

Sexually similar to her mother, learning as a child to identify with and imitate her ways, a daughter must contest this similarity and work for contrast during adolescence if she is to adequately differentiate herself as an individual and establish more independence. The conflict she typically has with her mother during the adolescent passage is between wanting to stay connected but not wanting to be a replica of her same-sex parent: "How can I stay close with you and still separate enough to become my own person?"

Questions That Trouble

There are many conflicts between mother and daughter during adolescence arising from questions that illuminate how developmentally torn the teenage girl has become. Consider just a few:

- "How can I be sexually similar to you and not just be an imitation of you?"
- "How can I remain connected to you while separating from you?"
- "How can I become different from you and still be accepted by you?"
- "How can I fight for my individuality without pushing your love away?"
- "How can I become different from you without losing you to the distance between us?"

Question?

What is the message the adolescent daughter often sends her mother?

"I'm not you, I'm not going to be like you, and I need you to love me all the same!"

The Single Mother's Challenge with Her Daughter

The challenge for a single-parent mother is to give her adolescent daughter sufficient room for separation and permission for individuality while still holding the young woman accountable for responsible conduct at home, at school, and out in the world.

As for managing conflict—and conflict between mother and daughter can be particularly intense because the connection from attachment and similarity are so strong—remain calm and reasoned, not explosive and attacking. It serves no good purpose to pour the gasoline of your own irritation at resistance onto the fire of your daughter's frustration with restraint. Such a choice risks leading you both into harm's way, saying in the heat of the moment what cannot be retracted but is later regretted for the hurt it has done.

Model the conduct in conflict that you would like her to model in return, and hold her to constructive account. "I don't call you names when we disagree, and I expect you not to call me names." Every time you do conflict with your daughter, you are teaching her how to do conflict, not just with you now but with significant others later on.

Alert!

> The dance of mother/daughter differentiation is hard to do. Disagreement with your daughter's choices is okay; criticism of her as a person is not. Cautioning her about consequences of her choices is okay; dooming her future with dire predictions is not. Sharing your history growing up is okay; expecting her to grow up just like you is not.

Be accessible for inconvenient communication when you are busy, relaxing, or tired. If she is inclined to talk and ready to share, you must be ready to listen. Also, create "vacation times" doing activities you both enjoy (eating out, shopping, going to a movie) to create a cessation in what can seem like ceaseless hostilities. If you are going to be her loyal adversary when she needs it, you must also have times of fun companionship. Remember, through conflict with you she is not so much fighting against you as she is fighting for the freedom to establish and lead a more individual and independent life.

How a Mother Can Wound a Daughter

When a mother is unwilling to bridge the difference between herself and her daughter and refuses to accept the individual her daughter is striving to become, the price for individuality the daughter can pay is loss of maternal understanding and even love. "My mother won't accept how I have grown to be different from her."

Faced with a daughter unlike herself, a mother can feel the definition of woman that she has modeled, that she has offered, that has been rejected, and so in hurt and anger reject back: "How can you act so ungrateful after all I've given you?" And now the daughter can feel torn between the need for individuality, and guilt for not providing the return of similarity her mother wanted, creating a common wound that can be hard to heal—being considered an undutiful daughter.

Advice to a single-parent mother about an adolescent daughter: Let your daughter have sufficient conflict with you to separate and assert her own individuality, welcome opportunities when she is able to connect with you, and do not blame, but respect, the differences between you.

Mother and Son: Distinction Versus Closeness

Sexually different from his mother, a son must not allow this dissimilarity to obstruct building a bond with his mother that he needs to feels securely attached as a child. Come adolescence, however, he doesn't want that closeness to diminish the growing sexual distinction between them. The conflict he typically has with his mother during the adolescent passage is between maintaining interpersonal closeness and establishing sexual difference: "How can I get you to treat me as sexually different from you but still connected to you?"

Questions That Trouble

There are many conflicts between mother and son during adolescence arising from questions that illuminate how developmentally torn the teenage boy has become. Consider just a few:

- "How can I stay close to you and still preserve the sense of sexual difference between us?"
- "How can I get your love without having to take your affection?"
- "How can I lose an argument with you and not lose face?"
- "How can I treat you like a woman and feel like a man?"
- "How can I act like I don't care about your love and let you know I really do?"
- "How can I enjoy what we have in common without diminishing my manliness?"

The Single Mother's Challenge with Her Son

For a mother and a son, there can be ongoing tension in adolescence. The teenage son wants to be close enough to feel connected with his female parent, but distant enough to preserve his growing maleness. This dance of closeness and distance is often expressed through conflict, which satisfies both needs at once—being in close communication over a difference that sets mother and son apart. In addition, conflict can be how the teenage boy asserts his maleness with his mother, standing up to the most powerful female force in his life, often challenging her to argue to see if he can win.

More conflict and more distance are what a mother frequently experiences during her son's adolescence, finding less time spent together, less personal confiding from her son, and less time together spent on a harmonious middle ground. For the son, more conflict and more distance can serve his developing male definition.

Sometimes, in frustration at the distance her son has put between them, a mother will use questions to elicit information, to encourage more sharing, and to close the gap of ignorance lack of communication has created. Unfortunately, these questions often don't encourage more communication; instead, they provoke more silence because of two problems with questions at this age. Questions can be invasive of privacy ("My business is my own to keep!"), and questions are emblematic of authority ("I won't be interrogated!").

So if questions to get more dialogue only seem to get less, consider using requests instead. "If you ever feel like telling me some about last night, I would love to hear." "It would really help keep me from imagining the worst if you could tell me just a little about what is going on."

How a Mother Can Wound a Son

When a mother is unwilling to allow sufficient interpersonal distance for her son's sense of male definition to develop, her son may forsake closeness to her to claim his freedom to grow. "I'd rather keep my distance than be controlled."

Faced with a son who avoids contact with her, who won't talk with her, a mother can feel undeservedly put off in spite of her constant efforts to communicate. In grief at what feels like his loss of caring, she can complain, "How can you pull away and cut me off after I have given you so much?" And now the son can feel torn between the need to preserve male definition and disloyalty for abandoning the woman who gave him life, creating a common wound that can be hard to heal—being considered a cold-hearted son.

Advice to a single-parent mother about an adolescent son: Give your son the space he needs to preserve his emerging male definition, express your love across that distance between you and keep communicating, and don't take his unwillingness to talk more as a personal rejection. It is done for him; it is not done against you.

**Fact**

Many teenage daughters pull away and fight their mothers to assert essential separation; many teenage sons pull away and fight their mothers to defend against excessive closeness.

Father and Son: Acceptance Versus Comparison

Sexually similar to his father, inclined as a child to identify with and imitate his ways, a son often directs his efforts to being like his father by doing like his father, wanting to follow the path of interest and performance that the man has set. The conflict he typically has with his father during the adolescent passage is wanting to declare independence by establishing a different path: "I don't have to compete and measure up to you!"

Questions That Trouble

There are many conflicts between father and son during adolescence arising from questions that illuminate how developmentally torn the teenage son has become. Consider just a few:

- "To have your approval, do I have to do like you?"
- "If we disagree, does one of us have to win?"
- "To do well, do I have to do better than you?"
- "If I do better than you, will we still be friends?"
- "If I choose not to follow your way, will I still have your blessing?"

The Single Father's Challenge with a Son

The challenge for the single-parent father is to allow his son to go up against the father in safe disagreement in order to define honest differences between them, and to approve departure from the father's path in search of sufficient individual variation.

Looking up to his father as a child, during adolescence the young man wants to establish himself on his own terms and have those terms respected, not rejected with disapproval. This is why criticism by the father can have such negative effect, conveying a failure to measure up to the model that father has set, while sarcasm and ridicule can drive humiliation and resentment very deep. Better to neutralize any correction you have to give your teenage son by being nonevaluative: "Often I don't understand your choices, but I do respect that they are yours to make, as is coping with whatever consequences then occur."

Sometimes a father can free up his son's struggles to grow by honestly cutting himself down to his son's human size by admitting his own frailties and failures, and by praising competencies he sees in his son. "I continue to make mistakes as always, and I see capacities in you I will never have."

Alert!

> Don't get into conflict with your son to prove who is the most right, better, or stronger man. You will only create a losing competition, where your victory is at the expense of your son's losing face. Better to treat disagreement as a chance to discuss and understand honest differences than as a contest where all that matters is arguing to win.

How a Father Can Wound a Son

When a father is unwilling to support any significant deviation from the father's way, the price for independence a son can pay is rejection from the man. "My Dad won't forgive me for refusing to be like him."

Faced with a son who seems to be growing "wrong" by not following in his father's footsteps, the man can feel disappointed and blame the feeling directly on his son: "You've really let me down!" Now the son has lost loving standing in his father's eyes, feeling torn between being his own man and not being the man his father wanted him to be, creating a wound that can be hard to heal—being considered a failure as a son.

Advice to a single-parent father about his adolescent son: Bridge the differences between yourself and your son with interest and appreciation, credit his efforts to make his own way in the world, and do not measure how he is growing up by comparing him to the man you have become.

Father and Daughter: Devaluing Versus Affirmation

Sexually different from her father, inclined to be his pleasing "little girl" when a child, she strives to outgrow that role and become more womanly during adolescence. The conflict she typically has with her father during the teenage years is between wanting to hold on to his admiration for the child she was and wanting to be taken more seriously now that she is older. "How can I stop being treated as your little girl and start being respected as a young woman?"

Questions That Trouble

There are many conflicts between father and daughter during adolescence arising from questions that illuminate how developmentally torn the teenage girl has become. Consider just a few:

- "As I grow up, will you still love me as much as when I was your little girl?"
- "If I'm your daughter, can you value me and treat me as seriously as you would a son?"
- "If I need you in a time of trial, will you be there for me?"
- "If I don't like doing what you like to do for interest or for fun, can you still enjoy my company?"
- "If I'm sexually different from you, can you still try and understand and appreciate the woman and person I have become?"

The Single Father's Challenge with His Daughter

The challenge for the single-parent father is to fully value his daughter when the conduct and focus of her life diverge from his own, as they usually begin to do in adolescence. If she is primarily concerned with relationships among her community of friends, he can dismiss the merit of her path through life because it is not more ambitious and performance based like his own.

Even worse than being rejected is being dismissed. Not to be liked can hurt feelings, but not to be considered a person worth taking seriously can injure self-esteem. How a child is treated influences how she comes to treat herself, and so a daughter treated as unimportant or insignificant or not worthy of serious attention can come to treat herself in a similar way. It's not that she feels his disapproval so much as she feels discredited in her father's eyes. So the father must take his daughter seriously as a person and a young woman.

In addition, through his treatment of his daughter, he shows her how to be well treated by a man. If she is valued and respected by her father, then she is more likely to expect similar treatment from the young men who become increasingly important in her life.

Pleasing him as a young woman and a person, she feels confident in herself. This is in contrast to the daughter of a father who could not be pleased, a young woman who may place herself at a continual disadvantage trying to compensate for credit not received from her father by doing anything to please other men.

 **Fact**

How a single-parent father treats the young men who date his daughter is important. So a dad may take a young man aside before the couple go out to explain the father's expectations. "I am entrusting you with my daughter's welfare tonight and I expect you to respect it, returning her by the time agreed, in as good condition as when she left. Have a good, responsible time."

How a Father Can Wound a Daughter

When a father, who has been socialized to believe that performance is the major contributor to self-esteem, is unwilling to credit his daughter's path because she is more relationally inclined, the daughter is at risk of feeling like a "second-class child" because of sexual dissimilarity. She is not following the male way. "My father never took me seriously." And so she stops taking him seriously back.

Faced with a daughter for whom he seems to matter less than he would like, despite having provided for her growing up, a father can act displeased, particularly when she seems more connected, communicative, and intimate with her mother: "How can you act so superficial with me?" And now the daughter, as much at sea about how to develop a relationship with him as he is with her, can feel torn between missing a deeper connection and resenting not feeling fully valued, creating a common wound that can be hard to heal—being discounted as a daughter.

Advice to a single-parent father about his daughter: Continually affirm the worth of your daughter as a person and as a young woman, treat her as you would like other men to treat her, and do not dismiss her relevance in your life because she is ignorant of, or not interested in, what matters to you as a man.

Question?

What is the greatest source of misunderstanding between mother and son and between father and daughter?

Sexual ignorance. A mother has no more experiential basis for understanding the male passage of her son than a father does for understanding the female passage of his daughter. Each adult must manage this relationship so that anxiety from ignorance does not cause the parent to seek excessive control to cope with excessive worry, creating unnecessary conflict that only pushes the son or daughter further away.

CHAPTER 18

Relationship with One's Ex-Spouse

W hatever personality and preference differences divided the marriage, they tend to grow more pronounced after divorce when each partner is freed to pursue life on his or her individual terms. Now there is no concern about giving offense by following inclinations and indulging habits the ex-spouse doesn't like, or fitting into the other partner's ways. The longer they now live apart, the more diversity develops between them, increasing lifestyle differences that will sometimes require tolerance from them both when communication and cooperation are required for the sake of their children.

Communicating Effectively

These lifestyle differences, unless clearly harmful to children by creating danger from neglect or abuse, need to be respected, not contested. Lifestyle differences will create parenting differences, children living on different family terms with each parent, and that's okay. The two households do not have to be entirely consistent. Each parent's sphere of family influence stops where the other's family household begins. Neither of them has to govern his or her personal life out of consideration for the other any more. Some common parenting responsibility is all they share.

Where consistency between households is in a child's bests interests—like maintaining a regular regimen of medication, dietary requirements, or schedule of remediation, for example—parents do need to discuss to what degree consistent support can be provided.

 **Fact**

Ex–marriage partners who cannot manage to work around and through individual differences between them without tension and conflict only create stress for their children. Ongoing parental bickering and animosity divide children's loyalties to painful effect. "They both blame the other and want me on their side. I'm torn in between because they still can't get along!" Conflict becomes pointless when it neither relieves tension nor resolves differences.

Communication is the tie that binds. By exchanging accurate and adequate information, you and your ex-spouse can stay on the same page about the children's well-being. "Over the week with me, he wet his bed two nights, but not the other three. That's better than he did before." Because each of you now sees the children separately, you each have different samples of their behavior to observe and concerns to hear.

Each of you are privy to different parts of the children's lives, and by combining what you know, the two of you become smarter than one of you. "The bed-wetting mostly occurs during the first couple of days of the school week, and not the rest. That being so, maybe we need to work with him on starting the week less anxiously."

It is in the best interests of the children for parents to form a working partnership on their behalf, and that means communicating with your ex-spouse in ways that maximize understanding and minimize offense, and treating your ex-spouse how you would like to be treated in return. You don't have to like each other to do this. You need only love your children enough to do this.

Alert!

Do not compete for "most important parent" with your children. You are both "most important," because you each provide some influences the other cannot. A father can no more replace a mother than a mother can replace a father. Each has a distinctively different role to play in the lives of the children, and hopefully each values the unique contribution the other has to make.

Positively Sticking to Specifics

In general, when it comes to discussing business about the children, no abstracts allowed. "I wish you'd be more responsible with the children," you say in hopes of encouraging your ex-spouse to do more house-keeping for the children when on visitation. But is that what you really communicated? No. The only information you have conveyed by the general term *responsible* is your disapproval of his conduct about something that bothers you but that has not been disclosed to him. What is it he is doing or not doing that you have labeled as "not responsible"? If your answer is, not getting the children back on time, then talk about that behavior. "I really need to have you get the children back by the time we agreed." Use operational language, not abstract terms, when describing what you'd like. What is it specifically (in the form of happenings or events) that you want or do not want to have happen?

Essential

Operational language is nonjudgmental. Being only descriptive and not evaluative, not only is it less likely to give offense, but it is explicit enough so that there is little room for misinterpretation. Instead of saying, "Be sure the kids bring everything for the weekend," be more precise. "When I pick up the kids, I need them to each bring a complete change of clothes, and that includes an extra pair of shoes."

When there is some behavior of your ex-spouse you want to take issue with, rather than talking about what's been happening that you don't like and how you want it to stop, talk about what you want to have happen and how you would like that to begin. Instead of saying, "Stop sending the kids home with dirty laundry," try, "It would really help if the kids came back with their clothes washed and clean." In general, a positive declaration motivates more cooperation than a negative complaint.

Question?

Why would I want to treat someone well whom I wanted to divorce and am glad I did?
The answer is, you wouldn't, except if you have children. In this case, you must divorce as partners but remain married as parents, finding ways to work harmoniously together for the sake of your kids.

Treating Your Ex-Spouse as an Ally

What is the best way to treat your ex-spouse? Treat your ex-spouse as a valued ally on whom you depend to work toward a common objective—the welfare of the children. To maintain and cultivate this alliance, treat him or her diplomatically by demonstrating acts of consideration that convey the value you place upon this relationship.

Alert!

If you are remarried, explain to your new partner how important it is to maintain a working alliance with your ex-spouse. Explain how showing consideration for your ex-spouse is not a matter of romantic caring for him or her. Consideration for your new spouse is a matter of love. Consideration for your ex-spouse is a matter of maintaining a well-working alliance for the sake of the children.

It may sound too old-fashioned and trivial to matter, but the quality of the divorced parent relationship has a lot to do with the courtesy each parent shows the other. Courtesy refers to specific acts that signify consideration. Successful alliances are maintained by a meticulous show of consideration, and they quickly deteriorate without it.

Subscribing to the "Articles of Consideration"

Obviously, the course of divorced-parent relationships does not always run smoothly, any more than does the course of true love, which in this case ended in divorce. However, with effort and attention, there are some specific acts of courtesy that signify consideration and tend to support a strong working alliance. To help start you thinking about what these acts are, reflect on the ten "Articles of Consideration" below, and see if you are willing to sign them for the sake of allying with your ex-spouse for the sake of your children.

1. "I will be reliable." I will keep the arrangements I make with you and the children. You can count on my word.
2. "I will be responsible." I will honor my obligations to provide for the children. As agreed, I will provide my share of their support.
3. "I will be appreciative." I will let you know ways in which I see you doing good for the children. And I will thank you for being helpful to me.
4. "I will be respectful." I will always talk positively about you to the children. If I have a disagreement or concern, I will talk directly to you.
5. "I will be flexible." I will make an effort to modify child-care arrangements when you have conflicting commitments. I will try to be responsive to work with unexpected change.
6. "I will be tolerant." I will accept the increasing lifestyle differences between us. I will accept how the children live with us on somewhat different terms.

7. "I will be supportive." I will back you up with the children when you have disciplinary need. I will not allow them to play one of us against the other.

8. "I will be involved." I will problem solve with you when the children get into difficulty. I will work with you to help them.

9. "I will be responsive." I will be available to help cope with the children's emergencies. I will be on call in times of crisis.

10. "I will be reasonable." I will talk through our inevitable differences in a calm and constructive manner. I will keep communicating until we work out a resolution that is acceptable to us both.

Essential

By subscribing to the ten Articles of Consideration, you model behavior that you encourage in return, and you strengthen the alliance with your ex-spouse, as he or she is encouraged to do with you.

Four Categories of Differences

It behooves ex-partners to tread lightly around differences, being both sensitive and wise in response to traits that set them apart as individuals—distinct and unique. The key is to understand how categories of differences vary from each other according to their susceptibility to change, and which differences are to be worked through, and which are to be worked around.

Consider four categories of human differences that exist between any two people, in this case a divorced couple, with categories listed from least to most easy to change.

Characteristic differences. These differences are non-chosen dimensions of being such as family history, physical features and sex, and inborn traits such as personality, temperament, and aptitudes, and normally they do not change. So by temperament, one parent tends to do unpleasant tasks as soon as they arise, whereas the other parent is more temperamentally inclined to put them off.

Value differences. A little less fixed than characteristics, value differences are still pretty inflexible. Deeply embedded beliefs about right and wrong, good and bad, appropriate and inappropriate, appealing and unappealing, are very hard to change. Acquired so long ago a person cannot remember when, when challenged to justify them, a person can run out of reasons to defend them and yet still cling to his or her original allegiance. So one parent believes routine should be firmly followed, whereas the other believes it should be flexibly managed.

Habit differences. These differences are patterns of learned behavior practiced over a long time, and they require a lot of effort to change. They are so familiar a person does them automatically, without thinking, which is why it takes acting intentionally in unfamiliar ways to break a habit. So one parent is more used to working than relaxing at home, while the other is used to treating home as a place to relax after work.

Want differences. These differences are based on what people desire to have happen or not to have happen, and of all four classes of differences, these are the most susceptible to change because they are most easily controlled by choice. What can make even these differences hard to alter, however, is that they are wed to what satisfies or makes a person happy. Thus changing a want may mean giving up some enjoyment or fulfillment. So one parent wants to start the weekend with children's getting homework done right away, while the other wants to put recreational time first and leave homework for later.

These differences, while they probably existed in marriage, may have been accommodated or ignored. After divorce, however, parents can be impatient with what they put up with before.

So how should these differences be treated? If differences are viewed as failings to be criticized, parents can attack the problem by attacking each other. "Well, if you'd just get them to get homework out of the way, they wouldn't be rushing through it Sunday night! You're still all play and no work!" To which the other parent takes offense and attacks back. "Relaxing and having a good time together on the weekends is more important than starting it off with more school. You're all work and no play, just like always!"

Alert!

> If you have such a contentious relationship with your ex-spouse that issues about cooperation or financial responsibility are sources of ongoing conflict, do not deputize your child to deal with the other parent to resolve these matters. Get outside help instead. Keep the child out of the adults' business.

Managing Differences

So what is a couple to do when differences of a bothersome kind emerge after divorce? First, understand that any characteristic, value, habit, and want differences that arise between them are a reality. Individuality of each parent makes human diversity inevitable. Second, when any of these differences offend either partner, do not engage in blame, but treat the difference at issue as a no-fault collision, as another unavoidable incompatibility that is bound to exist as differences between ex-spouses after divorce become more varied and pronounced. And third, learn to resolve the difference below the rejection line.

The Rejection Line

What is the rejection line? In the hierarchy of differences from least to most susceptible to change—characteristics, values, habits, and wants—the rejection line separates wants from the other three categories of differences. Although characteristics, values, and habits are very hard to change, wants are more flexible and amenable to choice.

The trap that divorced couples fall into is one parent's demanding that the other alter a characteristic, value, or habit that is unlikely to be changed, or face disapproval if he or she cannot. Then the other parent, resenting and resisting what feels like rejection, and fighting back, helps provoke a pointless conflict that neither relieves frustration nor resolves the difference at issue, but only generates ill feeling between them, with which children must now contend.

 **Essential**

> Neither parent should get in the business of changing each other's characteristics, values, or habits, because any demand to alter these intractable traits will usually be experienced as rejection and will lead to pointless, and often painful, conflict.

In the interests of the relationship, each parent needs to do the following: Accept in each other those characteristics that are part of that person's human nature. Respect those values in each other with which one disagrees. Tolerate a lot of habits in each other that one may sometimes wish would go away. Contest differences only on the level of wants because they can be negotiated below the rejection line. For partners to say they *want* something different does not inflict rejection; it only creates disagreement.

Resolving Differences below the Rejection Line

If criticizing differences above the rejection line creates injury and ill feeling but these differences will always exist, what is the couple to do? The answer is, translate incompatibilities arising from characteristics, values, and habit differences into disagreements over the wants these differences dictate, and then negotiate and resolve them below the rejection line.

For example, suppose there are two parents who have very different family priorities when beginning a weekend with the children. One parent's value is work before play; the other parent's value is play before work. In consequence, in one setting, homework is gotten out of the way Saturday morning, and in the other, it is left until Sunday night, each priority offending the other parent. Who is right?

They both are. And the more they argue the merits of their respective values, the "righter" each will feel. What to do?

Rather then getting into a conflict over which parental value is "right" and allowing argument to further polarize the difference between them, each parent can discuss the wants each value dictates, and then negotiate the wants, leaving the values alone. So, a compromise is reached. The "play first" parent and the "work first" parent agree to schedule homework on Sunday morning. This way, Saturday is left free and clear for play, and there is no rush to finish homework Sunday night.

So the contract for treating individual differences runs like this: "We understand that there will be inevitable incompatibilities (no-fault collisions) based on growing family and lifestyle differences between us that are unlikely to change. We understand that learning to live with these differences between us is the lifelong challenge of our relationship, as we work through some, but work around more. We understand that criticizing differences only creates hurt feelings, and arguing about those differences only makes them more intractable. We agree to translate any incompatible differences in characteristics, values, or habits into the opposing wants they dictate, and then negotiate a compromise in wants we can both agree to support."

 **Essential**

Never attack differences over characteristics, values, or habits between you and your ex-spouse. Since these traits are mostly unchangeable, you will only end up criticizing who and how the other person is, causing damage to the relationship, creating tensions between parents with which children must live. Instead, translate differences rooted in unchangeable traits into the wants they dictate, and resolve them below the rejection line.

Resentment of the "Good Time" Parent

Resentment toward one's ex-spouse not only strains that relationship, but it creates emotional strain for children, who often feel they cannot have a good time with the resented parent without offending the resenter. And when the noncustodial parent becomes the "good time" parent, the custodial parent can be at significant risk of grievance over what seems an unfair return for effort invested and responsibility taken.

The Problem of Envy

Simply put, it can be easy for a custodial parent to resent the good and easy time the ex-spouse has with the children on visitation. Beforehand, the children get excited; during the visit, they seem to have nonstop fun; and returning home, they are grateful for everything that the noncustodial parent did to entertain and make them happy. How can the custodial parent compete with this performance? The custodial parent can't. By comparison, home can sometimes seem dull and ordinary, boring and routine, taxing and irritating.

To the custodial parent, who feels overworked and undervalued, this unfavorable comparison to the ex-spouse can feel distinctly unfair. After all, who does the drudgery of daily supervision? Who keeps the home stocked and supplied? Who asserts demands, defends limits, enforces rules, and disciplines violations? Who settles fights, soothes upsets, attends sickness, and solves problems? Who bears primary responsibility for the children's care? Where is the appreciation for doing all this? Nowhere!

 **Fact**

Custodial parents often feel taken for granted by their children, or feel blamed for being moody and irritable when they're tired. Although children expect far less from the noncustodial parent, they seem to appreciate him or her more. Although they expect much more from the custodial parent, they seem to appreciate his or her constant effort less.

Putting Noncustodial Parenting into Perspective

Before a custodial parent gives in to resentment, however, he or she might want to consider this inequity from another perspective. In terms of trust and openness, the children's relationship with each of the two parents can be very different. Between children and noncustodial parent there is sometimes something missing—authenticity.

Wanting so much to make their visit a success, the special effort to please each other that children and noncustodial parent make often gets in the way of expressing hard feelings that normally arise. Neither adult nor children, for example, may feel comfortable expressing anger or dissatisfaction with the other, or making demands that would spoil their limited time together. This is often a "best behavior" relationship on both sides, the more so the less frequent contact is, neither party wanting to displease or disappoint the other. For this reason, some degree of authenticity is sacrificed for the sake of harmony, openness is partly guarded, and children and noncustodial parent can sometimes come away from visitation feeling mixed. They had a good time, and yet they feel dissatisfied because they did not connect as completely as they longed to do. Often, the relationship between children and noncustodial parent is more constrained than with the custodial parent, with whom more emotional intimacy feels allowed.

How the Custodial Parent Gets the Best

In one way, it is true that the noncustodial parent gets the best behavior from the children, and the custodial parent gets the worst. But on a deeper level, this statement can be false. With their custodial mother or father, the children have an open enough relationship to risk sharing their worst sides, unafraid that by doing so they will jeopardize their standing with the resident parent.

Although being taken for granted can be irritating at times, the custodial parent can also treat this assumption as a compliment and statement of trust. The children are implying, "Because you are always here, and because you will always love and accept us, we don't have to worry about our bad moods or misbehaviors driving you away. Because we live together, we don't have to act like it's a visit. We don't have to act special with you. We can act ordinary. We can just relax and be ourselves."

 **Fact**

> What custodial parents get is usually an honest mix of good and bad from the children, whereas the noncustodial parent is often limited to "the best."

Taking Hard Stands with the Ex-Spouse

Circumstances can arise when custodial parents must act for the child's best interests in ways their ex-spouse may not like. In the process, anger can be provoked and conflict created, with custodial parents taking stands that the ex-spouse may consider offensive or unjust.

What kinds of stands? The most common two are for child safety and for child support. In both instances, custodial parents (because they have custodial responsibility) must look out for the child's welfare by monitoring conditions and treatment while on visitation and by assessing ongoing financial needs at home.

Taking issue with the noncustodial parent's conduct is not easy when that former partner feels that what happens during visitation is none of the custodial parent's business. Nor is it any easier to take issue with monetary contribution when the former partner believes the initial settlement for child support should remain the final one. The noncustodial parent is wrong on both counts. Custodial parents have ongoing responsibility for evaluating safety of visitation and for ensuring the child's adequate support at home.

Child Safety

Custodial parents need to speak up to their ex-spouse about visitation concerns that the child feels secure voicing only at home. "I'm left alone too much. I get frightened about what might happen."

These kinds of statements must be taken seriously. Custodial parents should first listen and then ask the child to specify what is happening or not happening to cause these feelings.

After telling the child what they are going to do, custodial parents must then inform the noncustodial parent about conduct and circumstances that are causing the child to feel unsafe. These concerns should be expressed in terms of reported behaviors and reported situations that occur. Although the noncustodial parent may respond with information that modifies the child's report, it is with the child's feelings that the custodial parent is most concerned.

The custodial parent is not interested in making accusations against the ex-spouse but wants to help make visitation feel as comfortable as possible for the child. To this end, the custodial parent is giving the noncustodial parent information that may be useful in making visitation a more positive experience. The custodial parent needs to send his or her ex-spouse this message: "I want you to know that I value your time with our child and want that time to be beneficial to you both. That is why I am sharing this information with you now." Approached in this supportive manner, in many cases the noncustodial parent will make modifications that improve the quality of visitation. Of course, what the child reports works well on visitation should also be shared with the noncustodial parent so he or she can be aware of what positive practices to continue.

Question?

What is one of the most powerful ways to build a positive parental relationship with an ex-spouse?

When children mention events or activities they found particularly meaningful or enjoyed on a visitation, share that information with the ex-spouse. This kind of credit sharing not only expresses your appreciation of his or her role in the children's lives, it gives your ex-spouse information on what parts of visitation are working particularly well.

Where the noncustodial parent reacts in denial about the child's reported sense of danger, however, stubbornly refusing to admit that visitation is exposing the child to risk of injury, custodial parents may have to take a protective stand by enlisting the help of relevant social authorities. Sometimes just knowing that outside officials have been notified is enough to cause the noncustodial parent to behave more responsibly.

To knowingly place the child in visitation in spite of knowledge of neglect, abuse, alcoholic drinking or other substance problems, or recklessness on the part of the noncustodial parent is irresponsible. The custodial parent, aware of the dangers, is sending the child into potential harm.

Child Support

Being asked to raise existing support payments often affronts noncustodial parents. They feel they are already giving enough. Besides, if they raise their contribution, they don't get any more benefit in return (to see the child more, to have more say over the child's life). If remarried, their new spouse may resent this additional drain on resources he or she feels should be devoted to the new family, not the old.

In making this request, the custodial parent is best served by documenting the existing need. Present the following:

- The schedule of basic expenses required to support the child at the time of divorce.
- A revision of these expenses based on how they have increased as the child has grown older and inflation has raised the cost of living.
- An addition of special unanticipated expenses that have arisen since the original settlement.
- A statement of how the custodial parent has had to spend more on the child too.

A request to raise child support is evidence that the custodial parent also has to contribute more than before. All he or she is really asking is for the ex-spouse to share in this increase.

Two-Household Family Living

I t's a big adjustment for children of divorce, learning to live in two parental households instead of one. As time goes on, lifestyle and value differences between each home become more pronounced, particularly so when either or both parent remarries and the influential effects of stepparents begin to be felt. As one child of divorce put it, "I grew up living in two separate family worlds. I got to do things in one that I couldn't do in the other, and I was expected to follow a different set of rules and routines in each place." The increased diversity of family values, interests, and practices in separate households usually broadens a child's experience and opportunities for growth. With dual-family living, a child tends to develop and actualize more parts of himself or herself than single-household living would normally allow. The longer parents live apart, the less they have in common, the more distinctly different from each other the child's two household worlds become.

Visitation Adjustments for the Child

No matter how well parental divorce is managed, visitation between separate households can still be a complicated experience for parents and children alike. Understand some of these complexities, and the adjustments can be eased.

When considering visitation, remember differences. It was irreconcilable differences between partners' ways and wants that caused the marriage to dissolve. After divorce, those incompatibilities that initially drove the couple apart usually grow more pronounced, becoming evident in different lifestyles that former partners lead, and different households that they run.

 **Fact**

Visitation puts children in the export/import business. To some degree, parental influences and household practices will be exported from one home and imported into the other, and parents must accept this interhousehold trade. When what is learned in one home is inconsistent with what is desired by the parent in the other, simply reassert what is acceptable for you. "I know you don't in your father's house, but in this household, we go to church on Sunday."

Because visitation requires children to bridge these differences, going back and forth takes getting used to. The transition is complicated. It requires more than simply walking out of one door and in through another. Children must let go of one family frame of reference and then reengage with another. Out goes one parent's family agenda and in comes the agenda of the other. "I have to learn to live two different ways, depending on which parent I'm living with. And when I don't keep the differences straight, sometimes the parent that I'm staying with gets mad."

To some degree, visitation causes a child to create a divided self—living one way with one parent and another way with the other. Most important, neither parent really understands the two-household adjustment the child is continually forced to make. "They only have to live one way, and I have to live two. And neither one appreciates the extra effort it takes for me to do both."

Managing Reentry

Management of their children's reentry into the home is one of the most complicated tasks custodial parents have to master. Pressures of getting back together, and possibilities for misunderstanding, create an increased vulnerability to hurt and conflict.

Consider the problem of timing. A custodial parent, happy to see the children after a weekend, holiday, or vacation separation, wants an immediate affectionate and communicative reunion. One child, however, remains distant and cool, wanting only to be left alone. The custodial parent thinks, "Why am I being treated this way? Haven't I been missed at all? Isn't the child glad to be home?"

Alert!

It is important for the custodial parent to be sensitive when the child has had to say a hard good-bye to the other parent. The boy or girl must manage a mix of grief and gladness. There is grief at letting go of a good time with the visitation parent, there is gladness at seeing the custodial parent again, and there is a need to honor grief before gladness can be expressed. "Sometimes coming back feels like I'm being torn apart." Divorce means never having your parents share the same home again.

The answer to the last two questions is yes. The child has missed the custodial parent and is glad to be home. However, he or she has not let go of the visit with the other parent and still wants to reflect on the memory of their being together. Thus preoccupied, the child acts removed and unresponsive, wanting time to emotionally close out the visit. He or she loves the custodial parent but is not ready to reconnect and open up just yet.

In this situation, custodial parents are well advised, after communicating welcome, to give the child privacy and space. Rather than treat this aloofness as rejection, respect it for what it really is—a period of difficult adjustment for which the child needs some time alone, to let the visit go.

When the child is nonresponsive to the single parent's welcome after visitation and seems to only want to be alone, give the child time and space apart to work through his or her letting go of valued time with the other parent. Also, be prepared for some testing of your family structure by a child who may try to carry over special indulgences (no chores) and personal freedoms (staying up late) enjoyed on visitation.

Recovering from a Hard Visit

This strategy is even more important after a hard visit, when the child's expectations were disappointed or some troublesome incident occurred. In either case, the child may have avoided speaking up, not wanting to make a disagreeable situation worse. As soon as he or she returns home, however, out come the injured feelings. The unhappy child picks on a sibling or the custodial parent, looking for a fight to get out that pent-up anger, disappointment, or frustration.

Again, the custodial parent needs not to take this treatment personally. Instead, say to the child, "It sounds like you may have had a hard visit. Take some time alone to settle down; then we can talk about what happened if you like." Over the course of many visitations, not every one will go well. When they don't, the child may bring hard feelings home. Acting them out in hurt or anger, however, although understandable, is not acceptable. The child must learn to talk them out in such a way that communication brings relief without inflicting harm on others. His or her custodial parent is happy to be a sympathetic listener, but not a whipping post.

 **Alert!**

Beware other-household extortion. Children will use some norms for living in one household to influence norms for living in the other. "But we all eat in front of the TV over there!" Without criticizing practices in the other home you do not want followed in your own, simply explain, "At this home, I want us to eat together with the TV off so we can have a chance to talk." One home does not have to replicate the other.

Visitation in an Embittered Divorce

Probably the most painful reentries occur when parents remain actively embittered. In this unforgiving circumstance, the child cannot act pleased to see one parent without offending the other. Constant pressure to take sides is increased by visitation when parents treat leaving their home as a betrayal of loyalty, as though the child were taking up residence in the enemy's camp. For the child in this situation, visitation is a no-win proposition.

In an embittered divorce, the child may feel resentment and hear slander from one parent toward the other in both households. One can sympathize with the weary twelve-year-old who angrily declared, "Sometimes I wish I could just divorce both of them and live alone!"

In this situation, warring parents may want to ponder the question, "Which do you love more—loving your child or loving to hate each other?" It takes parents who have emotionally reconciled the differences between them to honestly support the child's contact with each other, blessing the child's passage back and forth between two homes, wanting the child to have time with the other parent, and wanting that time to be good.

 **Essential**

At worst, embittered parents can try to get revenge on each other, using time with the child to poison the child's mind against the other, or deliberately sabotaging the good the other parent is trying to do. Now the child becomes a pawn in the vindictive game both parents are determined to play, a losing game because of the love the child loses for them each.

Visitation Adjustments for the Single Parent

In addition to visitation adjustments faced by children of divorce, a custodial single parent can have adjustments of his or her own. When it feels hard to let the child go on visitation, or when it feels hard to get the child back from visitation, the single parent can be put to certain adjustment tests. Should either adjustment occur, it is important to know that nothing is "wrong" with you or your relationship with the children.

When It's Hard Letting Children Go

The letting-go dilemma might be described in these words: "I really miss my daughter when she goes to see her father, because I have to stop acting like a parent now that she is away. We've grown so close since the divorce, and I miss that parental connection when she's not here. I know I should enjoy free time to do things for myself, but I haven't yet found a good-feeling way to do that. So those times when she is gone are empty, frustrating, lonely times for me. What makes it even harder is that I know how much fun she is having with her dad and how much she looks forward to seeing him. I'm glad she does, but it makes me almost jealous to have to share her with him, and resentful that she can enjoy times apart and I can't. So I am cooler to her when she returns than I would like to be."

For this single parent, the child's reentry from visitation can be an emotionally mixed experience—happy to have her daughter back, but put off that her daughter had wanted to leave in the first place. Also, each departure of the child only reminds the mother of how much she depends upon single parenting to give structure and meaning to her life, and how little of herself, at this point, she has outside of the parental role.

When It's Hard Getting Children Back

The getting-back dilemma might be described in these words: "I feel so relaxed when the kids are gone to see their mother. It's like the whole single-parent role—responsibilities, restrictions, and all—is just lifted from me. I suddenly feel free to do with myself what I want, without having to consider anyone else's needs for a while. But that elation has a real catch to it. When the kids come home, I can really come down. Happy as I am to see them again, I have some regret at losing the freedom I enjoyed when they were gone." For this single parent, the children's reentry from visitation can be an emotionally mixed experience—happy to have them back, but sad to lose the freedom their absence gave. Also, each departure of the children only reminds the father of how much is tied up in single parenting, and how hard it is creating personal space and time apart for himself.

Essential

It's not just children who have adjustments to make to visitation as they travel back and forth between separate households. Each single parent has adjustments to make too—from normal ambivalence about letting children go on visitation to normal ambivalence about having them return.

When Your Child Acts Like Your Ex

Although divorce is meant to free up partners from painful exposure to each other, when there are children, that exposure continues to be felt, directly through ongoing contact as parents, and indirectly by how each parent, by instruction and example, continues to influence how children grow. Like it or not, through visitation, the child can become a carrier of each parent's influence back to the home of the other parent, serving as a painful reminder about how marriage to that person was.

Unwelcome Influence of the Other Parent

When a child demonstrates parental influence through imitation of one parent that affronts the other, the offended parent may object: "You're behaving just like your father!" (The child is picking up some of the quick, sarcastic repartee that the single parent hated in her ex-husband.) "Well," demands the child, proud to be acting like her father, "what's wrong with that?"

It's a hard reality for many single parents to accept that they can divorce a spouse, but not his or her influence on the child. "I know it's not her fault," confesses one single father, "but sometimes I feel angry at my daughter, not for anything she's done, just for the way she is. She even looks like her mother. I want my daughter to see her mother, to love her mother, but I don't want her to turn out to be a complainer like her mother. Yet my ex-wife is the major model for womanhood in my daughter's life."

Alert!

Criticize a child for acting just like the other parent and the child is placed in conflict between wanting to emulate the absent parent (who talks loudly to convince) and not wanting to offend the resident parent (who will no longer be bullied by a loud tone of voice). Take issue with your child's behavior, not with its similarity to your ex's. "I need you to talk to me in a quiet voice."

Or the single mother may have her say. "I am determined to bring my son up so he is not like his father! But I can't deny visiting rights just because I can't stand the kind of man my ex-husband is. So when my ten-year-old son swaggers back into the house after a visit, using that loud manner of speech that his macho father does, it makes me sick. I just hate to see that influence happening and not be able to stop it. And when my frustration shows, my son ends up hurt because he doesn't understand why I'm not happy to see him showing off mannerisms he's learned from his dad, whom he idolizes more the less they are together."

Criticizing Similarities

Parental criticism of similarity can create problems of guilt and fear for the child, particularly when he or she is very young. Two trains of thought can lead to injury.

- "My mom criticizes my dad for being bad. I am told I am just like my dad. Therefore, I am also bad." So the child feels guilty: "I am no good, just like my father."
- "My dad divorced my mom because he didn't love her anymore. He tells me I am just like my mom. Therefore, maybe he will stop loving me." So the child feels afraid. "Is my dad going to divorce me too?"

Essential

Divorce, when children are involved, is never "final." Not only will you and your ex always be connected as parents through your mutual offspring, but the children will continue to remind you of your ex-spouse through certain similarities to that parent, some of which you will like, and some of which you will not.

Criticism of the absent parent, even when no similarity to the child is attached, can be harmful. "Your father is just lazy, feeding you nothing but fast food the way he does." Because children partly identify with their noncustodial parent, any criticism of that father or mother will be taken personally as a reflection on them. You cannot criticize a child's other parent without the child's feeling criticized.

Adolescence—the Enemy of Visitation

Visitation during the teenage years can be frustrating not only for noncustodial parents, but for the adolescent as well. Consider the teenager's predicament. As an adolescent, she has separated from childhood and begun to form a social "family" of friends with whom to share companionship and adventures while exploring a more independent world of growing up. These friends understand what it's like to be adolescent in ways no parents can. It is support of these friendships that enable her to develop more social independence. So it is not surprising that the teenager wants to spend more time with friends than with parents.

Visitation Frustrations

Visitation becomes frustrating for the teenager because it is so often at the expense of time with friends. "Well then," suggests the custodial parent, "why don't you just plan to be with your father when you have nothing else going on?" Sighs the teenager, "You don't understand. Planning is not the way we do things. My friends and I don't decide what to do and then get together. We get together and then decide what we're going to do."

That's right. Unhappily, such a spontaneous social life is automatically in conflict with the scheduled contact of visitation with a noncustodial parent who has to organize his busy life to create times to see his child. Neither the teenager nor the noncustodial parent wants to be let down—the teenager by making a commitment to him that will cause her to miss a good time with friends, the noncustodial parent by having a commitment broken after he has gone to the trouble to plan for it.

Essential

When it comes to visitation during adolescence, there is increased potential for frustration on both sides—for the teenager not wanting to be tied down, and for the noncustodial parent not wanting to be let down.

Managing Visitation During Adolescence

It can take a lot of maturity for the noncustodial parent to maintain contact with a teenage child under such trying circumstances. It is tempting to feel hurt and act resentful, to take the teenager's social preference as a personal rejection, when it is usually not. It is normal for a boy or girl to feel ambivalent about visitation during adolescence. In most cases, that ambivalence does not reflect a lack of love for the noncustodial parent, only the teenager's healthy need to stay primarily connected to friends.

Therefore, the noncustodial parent may want to consider some suggestions for helping visitation work during this socially competitive time.

Don't get into a bidding war with your teenager. Don't try to materially enhance your time with her with costly activities in an effort to woo her away from friends. You risk feeling used in the process and ending up resenting her for the expense.

Do invite her to include friends in visitation because that allows her to have it both ways—time with you is also time with friends.

If you are remarried or romantically attached, make sure you take some separate time to be alone with your teenager during some of the visitation. Just as you want her to take time away from friends to be with you, she values time alone with you away from your significant other.

Do not limit all contact with her to agreed-upon visitations. Take the initiative to keep in touch between visitation times by other communication—by e-mail, phone, and letter. Take her out for an unplanned time to eat together. Attend her performance events. Such shows of interest and caring are usually appreciated by the teenager and take advantage of her openness to spontaneous contact.

Alert!

Sometimes a noncustodial parent will blame the custodial parent for the adolescent's reluctance to abide by a fixed visitation schedule. "This is your doing. You just don't want me to see our child!" Usually not so. Now visitation is in competition with the teenager's other social needs. Adolescent socializing often competes with visitation.

Try increasing the frequency of short contacts and reducing longer ones that are more likely to be socially costly to her. And when she is with you, support her communication with friends.

Finally, be willing to be more flexible around her social needs and do not burden her with disappointment or anger when she wishes to change agreed-upon visitation plans. Do, however, let her know that you have commitments too and that you expect the courtesy of due notice so you have time to make other arrangements, the same courtesy she can expect if you must change visitation plans.

Chapter 20

Giving Marriage Another Try

Having divorced, most adults, with children or without, elect to date again, and a majority of these choose to remarry. Whether motivated by a marriage gone bad to marry better the next time or because "hope springs eternal" or because life with a partner is how they still want to live, most divorced adults desire to try marriage again.

Dating and the Children

No divorced marriage was entirely bad. Looking back, there were good times that were enjoyed, there were parts of the relationship that worked well, and there was some shared history that will be positively remembered. So in general, divorce does not usually sour adults on future companionship. What it does do, however, is cause adults to engage in an activity in which they are long out of practice—dating! Now that they are older and have been married, what approaches should be taken and what social rules apply? Where does one go to meet eligible people? How does one keep dating casual? How does one find a relationship with serious potential?

A change a single parent must discuss with children is when he or she starts dating, because the implications for children are too important to ignore. For younger children, make it very clear that early dating is social and recreational, satisfying a need for adult companionship.

Should it ever become serious and romantic, fulfilling the parent's need for adult love, then the children should be told that this is a significant relationship.

Be cautious about including children on a social date because they may assume the relationship is serious when it is not. Should they begin to develop affection and become attached to the parent's companion, a breakup of that relationship may bring them disappointment and another experience of loss.

For teenage children, parental dating raises additional concerns. At a time when they are coming into their own sexuality, beginning to date, and entertaining thoughts of romantic love, now their parent is acting like a sexual, dating, and romantic person too. This can be threatening: "My parent is acting my age!" This can be embarrassing: "My friends think it's funny that I have a parent who dates!" This can be worrisome: "How do I know that the person my parent is dating is safe to be with?"

Essential

The single parent who has begun to date needs to talk with young children about the difference between social and serious dating. With adolescents, he or she needs to discuss how to conduct parental dating in such a way that they grow comfortable with this new behavior.

Handle your own social dating with the same respect you would expect from your older children if they were starting to go out. Give them adequate information about where you are going and with whom, and a means to contact you should the need arise. Tell them when you will return. Promise that if there is any change in plans, you will call and let them know.

If the children are very young and you have not gone out since divorce, understand that your leaving is an act of separation. This temporary absence will take some getting used to by the children.

Initially, they may need assurances before you go, and a phone call while you are away. In addition, they must feel comfortable and secure with whoever is charged with their care while you are gone.

In order not to feel entirely captive of one's responsibilities as a single parent, a mother or father needs a separate social life from children, who need to feel safe when that parent goes out and they are left behind.

Alert!

When your ex-spouse develops a new romantic attachment, it is natural to feel threatened and insecure about how this family change may compete with your role as parent and possibly lessen your standing with your children by winning them over. To reduce this threat, simply resort to common sense: a new love interest, even a stepparent, is only an additional adult in your children's world, never your parental replacement.

Handling an Ex-Spouse's New Relationship

"Oh, I assumed my ex would get into a serious relationship before long, but now they're talking about marriage. The kids come back and say how wonderful this new person is, about how they are all excited about the new home for everyone, with a special room to fix up when they visit. It's hard hearing all this. It's scary. Maybe the new home and stepparent will be so good they won't want to be with me anymore."

Often, when one's ex-spouse starts a new serious relationship, it is threatening to the other single parent, particularly if he or she has yet to form a comparable attachment. Objectively, the threatened single parent knows that the ex's new love interest, the children's possible stepparent, cannot really replace a biological mother or father, but she or he still fears that nonetheless. And now an emotional tangle can occur that puts both single parent and children in a very hard place.

Sensing their parent's discomfort with the romantic changes in the other parent's life, and with a significant new adult in their life, the children may try to downplay how much they like this new person, or give expressions of caring to help their parent feel more secure. Unfortunately, such comfort often only makes the threatened single parent feel worse. "They're only reassuring me to cover up how much they like the new person."

Now the children are caught in conflict. They want to like the one parent's new love interest, but not so much they hurt the other parent's feelings. As for the threatened parent, he or she would like to share emotional discomfort with the children at this unwelcome turn of events, but doesn't want to burden them or interfere with their adjustment to this family change in the other parent's life. And that adjustment is often conflicted because now they have to share their other parent with another adult. "We can't ever see our other parent without the new friend!" But they don't want to risk offending that parent, so they complain or even act out their complaints with the unattached parent, who resents being the recipient of hurt feelings or mad behavior that should properly be addressed to the other parent.

Alert!

When a parent remarries a partner with children, the parent's child can feel threatened by these step relationships: "I only get to see my dad on visitation, but my stepmom's kids see him all the time. Maybe he'll love them more than me because they spend more time with him than I do now!"

To reduce the likelihood of all this emotional entanglement when your ex develops a new romantic attachment, consider the following suggestions.

When this change proves difficult for you to easily accept at first, tell that to the children so they know your hard feelings are about you, not about them. Declare that you want to be able to hear about when this change is good or difficult for them, but that sometimes you may want to limit these discussions to take care of your own feelings about the issue.

If you have the need to talk out sadness, frustration, or anger with this turn of events, do not do so with the children, but with your own adult support, be that a friend or a counselor. Do not accept displaced hurt or anger acted out by children in response to the romantic change in the other parent's life, but offer to listen (to the degree you can) to whatever emotional discomfort they feel, or find a counselor for them to help them work this adjustment through. Finally, put this change into a time perspective. Say to yourself, "What feels so hard to accept at the beginning will trouble me much less in a year."

Role Conflict in Being a Single Parent

Most single parents, unless so badly burned by marriage that further attachment is forsaken, still hold out the hope of finding a romantic relationship for themselves, which is why the majority of single parents remarry. But finding this attachment is complicated when they have a custodial (as opposed to a noncustodial) role.

The complexity is evidenced in the title "single parent," because within it lies a crucial role conflict between wanting to be a *single* person free to date and find a significant other, and wanting to be a responsible *parent* by honoring family commitment to one's children.

This conflict feels like a double bind because it often is—satisfying one want sometimes comes at the expense of satisfying the other. Making time for dating and developing a serious relationship can mean taking energy and attention away from parenting; putting offspring first, treating children as a top priority, can mean placing romantic interest second or on hold. "Sometimes I feel guilty putting myself first, and other times I feel resentful putting my children first."

For custodial single parents, this conflict can be even more acute when they find themselves envying how the noncustodial parent has much more freedom to act single because of having less daily responsibility to parent. How the acting single versus acting parent conflict is resolved can affect the relationship with one's ex-spouse, generating resentment that does no one any good. "It's not fair! Their father flies so free while I'm tied down to family!" Even worse, that resentment can be directed toward the children. As one divorced single mother in her early twenties expressed it, "If it wasn't for having to take care of them, I could be out having a good time!"

Rather than envy and resent the noncustodial parent because of his or her greater freedom to act single and to pursue a romantic relationship, the custodial parent needs to use this inequity in personal freedom to better understand the single versus parent tension. This conflict has important implications for the custodial parent's managing his or her own significant romantic relationship should it come along.

 ## Essential

Single parents need to understand the unavoidable tension between wanting romantic companionship and wanting to care for one's children, and how this conflict plays out after divorce with children occurs, particularly for the parent with major custodial responsibility. It is not a grievance to resent. It is an ongoing fact of single-parent life, a fact that gets more complex and conflicting once a single parent becomes romantically attached.

Honest Ambivalence

One outcome of the single versus parent conflict can be an honest ambivalence. Sometimes the single parent may feel like having children is a mixed blessing, when their needs or demands make it difficult or impossible to cultivate a serious adult relationship. Other times, the single parent may feel the significant other is a mixed blessing, when that person's needs and opinions complicate or conflict with parental management of the children.

Resolution of this conflict by resorting to one extreme or the other can be costly. Total focus on the children can deny the single parent of loving adult companionship, create undue dependency for love on children, and cause great pain from loss when it is time to let grown children go. Total focus on a significant other can deny children of needed parental attention, cause actual neglect, and foster feelings in children of emotional abandonment. So what resolution should the single parent seek? There are two. One is making a compromise about attention and the second is making a distinction about love.

The Compromise about Attention

The compromise involved in balancing needs for adult companionship and parental responsibility requires understanding that between the extremes of total absorption with children and total romantic preoccupation with another adult is a middle way. Children have to understand that it is important for their single parent to have loving adult companionship so that child love is not the only love that mother or father is bound to have. The significant other has to understand that the single parent is married to a previous and ongoing commitment to children that will not be forsaken for romantic love.

To find the middle way, the single parent must honor relational needs with children and with significant other by dividing availability. "Neither one of you can have all of my attention, but there will be sufficient to go around. You can't always have as much from me as you ideally want to get. I can't always provide as much for each of you as I ideally want to give. Many times, none of us will be totally satisfied. And that is okay." Resolution of the acting single versus acting parent conflict means that all parties concerned—single parent, children, significant other—will have to be content with the compromise: some attention is enough.

 **Fact**

> Resolving the single-parent conflict (acting single versus acting parent) means compromising on how attention is given, and maintaining the distinction between partner love and parental love.

The Distinction about Love

Sometimes, in the conflict between wanting to act single and wanting to act parent, the single mother or father can feel torn—love for the romantic other in seeming conflict with love for one's children. On these occasions, it helps if the single parent can separate the concept of love from the concept of attention. Showing one party less attention on a particular occasion than the other does not signify less love for one and more for the other. As mentioned earlier, compromising how attention is given is the best a single parent can do. Attention wanders, but love is constant. Inequality of attention does not signify inequality of love.

Not only is love a constant, but there is an important difference between partner love and parent love. They are not the same. They are not in competition. Neither one need be or should be at the expense of the other. Partner love is committed to deepening adult intimacy. Parent love is committed to nurturing a growing child. To give partner love to a child inappropriately treats that son or daughter as a source of adult intimacy. To give parent love to a significant other inappropriately treats that man or woman as a dependent child.

Stepfamily Adjustments

With parental remarriage with children comes the beginning of step relationships, a family change that for many children brings a sense of feeling dispossessed. They may never have quite the sense of belonging in the reconstituted family as they did in their family of origin or single-parent home. There is a certain awkwardness created by inherent tensions in step relationships that makes it hard to entirely relax as one did with two, or even one, biological parents in the home. This awkwardness is natural considering the family adjustments that are being made.

Family Adjustments

Consider just a few of the changes everyone must manage when the stepfamily is created. Everyone must learn to share a common living space, belongings, and resources in that space, and maintenance of that space.

Everyone must manage more personal exposure to each other, sometimes seeing each other tired or irritable, acting at their worst in ways not displayed before.

Everyone will coexist around some human differences (in characteristics, values, habits, and wants) that each will sometimes find hard to tolerate.

Everyone will sometimes find him- or herself in conflict over competing desires and opposing points of view.

Everyone will encounter disagreements about what rules and responsibilities are going to define membership in the new family.

 **Fact**

Because of tensions from the complexity of living together in step relationships, some loving couples decide to keep their respective households separate and to delay remarriage until after all the children are grown and gone.

None of these complexities are problems to be eliminated. They are a continuing reality to live with. Remarriage with children is not for the uncommitted, inflexible, or faint of heart. It takes commitment to forge caring relationships between family members who are not historically and biologically connected. It takes tolerance to embrace unfamiliar differences that are inconsistent with one's experience and values. And it takes steadfast courage to work around unavoidable incompatibilities and work through necessary conflicts to create a family in which everyone has a stake and all feel accepted.

Child Adjustments

Sometimes a single parent, recently remarried, will get impatient with children who seem slow to get on board with the new family program. Rather than hurry the children up, it's better to appreciate the multifaceted change they are being asked to make. Consider just a few common adjustments.

 *Question?*

What is the biggest challenge in managing step relationships?
Acceptance. For the stepparent, how much family diversity from what you've known and what you value can you accept? For the parent, how much incompatibility between your view and the stepparent's view of your parenting and of your children can you accept? For the children, how much outside direction, influence, and authority from the stepparent can you accept? The key attitude for making step relationships work is tolerance.

When parents were married, the child got used to living around two closely connected and familiar adults. When parents divorced, the child got used to living around familiar parents living in an unfamiliar way—separated and disconnected. With remarriage, the child must get used to living around their familiar parent who is now cohabiting with another adult who is much less familiar. "Living with a stranger in the family, it doesn't feel as much like home anymore!"

When parents were married, the child got used to simple, unconditional caring from both parents. When parents divorced, the child questioned the commitment of parental caring. With remarriage, the child must get used to receiving more conditional caring from the parent's new spouse and receiving more conflicted caring from the parent. "My stepparent only really likes me when I do what she likes, and my dad often gets angry when I don't!"

When parents were married, the child felt sufficient connection (from time and attention) with both parents. When parents divorced, there was a loss of connection, with only one resident parent (who is now busier) present and with the other parent (who is now seen only on visitation occasions) absent. With remarriage, there is further loss of connection with the resident parent because of competition for time with the parent by the new stepparent. "I don't get much time alone with my parent anymore!"

Essential

Changes in family that remarriage brings, and the adjustments that children must make, can and should be discussed with children. Why? First, to recognize demands being made. Second, to give children credit for having to make a hard adjustment. And third, to explore actions parent and stepparent can take to moderate the difficulty of these demands.

When parents were married, the child believed parents would always stay together. When parents divorced, the child had to accept that parents would never be together again. With remarriage, the child now has to get used to having a parent intimately together with another adult who is not the child's parent. "It doesn't feel right when Mom cuddles and kisses a man who is not my dad!"

When parents were married, the child had a mother and father who stayed pretty much the same as the child had always known them. When parents divorced, the child got to see parents start growing more different from how they used to be when they lived together. With remarriage, the child now has to get used to seeing the parent become more different still, as he or she to some degree falls under the influence of the new spouse and in some ways starts to grow more similar to that person. "Once they got remarried, my parents and my family really started to change!"

Common Stepfamily Tensions and Conflicts

Romantic expectations about remarriage, such as "Our love for each other is enough to see us through any problems with the children" and "Once everyone's adjusted, our stepfamily will live happily ever after," will not serve remarriage well. Realistic expectations are what are needed: "We both understand that there will be predictable tensions and conflicts that are built into the stepfamily relationships we are putting together."

To know if your relationship is worth remarriage, you must honestly answer three questions: "Do I like how I treat myself in the relationship?" For example, do you act in ways that create self-respect? "Do I like how I treat the other person in the relationship?" For example, do you treat the other person in ways you would like to be treated in return? "Do I like how the other person treats me in the relationship?" For example, do the other person's actions cause you to feel safe and valued? Unless you answer yes to all three questions, don't commit.

Predictable Stepfamily Tensions

When step relationships become strained, it doesn't mean family members can't get along, it means there will always be some hard times getting along. Certain tensions are simply part of living in step relationships where the foundation of biological attachment, historical love, and social similarity is lacking.

For example, parent and stepparent will sometimes see the children through a different lens. What seems like a normal irritation to the parent, who is used to this behavior and has learned to tolerate it, can be highly offensive to the stepparent, for whom this conduct is foreign and unacceptable. "Don't your children have any table manners?" fumes the stepparent, who was taught to obey certain rules of conduct when eating together. "Responsibilities are major, but manners are minor," replies the parent, offended by this "misplaced" order of priorities.

Parent and children will sometimes see the stepparent through a different lens. An expression of opinion that seems like a demonstration of the stepparent's caring to the mother or father can seem inappropriately intrusive to the children, who complain to the parent, "You're the only one who should be judging what is best for us!" Replies the parent, "That opinion was for your benefit, can't you see?"

Stepparent and children will sometimes see the parent through a different lens. "Don't you talk to your parent that way!" objects the stepparent, who believes the parent should be treated with the courtesy due a respected elder. "We always talk to our parent that way!" object the children, who believe their parent should be treated with the informality due an old friend.

Then there are inevitable insider/outsider tensions. Whenever any two of the three parties (stepparent, parent, and children) are together, the third can feel left out. When parent and stepparent take time to be together, children can feel jealous and left out: "You'd rather be with him (or her) than with us!" When parent and children take time together, the stepparent can feel jealous and left out: "Your children matter more to you than I do!" And when stepparent and children are left together, the parent can feel anxious: "What's going to happen if they get into a disagreement and I'm not there?"

Predictable Stepfamily Conflicts

There are predictable grievances that give each party (stepparent, parent, and child) cause for frustration and anger and often precipitate conflict in the reconstituted family. These grievances are nobody's fault because they are rooted in the nature of stepfamilies, in the family dynamics that remarriage with children create. Each party has times when he or she feels misunderstood and unappreciated by the other two.

For the parent, there is frustration at not being able to make everyone happy, feeling caught between competing demands of stepparent and child and not able to satisfy one party without disappointing the other, and having divided loyalties when it comes to brokering conflicts between the two. "Nobody else in the family knows how painful it is to be caught in the middle of a conflict between two people I love who do not, at least at the moment, like each other, both wanting me to take their side."

For the stepchild, there is resentment at having to share family space with someone who isn't family, seeing one's parent acting affectionate with this nonparent, and having to accept an additional authority who makes new rules and demands that did not exist before. "Nobody else in the family knows all the changes I have to make to get used to someone new in the family, fitting into how that person likes to live, that person telling me new things I must and cannot do, while my parent mostly agrees and expects me to go along."

 **Fact**

You can't happily marry or remarry anyone until you are happily married to yourself. An unhappy person cannot make a happy marriage because he or she is ruled by painful discontent. Demanding that unhappiness be shared only proves the old adage that "misery loves company." To scapegoat step relationships for personal or marital unhappiness is not the answer either. It takes two people, each happy within him- or herself, to create a happy remarriage.

For the stepparent, there is resentment from feeling constantly exposed to unfamiliar and irritating parenting and child behavior, and feeling taken advantage of because so much effort made seems invisible to others, and so many contributions made seem taken for granted and not reciprocated. "Nobody in the family knows all the restraint it takes to tolerate parenting practices and conduct in children with which I don't agree, but about which I mostly keep silent and accept for peace and quiet's sake, just another way I give that no one appreciates."

All parties in the reconstituted family need not take these inherent grievances personally but must honor them with respectful discussion when they arise—declaring them without blame and listening without defensiveness. These grievances are built into stepfamily relationships and will not go away.

Helping Step Relationships Work

Given all the complexities, tensions, and conflicts built into step relationships, can remarriage with children work? Yes. What it takes is commitment of the two adults to make two marriages at once—as partners and as parents as well. In addition to accepting and defining the roles of husband and wife, they must simultaneously accept and define the roles of parent and stepparent. For this reason, remarriage with children is at least twice as complicated and challenging as marrying with no children at all. The learning curve of adjustment is very steep because there is so much complexity to manage right away.

Alert!

When a child objects to a stepparent, "You're not my real parent!" it is important for that adult to agree. "That's right, and I have no intent to be. But I am your real stepparent, just as you are my real stepchild. Together we can choose to define what these terms actually mean so how we are together works for both of us."

Because there will be so many human differences to manage—between parent and stepparent about parenting, between parent and children about family changes, between stepparent and children about how things will be done—each partner must commit to ongoing communication to understand each other's point of view, and to flexibility in resolving opposing wants.

For the well-being of children, the goal of remarriage is to create a functional parental unit on which the healthy operation of a family can depend. This means that to put children first, parent and stepparent must in a way put them last.

The order of priorities is as follows.

- Parent and stepparent take sufficient care of themselves individually so they have positive energy to invest in the marriage.
- Parent and stepparent take sufficient care of their marriage so they have positive energy to invest in the children.
- Parent and stepparent invest positive energy in the children so children are encouraged to respond positively in return.

Alert!

In early remarriage, it is particularly important that the stepparent exercise adequate restraint and self-care so he or she does not excessively give to stepchildren, over investing and then expecting an unrealistic return. What usually happens is that children happily take for granted what they are given, leaving the stepparent exhausted from extreme effort and resentful at not getting adequate appreciation or equal effort back.

In a remarriage, when parent and stepparent become focused on parental responsibilities at the expense of maintaining personal and partnership needs, then the deterioration of family begins. Children assume too much importance, and the adults enter a downward spiral of personal and partnership neglect. "I don't have time or energy to do anything for me!" "We don't have time or energy to do anything for our marriage!" Then, with the adults exhausted and more frequently in conflict, effective family functioning is undermined by stress. "The only thing my parent and stepparent aren't too tired to do is fight with each other and act irritable with us!" In general, when each partner and the marriage is well maintained, the interests and needs of children are best served.

Essential

For the sake of the children, parent and stepparent must take adequate care of themselves individually and of their relationship if a functional family is to be created and a successful remarriage is to be made.

Do's and Don'ts for Stepfamilies

What are some guidelines parent and stepparent can follow to sustain the family that remarriage has created? Many books have been written on this topic alone. To get you started thinking about helpful strategies, here are some do's and don'ts to consider.

What to Do

- If you are the parent, do give the stepparent appreciation for the visible and invisible efforts he or she makes for the children, and for the valued parenting perspective and ideas he or she brings.
- If you are the stepparent, do give the parent tact when expressing disagreement with the children's choices or the parent's response so that the parent does not feel criticized and put on the defensive about himself or herself on behalf of the children.
- Do take time apart to enjoy and nurture the marriage, and when you get away to relax as a couple, don't use that time to discuss the children.
- Do treat conflict about the children as a chance for parent and stepparent to share different views of the same problem, using this difference in perception to strengthen mutual understanding because two of you are smarter than one of you.
- Do allow all family combinations to have time together: time with parent and stepparent alone, time with parent and chil-

dren alone, time with stepparent and children alone, and time with everyone all together. Often, stepparent and step-children get along better when the parent is absent and they do not feel they have to compete for his or her attention.

- If you are the stepparent, do make clear to the parent that although there may be discouraging times when you do not care for the stepchildren, you always care about what happens to them and want the best for them.
- If you are the parent, do let the children know that neither by dislike nor misbehavior will they be able to drive away the stepparent and break up the marriage, which is here to stay.
- Early in remarriage, do have the parent be in charge of the corrective authority with children so the stepparent can build a positive relationship with them by exercising mostly contributive authority—in charge of giving valued resources, support, and permission that only an adult authority can provide.
- If you are the parent, as much as possible, do let stepparent and children work out their differences without mediating their disagreements. The more they learn to safely resolve their own conflicts, the more resilient their relationship will become.
- Do give the stepparent flexibility to disengage from parenting responsibility when he or she needs a break and then to reengage when energy and caring permit, because the stepparent needs more degrees of freedom in parenting involvement than does the parent, who must remain constantly involved and committed.
- Do take advantage of the diversity of experience, interest, opportunity, and new extended-family relationships that the stepparent brings into the lives of his or her stepchildren, and help the children appreciate these gifts.

Question?

What can be an important gift for children from parental remarriage?

When children see a happy remarriage after having witnessed how unhappiness between their parents ended in divorce, they are given an instructive example of how a mutually fulfilling marriage can be made.

What Not to Do

Do not expect teenage children to emotionally bond to a step-parent when they are already in the process of adolescent separation from their parents, pulling away and pushing against authority for more independence. Children up to about the age of eight have the best bonding potential with a stepparent because they feel more wed to family and more welcoming of a new caring adult in their lives.

Do not allow differences over the parenting of the children to become divisive of the marriage, but take whatever discussion time is required to come up with a decision you can both support, because when you can reach agreement as parents, you strengthen the marriage.

Do not blame yourself, your partner, or the children for the common tensions that are built into all step relationships; just discuss and resolve them on a situation-by-situation basis, understanding that these issues are nobody's fault and are not going to go away by themselves.

Do not attack personal and parenting differences by making critical judgments of each other's conduct, but be behaviorally specific and nonevaluative instead: "I disagree with the way you handled that situation, this is why, and this is what I would like us to talk about."

Do not undercut each other's authority with the children by allowing them to go around one of you to get a different decision from the other.

If you are the stepparent, do not create any "parent in the middle" confrontations by demanding, "It's either them or me!" Stepparent and children must learn to share the parent's loyalty, time, and attention.

If you are the parent, do not take the stepparent's visible and invisible efforts for granted. Keep recognizing the stepparent's efforts so you and the children can stay appreciative of the good he or she brings, and so the stepparent feels like a valued and noticed contributor to the family.

If you are the parent or stepparent, recognize with appreciation the adjustment and cooperation children make to act as a contributing part of the new family system.

These are just a few suggestions for helping reconstituted families work. Use them as a starting point to further educate yourself about the realities of step relationships so your new marriage has an improved chance to succeed. And to remind yourself of what it takes to make a marriage or remarriage work, go back and re-read the first chapter of this book.

Helpful Web Sites

✍ *www.carlpickhardt.com*
Helpful articles on parenting children and adolescents

✍ *www.divorcesupport.com*
Divorce forms, books, and articles

✍ *www.divorcesource.com*
General information for parents

✍ *www.divorce-kids.com*
Information for children about divorce

✍ *www.divorcedecision.com*
Help in making the divorce decision

✍ *www.womansdivorce.com*
Help for the divorcing woman

✍ *www.divorceonline.com*
Articles on all aspects of divorce

✍ *www.divorcenet.com*
Family law information

✍ *www.positiveparentingthroughdivorce.com*
Online instructional program for parents

Appendix B
Further Reading

Barr, Debbie. *Children of Divorce.* (Grand Rapids, MI: Zondervan, 1992).

Marston, Stephanie. *Divorced Parent.* (Fairfield, NJ: William Morrow, 1994).

Neuman, M. Gary. *Helping Your Kids Cope with Divorce.* (New York: Random House, 1998).

Pickhardt, Carl, Ph.D. *The Everything® Parent's Guide to Positive Discipline.* (Avon, MA: Adams Media Corporation, 2004).

Pickhardt, Carl, Ph.D. *Keys to Successful Stepfathering.* (New York: Barron's, 1997).

Pickhardt, Carl, Ph.D. *ROMANSWERS—Practical Answers to Common Questions Troubling Relationships, Romance, and Marriage.* (Xlibris.com, 2001).

Pickhardt, C. E. *The Case of the Scary Divorce—A Jackson Skye Mystery.* (Washington, DC: Magination Press, The American Psychological Association, 1997).

Wallenstein, Judith S., and Blakeslee, Sandra. *What About the Kids?: Raising Your Children Before, During, and After Divorce.* (New York: Hyperion, 2003).

Wallenstein, Judith S., Lewis, Julia M., and Blakeslee, Sandra. *The Unexpected Legacy of Divorce.* (New York: Hyperion, 2000).

Helpful Support Groups

Parents Without Partners
☎(561) 391-8833
Provides local support for divorced single parents

Parents Anonymous
☎(909) 621-6184
Strengthening families, breaking the cycle of abuse, and helping parents create safe homes for their children

Tough Love
☎(215) 348-7090
Providing program support and guidance for families in trouble, emphasizing problem solving and children growing into responsible adults

Al Anon
☎(888) 4AL-ANON
Helping families recover from a family member's problem drinking

Circle of Parents
☎(312) 663-3520
Providing mutual support groups in which parents can help each other

Index

THE *EVERYTHING*®
PARENT'S GUIDES SERIES

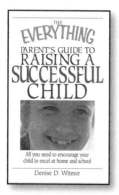

ISBN: 1-59337-043-1

A s parents struggle with these questions on a daily basis, *The Everything*® *Parent's Guide to Raising a Successful Child* helps put their fears to rest, providing them with professional, reassuring advice on how to raise a "successful" child according to their own standards.

F or parents of children with autism, daily activities such as grocery shopping or getting dressed can become extremely challenging. *The Everything*® *Parent's Guide to Children with Autism* offers practical advice, gentle reassurance, and real-life scenarios to help your family get through each day.

ISBN: 1-59337-041-5

ISBN: 1-59337-446-1

E xpert William Stillman discusses what bipolar disorder is and brings to light the many misconceptions, myths, and stereotypes associated with it. This comprehensive guide helps parents build a supportive family environment while learning to cope with the ups and downs of their child's unpredictable behavior.

Expert Advice for Parents in Need of Answers

All titles are trade paperback, 6" x 9", $14.95

Filled with helpful hints and practical guidance, this authoritative work is designed to provide parents with the latest information on the best treatments and therapies available, education options, and ways to make life easier for parent and child on a day-to-day basis.

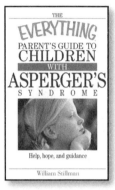

ISBN: 1-59337-153-5

ISBN: 1-59337-135-7

The Everything® Parent's Guide to Children with Dyslexia by Abigail Marshall—manager of *www.dyslexia.com*—gives you a complete understanding of what dyslexia is, how to identify the signs, and what you can do to help your child.

A child's tantrum can happen at virtually any time, but it's always inconvenient, frustrating, and embarrassing for a parent and sometimes dangerous for the child herself. *The Everything® Parent's Guide to Tantrums* teaches parents to identify various triggers that provoke extreme reactions and helps them strategize ways to calm down their children and minimize any long-term effect.

ISBN: 1-59337-321-X

Available wherever books are sold.
Or call 1-800-258-0929 or visit us at *www.everything.com*

ISBN: 1-59337-321-X

Rising obesity rates have become a national epidemic in America, and no age group is more affected than today's children. *The Everything® Parent's Guide to the Overweight Child* gives parents practical advice for helping their children develop the skills needed to lead a healthy, active lifestyle.

If you're looking for the facts about how this disorder may affect your child, it's hard to know where to turn. *The Everything® Parent's Guide to Children with ADD/ADHD*, written by child psychologist Linda Sonna, gives you the clear answers and accurate information about the signs, symptoms, and treatments of this disorder that you need.

ISBN: 1-59337-308-2

The Everything® Parent's Guide to Positive Discipline gives you all you need to help you cope with behavior issues. Written by noted psychologist Dr. Carl E. Pickhardt, this authoritative, practical book provides you with professional advice on dealing with everything from getting your kids to do their homework to teaching them to respect their elders.

ISBN: 1-58062-978-4

Strong-willed children push back against authority, exercise strong and often unwavering opinions, and try to impose their own rules. By examining its causes and effects, *The Everything® Parent's Guide to the Strong-Willed Child* enables parents to stop this pattern of behavior.

ISBN: 1-59337-381-3

Available wherever books are sold.
Or call 1-800-258-0929 or visit us at *www.everything.com*